UNDERSTANDING
FACULTY PRODUCTIVITY

UNDERSTANDING FACULTY PRODUCTIVITY

Standards and Benchmarks for Colleges and Universities

Michael F. Middaugh

Jossey-Bass Publishers
San Francisco

Jossey-Bass books and products are available through most bookstores. To contact Jossey-Bass directly, call (888) 378-2537, fax to (800) 605-2665, or visit our website at www.josseybass.com.

Substantial discounts on bulk quantities of Jossey-Bass books are available to corporations, professional associations, and other organizations. For details and discount information, contact the special sales department at Jossey-Bass.

Printed in the United States of America on acid-free, recycled stock that meets or exceeds the minimum GPO and EPA requirements for recycled paper.

Library of Congress Cataloging-in-Publication Data

Middaugh, Michael F., 1945–
    Understanding faculty productivity : standards and benchmarks for colleges and universities / Michael F. Middaugh. — 1st ed.
      p.   cm. — (The Jossey-Bass higher and adult education series)
    Includes bibliographical references (p.   ) and index.
    ISBN 0-7879-5022-X
    1. College teaching—United States—Evaluation.   2. Universities and colleges—United States—Faculty—Statistics. I. Title. II. M53   2001
378. 1′25—dc21
00-009571

FIRST EDITION
HB Printing   10 9 8 7 6 5 4 3 2 1

THE JOSSEY-BASS

HIGHER AND ADULT EDUCATION SERIES

CONTENTS

FIGURES, TABLES, & EXHIBITS

Tables

Figures

Exhibits

PREFACE

This book is about what faculty in U.S. colleges and universities do—and what they don't do. And let me say at the outset that faculty do far more teaching and research and perform far more public and institutional service than the American public perceives—all of which they do very well.

Unfortunately, colleges and universities have done a horrible job of communicating to external publics, particularly parents and legislators, what faculty are expected to do, what they actually do, and how well they do it. And postsecondary institutions have done little to communicate—even among themselves—that what faculty do has any day-to-day impact on students, let alone on people outside the academy.

In the hope of helping institutions correct some of these deficiencies and respond to increasing public criticism, I address the following questions in this book: How productive, in fact, are America's faculty? How do we know about their productivity? How can we measure faculty performance in ways that can be commonly understood and—most important—believed?

This book is not, however, an apologia for American faculty. It is a representation of my observations and reflections, as an administrator, from nearly a decade of research and study in the area of faculty activity. Although I have a joint faculty appointment at the University of Delaware, I am primarily an administrator and have been for all of my professional life in higher education. In my role as policy analyst, I bring the content and methodology of institutional research to an area—measuring faculty productivity—that has long been in need of those resources. Although some might view the notion of an administrator writing on the subject of faculty productivity as kin to the fox writing on optimizing poultry production, the simple fact is that clear, objective institutional research on faculty activity can provide a rich and textured picture of what faculty do—a picture that is long overdue.

Purpose of the Book

Why write a volume on the topic of faculty productivity? In part it is a response to criticism. For the past several years, higher education has been criticized severely for failing to provide information that speaks to issues such as productivity and accountability. Groups external to institutions of higher education are demanding clear, unambiguous descriptions of the ways colleges and universities conduct their business.

The U.S. Congress clearly perceives that a college or university education costs far too much for the value received. For that reason, in 1998 Congress appointed a National Commission on Higher Education Costs to study the issue and to make recommendations, which will be described in this volume. Suffice it to say here that the focus of congressional discussion has been solely on the issue of cost, with no linkage to college and university productivity.

In my view, however, any sensible discussion of costs must address the issue of return on investment. What value is received in return for expenditures? Or put another way, what are the tangible products of higher education in the core mission areas of instruction, research, and public service?

A number of state legislatures, most notably in South Carolina, have developed performance measures that are tied to ill-conceived data constructs intended to address institutional and faculty productivity but are, in fact, misleading, erroneous, and damaging to colleges and universities. These efforts by the states will also be described in this volume.

Finally, if they are to be responsible stewards of fiscal and human resources, higher education institutions themselves need consistent and reliable quantitative and qualitative information on institutional and faculty productivity and accountability.

So the basic question I address here is, How can colleges and universities effectively communicate credible information about productivity and accountability? Institutions of higher education, particularly in the public sector, are multipurpose entities. Their focus on undergraduate education is frequently augmented by graduate education, externally sponsored pure and applied research, and public service. And although most colleges and universities have platitudinous mission statements that embrace these diverse institutional functions, the order of priority and the reward system that underpins it are not always clear. The consensus outside higher education is that faculties frequently shape their activity to meet their own professional needs, as opposed to the needs and priorities of the institution that employs them.

Criticism of Faculties

Henry Rosovsky (1992), former dean of the faculty of arts and science at Harvard University, characterized American faculties, when viewed as social organisms, as operating "without a written constitution, and with very little common law. That is a poor combination, especially when there is no strong consensus concerning duties and standards of behavior. This situation has been made infinitely worse by the lack of information in the hands of [academic] deans concerning [the workload of] individual professors" (p. 3A).

Rosovsky goes on to say that he does not blame faculty for current behavior patterns and that they are indeed quite rational and understandable, given the absence of constraints. He continues:

> A wise senior colleague with whom I recently discussed our predicament strongly argued that the administration should assume most of the blame precisely because of our manifest unwillingness to set clear tasks and clear limits. The university setting and competition with other institutions make these assignments unusually difficult, but I am willing to agree that deans . . . have not displayed the required degree of leadership. [p. 2B]

I do not intend to lay blame on any constituency within higher education. That administrators lack the appropriate information to manage resources and ensure accountability is, however, a fair characterization of the state of affairs in many colleges and universities. Dean Rosovsky himself underscores this point:

> From the point of view of a dean, two observations are in order. First, the dean has only the vaguest notion concerning what individuals teach. Second, the changes that have occurred [in faculty workloads, over time] were never authorized at the decanal level. At least that is what I believe, and that is my main point. No chairman or group of science professors ever came to the dean to request a standard load of one-half course per year. No one ever requested a ruling concerning, for example, [workload] credit for shared courses. Change occurred through the use of *fait accompli,* i.e., creating facts. [p. 1B]

I have found Rosovsky's observations repeatedly reinforced during the past decade, as I have worked with academic administrators and institutional research personnel from hundreds of colleges and universities across the country.

Need for Productivity Data

In order to enhance precision in the development of data concerning faculty productivity, the data elements must be both inherently useful—and *used*. And there is no better way to ensure that data will be used than to tie information to resource allocation and reallocation decisions. If productivity and costs are inextricably linked and cost containment and efficiency are rewarded, then information that demonstrates productivity becomes incredibly powerful. The relationship between academic productivity and instructional costs is well documented (Brinkman, 1990; Brinkman, 1992; Hoenack, 1990; Middaugh and Hollowell, 1992; Middaugh, 1995; Middaugh, 1998).

Distilled to its simplest form, the more faculty teach, the lower instructional costs are. But if faculty are to pursue other legitimate academic interests, that is, the research and service that are directly related to the institution's mission, how can a balance be struck between teaching and other ancillary activities that takes cognizance of the issue of cost-efficiency? How can this information be assembled into reporting structures that have utility to deans, department chairs, and others interested in knowing what faculty do and whether faculty resources are being deployed in the most effective and efficient manner to accomplish both *institutional* and *departmental* objectives? And how can sufficient clarity and credibility be introduced into this information that it can be understood and used by those outside academe? It is precisely this information that constitutes the foundation for new paradigms in talking about faculty productivity.

But the mere quantitative demonstration of productivity and efficiency is not sufficient. If colleges and universities are to demonstrate that they are productive in the areas of teaching, research, and service, they must be prepared to describe not only *how much* faculty are teaching or *how much* research or public service they are doing but *how well* they are doing those things. How colleges can do so is the sum and substance of what this book is about.

Previous Research on Productivity

It is easiest to see the direction that discussions about faculty productivity must take by first examining the ways *productivity* has been described over the years. The opening chapter of this volume examines institutional and national efforts to describe faculty activity and clearly delineates the shortcomings in those approaches.

Once inadequacies in current analyses of productivity have been identified, the book then moves into a discussion of new paradigms for thinking about productivity and accountability. The starting point for this discussion is the national reporting effort begun in the mid-1990s under the auspices of the American Association of State Colleges and Universities (AASCU), the National Association of State Universities and Land Grant Colleges (NASULGC), and the American Association of Community Colleges (AACC). That effort grew into the Joint Commission on Accountability Reporting (JCAR), which attempted to describe what colleges do—including faculty activity—in terms of measurable institutional outputs. The JCAR methodology was the first serious attempt to look at both the process and outcomes aspects of higher education functions.

However, the JCAR effort was intended to provide reporting conventions for audiences outside higher education. Although useful, these conventions were never intended to be management tools that would address the concerns that Henry Rosovsky raised. An examination of the JCAR methodology identifies areas in which significant breakthroughs have been made with respect to productivity and accountability reporting, as well as identifying areas where additional work is needed.

The Delaware Study

At about the time JCAR was evolving, the University of Delaware received successive grants from the TIAA-CREF Cooperative Research Program and the Fund for the Improvement of Post Secondary Education (FIPSE), respectively, to support the development of a national data-sharing consortium, now known as the Delaware Study—a study that focused on instructional costs and faculty productivity at the academic discipline level of analysis. This approach to reporting is a direct response to the concerns of Henry Rosovsky and others, with respect to the need for reliable management data. This book examines the conceptual underpinnings for the Delaware Study and describes how institutions, system administrations, and governing boards are using the data to make better decisions. The book also delineates how the Delaware Study, when used with appropriate JCAR reporting conventions, provides a comprehensive picture of institutional and faculty productivity and accountability.

Although JCAR and the Delaware Study represent significant progress in quantifying productivity and accountability information, the qualitative dimension must also be addressed. A number of institutions across the country have established measures that describe not only how much activity faculty are engaged in but how well faculty perform in those activities. The final section examines these qualitative measures and offers suggestions for effectively combining quantitative and qualitative data into a single reporting package.

Audience for the Book

I wrote this book primarily for provosts, deans, department chairs, and those in state higher education coordinating agencies who have responsibility for accurately describing what faculty do. In fact, people in those positions are the colleagues with whom I have worked over the past ten years to develop new ways of talking about faculty productivity. Officials in federal and state governmental agencies, as well as in higher education associations wishing to take a serious look at the linkages between cost containment, productivity, and quality, will also find the book interesting. And it will have value for graduate students contemplating careers in higher education administration.

As I noted earlier, this volume is the result of a decade of collaborative research with colleagues from over three hundred colleges and universities across the United States. I could never have written it if these colleagues had not been risk takers who were willing to share sensitive data and willing to think in new ways about how to describe what faculty do. For their cooperation—and frequently their inspiration—I am in their debt.

Michael F. Middaugh

August 2000
Newark, Delaware

THE AUTHOR

Michael F. Middaugh is assistant vice president for institutional research and planning at the University of Delaware, where he has worked since 1985. Previously, he was assistant to the president at the State University of New York (SUNY) Institute of Technology at Utica and assistant director of institutional research at the SUNY College at New Paltz.

Middaugh received a D.E.D. in educational administration from the State University of New York at Albany, an M.A. in liberal studies from the State University of New York at Stony Brook, and a B.S. in biological sciences from Fordham University. He is the 2000–01 president of the Association for Institutional Research and was the 1999 international conference chair for the Society for College and University Planning.

Middaugh writes and consults extensively on the practice of institutional research and on measuring faculty productivity and instructional costs. He resides with his wife, Margaret Coupe, in Wilmington, Delaware.

CHAPTER ONE

DEFINING FACULTY PRODUCTIVITY

In the Preface to this book I offered a fairly harsh criticism of higher education. I said that colleges and universities have done a horrible job of communicating to both internal and external groups precisely what faculty do and how well they do it. There is an assumption among the general public—and this includes state and federal legislators and agency heads—that faculty are hired largely, if not solely, to teach. Other activity is either superfluous or self-serving. This is not simply a contentious observation on my part but a reflection on comments I have heard during the past decade by people who influence wide audiences, both inside and outside the academy.

Two of those commentators are Robert Zemsky and William Massy; they offer a scathing indictment of faculty who put their own career interests ahead of their duty to teach. Zemsky is professor of higher education at the University of Pennsylvania. For the past several years he has worked with the Pew Charitable Trusts on the Pew Higher Education Roundtable, as well as in the production of a series of related newsletters called *Policy Perspectives*. William Massy, professor emeritus of education and business administration at Stanford University, has spent the past decade writing on productivity and cost containment in higher education. In 1990 Zemsky and Massy coauthored a widely cited article in *Change Magazine* titled "Cost Containment: Committing to a New Economic Reality," wherein they describe their concept of the "academic ratchet." The article calls faculty to task in the following manner:

[The academic ratchet is] a term to describe the steady, irreversible shift of faculty allegiance away from the goals of a given institution, toward those of an academic specialty. The ratchet denotes the advance of an entrepreneurial spirit among faculty nationwide, leading to an increased emphasis on research and publication, and on teaching one's specialty in favor of general introduction courses, often at the expense of coherence in an academic curriculum. Institutions seeking to enhance their own prestige may contribute to the ratchet by reducing faculty teaching and advising responsibilities across the board, thus enabling faculty to pursue their individual research and publication with fewer distractions. The academic ratchet raises an institution's costs, and it results in undergraduates paying more to attend institutions in which they receive less attention than in previous decades. [p. 22]

The foregoing comments suggest that faculty are self-centered, that they are engaged in activity directed at self-aggrandizement, and that undergraduates are being cheated both intellectually and financially by the institutions that admit them. And Zemsky and Massy's critique of American faculty is not an isolated viewpoint. The National Commission on Educating Undergraduates, created in 1995 under the auspices of The Carnegie Foundation for the Advancement of Teaching, was charged with examining undergraduate education in the United States, most specifically at research universities. It was initially chaired by Ernest Boyer, president of The Carnegie Foundation, and was renamed the Boyer Commission following his death in 1995. Here is the commission's assessment of faculty at research universities:

To an overwhelming degree, they [American research universities] have furnished the cultural, intellectual, economic, and political leadership of the nation. Nevertheless, the research universities have too often failed, and continue to fail, their undergraduate populations. . . . Again and again, universities are guilty of advertising practices they would condemn in the commercial world. Recruitment materials display proudly the world-famous professors, the splendid facilities and the ground breaking research that goes on within them, but thousands of students graduate without ever seeing the world-famous professors or tasting genuine research. Some of their instructors are likely to be badly trained or untrained teaching assistants who are groping their way toward a teaching technique; some others may be tenured drones who deliver set lectures from yellowed notes, making no effort to engage the bored minds of the students in front of them. [Boyer Commission on Educating Undergraduates in the Research University, 1998, pp. 5–6]

Like Zemsky and Massy, the Boyer Commission strongly suggests that American faculty are more interested in pursuing their own research interests than in teaching undergraduates. They accuse research universities of false advertising, claiming world-class faculties in their recruiting literature but delivering a product that rarely, if ever, brings undergraduates into contact with those faculty. The Boyer Commission (1998) report states:

> Many students graduate having accumulated whatever number of courses is required, but still lacking a coherent body of knowledge or any inkling as to how one sort of information might relate to others. And all too often they graduate without knowing how to think logically, write clearly, or speak coherently. The university has given them too little that will be of real value beyond a credential that will help them get their first jobs. And with larger and larger numbers of their peers holding the same paper in their hands, even that credential has lost much of its potency. [p. 6]

Current Criticism of Higher Education

Current criticism of higher education faculty is not limited to academic and scholarly publications. The general public has, in recent years, become enamored with general trade publications that rank colleges and universities and suggest which of these are best buys. The appropriateness of the variables measured and the relative merits of the methodologies used in these rankings and consumer advocacies form the subject matter for another book. The bottom line, however, is that these publications sell; they reach wide audiences and are given enough credibility that institutions worry about their relative position in the ranking. Foremost among these trade publications is *U.S. News and World Reports' America's Best Colleges.* The following assessment of American higher education was taken from the 1996 edition of *America's Best Colleges:*

> The trouble is that higher education remains a labor-intensive service industry made up of thousands of stubbornly independent and mutually jealous units that must support expensive and vastly underused facilities. It is a more than $200 billion-a-year economic enterprise—many of whose leaders oddly disdain economic enterprise and often regard efficiency, productivity, and commercial opportunity with the same hauteur with which Victorian aristocrats viewed those in "trade". . . . The net result is a hideously inefficient system that, for all

its tax advantages and public and private subsidies, still exacts a larger share of family income than almost anywhere else on the planet. [p. 91]

Having suggested that colleges and universities are inefficient, less than productive, and generally badly managed, the same article goes further:

> For their part, most colleges blame spiraling tuition on an assortment of off-campus scapegoats—congressional budget cutters, stingy state legislatures, government regulators and parents who demand ever more costly student health and recreational services. Rarely mentioned are the on-campus causes of the tuition crisis: declining teaching loads, non-productive research, ballooning financial aid programs, bloated administrative hierarchies, "celebrity" salaries for professional stars, and inflated course offerings. If colleges and universities were rated on their overall financial acumen, most would be lucky to escape with a passing grade. [pp. 91–92]

Once again faculty are depicted as scapegoats who do little teaching and are involved in meaningless, nonproductive research. If, as the opening paragraph in the Preface suggests, American faculty are far more productive than they are generally given credit for being, how can this barrage of criticism from both inside and outside of higher education be justified?

Are colleges and universities a collective of charlatans who claim to be educators but whose functions are so diverse and whose priorities so confused that undergraduates will emerge with a virtually meaningless credential, knowing little more than they did when they entered? Or are colleges and universities simply complex institutions that are, in fact, performing quite effectively in every way *except* communicating and describing their productivity?

Need for a New Language

Even though colleges and universities have evolved in diverse ways over the past half-century, the language they use to talk about what they do has essentially remained unchanged. They have thereby done themselves significant harm.

Wounds of this sort are largely self-inflicted. Colleges and universities have, over the years, felt no sense of urgency in developing information that speaks to issues of productivity or efficiency. They have largely operated with an ivory tower mentality, as though they were above the need to be accountable for how their resources, both fiscal and personnel, were used. Attempts to describe faculty activity have been misguided, ill-conceived, and poorly executed.

When institutions have tried to talk about faculty productivity, they have spoken most often in terms of what faculty do. An example would be, "Faculty, on average, spend X percent of their time teaching, Y percent doing research, and so on." These may be important data, but they are not productivity measures. Quite candidly, it matters little whether a faculty member spends nine or ninety hours per week in the classroom or research laboratory unless there is some assessment of the quality of the product that comes from the time spent. Simply being busy does not mean being productive. The existence of "productivity data" implies that products have been examined; how those products have been defined and measured is the subject of this book.

Measurement of Productivity

Some would argue that institutions of higher education are different from other institutions and do not lend themselves to productivity measures. Colleges and universities claim to be in the business of producing knowledge—a difficult commodity to measure. But let's put that notion to rest once and for all. Consider my home institution as one of the three thousand colleges and universities against whom the foregoing criticisms have been leveled.

Example: The University of Delaware

The University of Delaware is an independent, state-related Research II university, with some 125 baccalaureate degree programs, 80 master's programs, and 40 doctoral degree programs. In academic and fiscal year 1999, the University of Delaware

- Took in $181.6 million in tuition and fees
- Had operating revenues totaling $465.8 million
- Expended $52.3 million in sponsored research and $15.6 million in sponsored public service
- Expended $178.1 million on instruction and departmental research
- Received private gift support in the amount of $45.7 million, much of which was added to the university's endowment of over $800 million
- Graduated 3,255 students with bachelor's degrees, 807 master's degrees, and 144 doctorates

These are not trivial numbers. Parents and students spend over $180 million in tuition and fees in a single year for instruction at the University of Delaware. What do they get for their money? Who teaches the courses—a tenured faculty member or a freshly minted graduate teaching assistant? Do the students learn?

Outside contractors paid the university close to $70 million for research and public service activity in a single year. What did they get in return for their investment? What impact does the research and service activity have on the university, the state, and the region? Are the benefits gained from research and service sufficiently important to society that faculty should engage in these activities in addition to, or in lieu of, teaching?

Benefactors gave the university $45.7 million in a single year, building on an endowment of $800 million. Why give to the University of Delaware? Why is this a solid investment?

And finally, in a single year the university awarded more than 4,200 degrees. What is the worth of a University of Delaware degree? Or as one of the university trustees, a CEO at a major Fortune 500 corporation, put it so eloquently and succinctly, "How do we know we're doing a good job at the University of Delaware? How do we demonstrate that?"

These are fair questions to which parents, legislators, donors, and others deserve complete and candid answers. And frankly, these are questions that those who manage multimillion-dollar institutional budgets should be able to answer.

Revenues at Other Institutions

To move from a single institution to a more global level, the National Center for Education Statistics (NCES) reports that parents and students spent $55.3 billion nationally in tuition and fees at colleges and universities during fiscal year 1996. (These are the most current national data available at the time of this writing.) Operating revenues at colleges and universities totaled $198.0.1 billion; $151.5 billion was expended on instruction; $23.8 billion was spent on research and public service; colleges and universities received $1.5 billion in gifts and endowment income in a single year. It is eminently fair to ask what the return has been on those investments. Because colleges and universities are in fact collegial, that is, run by faculty, it is fair to put the question more precisely: How productive *are* America's faculty?

Times have changed for higher education, and there is a new climate wherein colleges and universities must regularly demonstrate that they are reliable stewards. As noted earlier, it is the new language that higher education institutions must use that is the focus of this book.

The Faculty Member as Mr. Chips

The popular notion of a faculty member at a college or university has historically been a vision out of the 1939 film *Goodbye, Mr. Chips*. The pipe-smoking hero, seemingly absentminded and distracted, perpetually dressed in tweed, ever-accessible to his students, both in school and forever after, Mr. Chips became the object of adulation and adoration. He was the consummate teacher. Prior to World War II, postsecondary institutions, from the Ivy League university to the local state teachers college, were magnets for and home to armies of people who were like Mr. Chips—or were trying to be—until after the war. Scholarly and popular writers then became openly critical of college and university faculties. They have argued that students are grossly shortchanged by the self-serving pursuits of faculty who have little interest in activities other than those that win them promotion, tenure, and the opportunity for personal entrepreneurism.

The crucial point in such a perception of faculty is not simply whether it is accurate or inaccurate. The point is that the perception is there and policy is being developed on the basis of it. State legislatures are tying funding to performance and productivity measures without having a clear sense of what constitutes a productive faculty member.

It is essential that colleges and universities develop credible and accurate ways to talk about the nature of faculty work, and specifically, the products of that work. Writers from both inside and outside the academy will continue to be critical of an enterprise that refuses to respond to questions such as, Who is teaching what to whom, how well, and at what cost? If American higher education does not develop realistic and credible measures for responding to these issues, solutions will be externally imposed; most likely they will be ill conceived and potentially destructive.

Inadequacy of Performance Measures

In this volume I will examine some of the faculty performance measures already on the books in a number of states and will demonstrate that they measure neither performance nor productivity. Yet they are the basis on which funding decisions are being made in those states, sometimes with disastrous results. To see the totally illogical conclusion to which externally imposed performance mandates can lead, one need only recall the State Postsecondary Review Entities (SPRE) regulations of the early 1990s. These federal substitutes for higher education accrediting agencies were short-lived, largely because of the ill-conceived benchmarks against which they measured institutional performance in higher education. These will be described in Chapter Two, but the lesson to be learned should be underscored here. We now have national and state government officials who are eager to define productivity measures for higher education; the record demonstrates that measures imposed externally are often inappropriate. If higher education does not define credible measures on its own, then it will have to live with the consequences.

Evolution of Faculty Work

Productivity cannot be measured until the nature of the work being assessed is well defined. For better or worse, faculty work has changed dramatically in the last half of the twentieth century, and the rate of change has accelerated over the last three decades. Colleges and universities are no longer the quiet, ivy-covered bastions of teaching and contemplation that were popularized in books and motion pictures during the first half of the twentieth century.

Consider the following sketch of the evolution of faculty duties. During the first half of the twentieth century, faculty life at most institutions consisted largely of a heavy teaching load, with little or no research activity. The faculty member, more often than not, began and ended a career at the same institution. Faculty compensation lagged well behind that for others with postgraduate degrees. In return for the less-than-competitive paycheck and unquestioned commitment to the institution, faculty were given total autonomy over their out-of-classroom activity. At the same time, following a probationary period of employment, faculty were granted tenure, that is, a guarantee of lifetime employment at their institution. However, World War II and the postwar economic and political climate radically changed the mix in this equation.

It was not until the late nineteenth century that a small number of American universities began offering doctoral education. Most colleges and land grant institutions focused primarily on undergraduate teaching; the land grant institutions emphasized their mission of service to the state and region. With the onset of World War II, major universities like Harvard University and the Massachusetts Institute of Technology played the lead role in establishing a working relationship with the federal government to apply research in support of the war effort. With substantial financial support becoming available from the government, other doctorate-granting universities across the nation pursued programs of applied research. This explosive growth in research activity gave rise to the introduction of formal graduate education at large numbers of American colleges and universities.

Following World War II, graduate students whose training had emphasized research techniques, as opposed to teaching paradigms, moved into faculty positions across the nation. These newly minted Ph.D.'s were trained in specific academic disciplines, and they concentrated on developing research programs in their cognitive area. Academic departments took on clearly defined forms, with little in the way of intellectual interaction between or among departments. Perhaps most significant was that young faculty were hired as *teaching faculty* but were promoted and granted tenure based on their record as *researchers*. The cold war and the race for outer space in the 1960s and 1970s further reinforced this pattern.

Ernest L. Boyer, in his seminal report, *Scholarship Reconsidered: Priorities of the Professoriate* (1990), summarized the postwar changes in American higher education as follows:

> But even as the mission of American higher education was expanding, the standards used to measure academic prestige continued to be narrowed. Increasingly, professors were expected to conduct research and publish results. Promotion and tenure depended on such activity, and young professors seeking security and status found it more rewarding—in a quite literal sense—to deliver a paper in New York or Chicago than teach undergraduates back home. Lip service still was being paid to maintaining a balance between *collegiate* responsibilities and *university* work, but on most campuses the latter had clearly won the day. [p. 12]

In other words, if one had asked in the early part of the twentieth century what faculty do, the answer would simply have been, "They teach." The complexities inherent in mounting a successful war effort in the 1940s and in maintaining the peace in the decades that followed resulted in graduate education programs that produced highly trained researchers who, quite candidly, had little or no background in effective teaching paradigms. This changed not only the mission and complexion of major research universities but also the comprehensive and baccalaureate institutions where research-trained Ph.D.'s became faculty.

Boyer's analysis continues:

> Research *per se* was not the problem. The problem was that the research mission, which was appropriate for *some* institutions, created a shadow over the entire higher learning enterprise—and the model of a "Berkeley" or an "Amherst" became the yardstick by which all institutions would be measured. Ernest Lynton, Commonwealth Professor at the University of Massachusetts, in commenting on the new priorities, concluded that developments after the Second World War established too narrow a definition of scholarship and too limited a range of instruction. Ironically, at the very time America's higher education institutions were becoming more open and inclusive, the culture of the professoriate was becoming more hierarchical and restrictive.

Thus in just a few decades priorities in American higher education were significantly realigned. The emphasis on undergraduate education, which throughout the years had drawn its inspiration from the colonial college tradition, was being overshadowed by the European university tradition, with its emphasis on graduate education and research. Specifically, at many of the nation's four-year institutions, the focus had moved from the student to the professoriate, from general to specialized education, and from loyalty to the campus to loyalty to the profession. [pp. 12–13]

The foregoing discussion argues that the nature of faculty work was substantially transformed during the twentieth century. Any methodology that hopes to measure faculty productivity must first take cognizance of what faculty do. Clearly they do more than teach. But is this the case only at research universities, where the institutional mission is a complex combination of teaching, research, and service? Or is it true for multiple types of higher education institutions, regardless of formal mission statement?

Faculty Work Patterns

The first step in defining faculty productivity is defining and understanding what faculty do. What is the typical faculty work week? How do faculty spend their time? Do their efforts coincide with the work patterns postulated in the preceding pages? Are work patterns at universities different from those at comprehensive colleges and universities? If so, does this imply multiple measures for productivity as one moves across institution types?

There are, in fact, empirical answers to these questions. The National Center for Education Statistics (NCES) in the U.S. Department of Education has created a comprehensive vehicle for collecting information on faculty activity and creating a longitudinal database as the data are collected over time. The National Study of Postsecondary Faculty (NSOPF) was administered to a national sample of faculty in 1988 and again in 1993; a third data collection is under way at this writing. NSOPF used a detailed survey that asked faculty questions about the nature and volume of their work and about their satisfaction with working conditions.

The problem with data of this sort is that they are self-reported. One can either take the viewpoint that the half-million faculty who respond to the National Study of Postsecondary Faculty's "Faculty Survey" are either pathological liars who answer only in their own self-interests, or they are extraordinarily hardworking individuals, the nature of whose work is not well understood. Obviously, this book will argue for the latter.

Indeed, the manner in which we have historically talked about and reported faculty work has been inadvertently misleading and often confusing. Self-reported data about how work time is distributed over various categories of activity do not address the products of those activities, or even the extent to which faculty work smartly and efficiently. Keep in mind throughout the following discussion that NSOPF describes what faculty do, not how productive they are (which is precisely how these data are frequently misused).

How many hours per week do faculty work? The notion that faculty work less than members of other professions is clearly contradicted by the self-reported mean number of hours worked per week in both 1987 and 1992. The data in Table 1.1 are arrayed by Carnegie institution type; for the reader unfamiliar with the Carnegie taxonomy, the following definitions, taken from the 1994 Carnegie Classification, will prove helpful:

Research universities: These institutions offer a full range of baccalaureate programs, are committed to graduate education through the doctorate, and give high priority to research. They award fifty or more doctoral degrees each year, and in addition they receive *at least* $15.5 million per year in federal support. The volume of federal support is the basis for distinguishing between Research I and Research II universities.

Doctoral universities: These institutions offer a full range of baccalaureate programs and are committed to graduate education through the doctorate. They award *at least* ten doctoral degrees annually in three or more disciplines, or twenty or more doctoral degrees in one or more disciplines. The number of doctorates awarded and the number of disciplines involved form the basis for distinguishing between Doctoral I and Doctoral II universities.

Comprehensive colleges and universities: These institutions offer a full range of baccalaureate programs and are committed to graduate education through the master's degree. They award *at least* twenty master's degrees annually in one or more disciplines. The number of master's degrees awarded and the number of disciplines involved is the basis for distinguishing between Comprehensive I and Comprehensive II institutions.

Liberal arts colleges: These institutions are primarily undergraduate colleges with major emphasis on baccalaureate degree programs. Liberal Arts I colleges award 40 percent or more of their baccalaureate degrees in liberal arts fields and are restrictive in admissions. Liberal Arts II colleges award fewer than 40 percent of their baccalaureate degrees in liberal arts fields or are less restrictive in their admissions.

Two-year colleges: These institutions offer the associate certificate or degree programs and, with few exceptions, offer no baccalaureate degrees.

Specialized institutions: These institutions offer degrees ranging from the bachelor's to the doctorate. At least 50 percent of the degrees awarded by these institutions are in a specialized field. Examples of specialized institutions include theological seminaries, medical schools, law schools, and art colleges.

TABLE 1.1. MEAN NUMBER OF HOURS WORKED BY FULL-TIME INSTRUCTIONAL FACULTY AND STAFF, BY TYPE AND CONTROL OF INSTITUTION (FALL 1987 AND FALL 1992).

Type and Control of Institution and Year	Full-Time Instructional Faculty and Staff	Mean Hours Worked per Week
1992		
All Institutions[1]	528,261	52.5
Public Research	107,358	56.4
Private Research	32,164	57.6
Public Doctoral[2]	52,808	55.1
Private Doctoral[2]	28,684	53.4
Public Comprehensive	94,477	52.4
Private Comprehensive	38,561	51.9
Private Liberal Arts	38,052	52.5
Public 2-Year	109,957	46.9
Other[3]	26,200	49.0
1987		
All Institutions[1]	515,139	52.7
Public Research	102,115	56.8
Private Research	41,574	56.1
Public Doctoral[2]	56,294	54.7
Private Doctoral[2]	25,065	52.2
Public Comprehensive	97,131	52.7
Private Comprehensive	36,842	51.2
Private Liberal Arts	38,446	52.5
Public 2-Year	96,144	46.9
Other[3]	21,528	51.9

Source: National Center for Education Statistics, 1997.

[1] All accredited, nonproprietary U.S. postsecondary institutions that grant a two-year (A.A.) or higher degree and whose accreditation at the higher education level is recognized by the U.S. Department of Education.

[2] Includes institutions classified by The Carnegie Foundation as specialized medical schools.

[3] Public liberal arts, private two-year, and religious and other specialized institutions, except medical.

The data in Table 1.1 show that faculty work 46.9 hours per week at public two-year colleges, and the time worked increases progressively with moves up the Carnegie taxonomy, topping out at approximately 57.6 hours per week at research universities. The data show stability over both the 1987 and 1992 NSOPF data collection cycles.

Perhaps the most surprising numbers are the hours worked per week by full-time faculty and staff at four-year institutions. Despite the distinctly different institutional missions among research universities, doctorate-granting universities, and comprehensive colleges and universities, the hours worked per week are fairly consistent across institutional types. And Table 1.2 demonstrates minimal variation

TABLE 1.2. MEAN NUMBER OF HOURS WORKED BY FULL-TIME FACULTY AND STAFF IN FOUR-YEAR INSTITUTIONS, BY PROGRAM AREA (FALL 1987 AND FALL 1992).

Program Area and Year	Full-Time Instructional Faculty and Staff	Mean Hours Worked per Week
1992		
All program areas in 4-year institutions*	405,783	54.2
Agriculture/Home Economics	9,698	56.5
Business	28,895	52.7
Education	30,127	52.5
Engineering	20,381	56.7
Fine Arts	26,874	51.5
Humanities	54,093	52.0
Natural Sciences	79,663	55.2
Social Sciences	48,030	54.2
All Other Fields	44,346	53.8
1987		
All program areas in 4-year institutions*	414,832	54.0
Agriculture/Home Economics	10,104	55.4
Business	28,630	52.7
Education	31,812	51.4
Engineering	20,915	55.0
Fine Arts	27,628	52.9
Humanities	60,781	53.2
Natural Sciences	74,852	54.0
Social Sciences	47,324	53.5
All Other Fields	29,042	52.7

Source: National Center for Education Statistics, 1997.

*Health sciences faculty are included in the program area total but are not shown separately.

across disciplines. Poets and social scientists work roughly the same number of hours as biologists and engineers.

Although the foregoing data indicate that faculty work considerably more than the traditional forty-hour week across all sectors of higher education, the question remains, What do faculty do with their work time? Faculty have considerable autonomy and discretion in apportioning their time, to the point that critics of higher education argue that the partitioning of faculty time is self-serving and inappropriate.

The NSOPF data in Table 1.3 reflect self-reported faculty estimates of time spent in four categories of activity—teaching, research, administrative functions, and "other" activities. If one focuses on teaching and research, the distribution of faculty time fairly reflects institutional mission.

The highest proportions of time spent in teaching are found in two-year colleges, liberal arts colleges, and comprehensive colleges, where the primary institutional mission is teaching. There faculty report that they spend from two-thirds to three-fourths of their time engaged in instructional endeavors. Doctoral and research universities show significantly lower proportions of time spent in teaching, with commensurately larger proportions of time spent in research. Those university faculty, on average, report spending less than half of their time engaged in teaching, with research consuming one-third of a faculty member's time at research universities and one-fifth of their time at doctorate-granting universities.

It is important to note that, consistent with Boyer's earlier observation, research is an integral part of the job culture for faculty at any four-year institution where at least 10 percent of a faculty member's time is devoted to research. Obviously that proportion becomes substantially larger at universities where research (pure and applied) is central to the institutional mission.

It is also noteworthy that faculty at all institutions, regardless of Carnegie classification, spend roughly one-fourth of their time in administrative and other activities. This is not surprising to those in higher education. The very term *college* is predicated on *colleague*. Higher education institutions are, in fact, organized to be administered and governed in collegial fashion. Whether this is the most effective or efficient means of governing is not the issue here. The fact is that colleges and universities are collegial structures, and a significant portion of a faculty member's time goes into activity related to the operation and administration of the institution. Yet this form of governance is rarely discussed outside the academy, and it is an organizational concept that is completely foreign to those working in corporate America.

When the distribution of time spent in teaching and research is examined across the disciplines for faculty at four-year institutions, the data follow predictable patterns. Faculty in the humanities and fine arts spend the largest proportion

TABLE 1.3. ALLOCATION OF TIME, BY FUNCTION, FOR FULL-TIME INSTRUCTIONAL FACULTY AND STAFF, BY TYPE AND CONTROL OF INSTITUTION (FALL 1987 AND FALL 1992).

Type and Control of Institution and Year	Full-Time Instructional Faculty and Staff	Percentage of Time Spent			
		Teaching Activities	Research Activities	Administrative Activities	Other Activities
1992					
All Institutions[1]	528,261	54.4	17.6	13.1	14.7
Public Research	107,358	40.4	31.5	12.9	15.2
Private Research	32,164	34.6	35.3	12.8	16.8
Public Doctoral[2]	52,808	46.8	23.8	13.2	16.1
Private Doctoral[2]	28,684	44.5	21.7	15.7	18.1
Public Comprehensive	94,477	60.2	14.0	12.0	13.7
Private Comprehensive	38,561	59.5	11.8	14.6	13.8
Private Liberal Arts	38,052	63.5	9.6	14.7	11.8
Public 2-Year	109,957	68.7	4.5	12.0	14.6
Other[3]	26,200	60.8	10.7	14.9	13.5
1987					
All Institutions[1]	515,139	57.1	17.3	13.2	12.5
Public Research	102,115	43.6	30.1	13.9	12.3
Private Research	41,574	42.1	30.6	13.2	14.2
Public Doctoral[2]	56,294	47.8	22.8	14.7	14.7
Private Doctoral[2]	25,065	41.1	26.4	12.8	19.6
Public Comprehensive	97,131	63.5	12.3	12.8	11.4
Private Comprehensive	36,842	63.7	11.2	14.2	11.0
Private Liberal Arts	38,446	66.8	10.5	13.8	9.0
Public 2-Year	96,144	73.3	4.2	10.9	11.6
Other[3]	21,528	63.6	8.8	15.2	12.5

Source: National Center for Education Statistics, 1997.

[1] All accredited, nonproprietary U.S. postsecondary institutions that grant a two-year (A.A.) or higher degree and whose accreditation at the higher education level is recognized by the U.S. Department of Education.

[2] Includes institutions classified by The Carnegie Foundation as specialized medical schools.

[3] Public liberal arts, private two-year, and religious and other specialized institutions, except medical.

of time teaching, with the proportion declining as one moves through the science and engineering disciplines. The pattern for time spent in research is inversely proportional to the time spent in teaching.

The data in Table 1.4 likely reflect external funding support for research in the various disciplines. Engineering, natural and physical sciences, agriculture, and the social sciences are disciplines that still receive generous federal funding for research and development activities. The National Science Foundation (NSF) reports some $12.3 billion in federal obligations for research and development activities at colleges and universities in science and engineering fields in fiscal year 1997. No comparable data regarding funding activity are available from the National Endowment for the Arts (NEA) or the National Endowment for the Humanities (NEH). Consequently, research activity is heaviest where it is financially supported. Still it is important to underscore that research activity occurs—and in significant proportions—in disciplines that do not enjoy substantial external support. In order to be promoted and tenured, artists must still show, musicians must perform, poets and authors must write, and teacher educators must train.

How many hours are spent in the classroom, and what are the relative teaching loads for faculty? Table 1.5 shows NSOPF data for mean hours per week spent in the classroom and mean student contact hours. The latter is a measure of workload in that it reflects the hours spent teaching multiplied by the number of students enrolled in those classes.

Again the patterns are predictable. Faculty at research universities spend less time in the classroom than those at other Carnegie institutions; the teaching load at public research universities is heavier than that at private institutions. Time spent in the classroom increases as one moves from research to doctoral universities and on through comprehensive, liberal arts, and two-year institutions. With the exception of doctoral universities in the 1992 data cycle, public institutions teach heavier loads than private colleges and universities. This is not surprising, given the emphasis that many highly selective private institutions place on small class size.

The time that full-time faculty at four-year institutions spend in class is clearly related to the discipline. Engineers, natural and social scientists, and faculty in agriculture, as shown in Table 1.4, were all more heavily engaged in research than those in other disciplines. Not surprisingly, they spend fewer hours per week in the classroom than colleagues in other disciplines. Teaching workload appears to be a function of pedagogical delivery system (see Table 1.6). Those disciplines typically associated with large, group-lecture modes of instruction (for example, introductory classes of business administration, anthropology, sociology, biology, and chemistry) will have heavier teaching loads than courses that rely heavily on

TABLE 1.4. ALLOCATION OF TIME, BY FUNCTION, FOR FULL-TIME FACULTY AND STAFF IN FOUR-YEAR INSTITUTIONS, BY PROGRAM AREA (FALL 1987 AND FALL 1992).

Program Area and Year	Full-Time Instructional Faculty and Staff	Percentage of Time Spent			
		Teaching Activities	Research Activities	Administrative Activities	Other Activities
1992					
All program areas in 4-year institutions*	405,783	50.8	21.1	13.2	14.7
Agriculture/ Home Economics	9,698	42.1	30.7	13.0	14.2
Business	28,895	54.1	17.9	12.1	15.7
Education	30,127	53.8	13.1	16.5	16.2
Engineering	20,381	48.5	28.1	11.2	12.0
Fine Arts	26,874	56.5	15.4	12.3	15.6
Humanities	54,093	59.7	17.8	13.1	9.1
Natural Sciences	79,663	50.0	29.1	11.1	9.7
Social Sciences	48,030	50.5	23.6	13.4	12.2
All Other Fields	44,346	52.9	16.1	15.6	15.2
1987					
All program areas in 4-year institutions*	414,832	53.2	20.4	13.7	12.6
Agriculture/ Home Economics	10,104	50.4	27.6	13.4	8.7
Business	28,630	60.3	16.0	11.5	12.2
Education	31,812	61.5	11.2	16.2	11.1
Engineering	20,915	56.2	22.4	12.3	9.1
Fine Arts	27,628	55.2	19.3	11.9	13.6
Humanities	60,781	62.2	16.9	14.5	6.5
Natural Sciences	74,852	53.8	26.7	12.3	7.2
Social Sciences	47,324	54.3	22.1	14.0	9.7
All Other Fields	29,042	59.8	11.1	11.2	11.9

Source: National Center for Education Statistics, 1997.

*Health sciences faculty are included in the program area total but are not shown separately.

TABLE 1.5. MEAN NUMBER OF CLASSROOM HOURS AND STUDENT CONTACT HOURS FOR FULL-TIME INSTRUCTIONAL FACULTY AND STAFF, BY TYPE AND CONTROL OF INSTITUTION (FALL 1987 AND FALL 1992).

Type and Control of Institution and Year	Full-Time Instructional Faculty and Staff	Mean Classroom Hours	Mean Student Contact Hours[1]
1992			
All Institutions[2]	528,261	11.0	337.4
Public Research	107,358	6.9	281.3
Private Research	32,164	7.1	231.7
Public Doctoral[3]	52,808	9.7	337.1
Private Doctoral[3]	28,684	8.3	395.6
Public Comprehensive	94,477	10.9	337.0
Private Comprehensive	38,561	10.6	273.6
Private Liberal Arts	38,052	11.0	242.4
Public 2-Year	109,957	16.3	457.3
Other[4]	26,200	12.9	321.4
1987			
All Institutions[2]	515,139	9.8	300.4
Public Research	102,115	6.7	263.5
Private Research	41,574	5.9	225.5
Public Doctoral[3]	56,294	8.1	285.9
Private Doctoral[3]	25,065	6.7	200.1
Public Comprehensive	97,131	10.4	316.7
Private Comprehensive	36,842	10.8	276.1
Private Liberal Arts	38,446	10.5	234.5
Public 2-Year	96,144	15.1	420.8
Other[4]	21,528	10.8	322.6

Source: National Center for Education Statistics, 1997.

[1] Number of hours per week spent teaching classes, multiplied by the number of students in those classes.

[2] All accredited, nonproprietary U.S. postsecondary institutions that grant a two-year (A.A.) or higher degree and whose accreditation at the higher education level is recognized by the U.S. Department of Education.

[3] Includes institutions classified by The Carnegie Foundation as specialized medical schools.

[4] Public liberal arts, private two-year, and religious and other specialized institutions, except medical.

individualized lessons or on studio or laboratory work (for example, music, art, or engineering). That said, it is worth noting that teaching workloads, on average, increased across the disciplines from 1987 to 1992.

In describing faculty activity so far, NSOPF data look exclusively at the number of hours worked and the proportion of those hours engaged in various types of activity. These are largely "input" measures and, as I argue later in this volume, they are the wrong measures for discussing issues of faculty productivity, particularly with those outside the academy. These input measures have value but not as measures of faculty productivity.

Tables 1.1 and 1.3 reveal the following portrait of an American faculty member: he or she works, on average, about fifty-two hours per week, spending just over half of those hours teaching, just under 20 percent in research, and the rest of the time in other sorts of job-related activity. That's fine, but what are the concrete products of these hours spent in various activity, particularly teaching, which constitutes the greatest block of time? Which students are being taught by which faculty and with what results? Are undergraduates being taught by those faculty in whom a college or university has the greatest investment—tenured and tenure-track faculty? Are students graduating with marketable skills? Are they going on to graduate study? These are but a few of the questions that underpin the notion of faculty instructional productivity in the minds of parents and legislators and others who have a stake in financially supporting higher education. They are perfectly legitimate questions that are in no way addressed by the measures we have just examined.

The National Study of Postsecondary Faculty provides the opportunity to self-report productivity in major noninstructional categories of activity. Table 1.7 shows the mean number of publications and presentations over twenty-four months by faculty in each of the major Carnegie classifications. Productivity here is measured in terms of discrete categories: refereed or juried publications, reviews and nonrefereed publications; books and book chapters, monographs and technical reports, presentations and exhibits, and patents, copyrights, and software.

What is revealing in Table 1.7 is not so much the number of publications and presentations being generated per faculty but rather that *every* Carnegie classification is showing some degree of noninstructional activity. It is not at all surprising to see a significant amount of activity in doctorate-granting, research institutions. The "publish or perish" mandate clearly underpins promotion and tenure at these institutions. However, comprehensive and liberal arts four-year colleges and two-year community colleges, which are characterized by more time spent in the classroom and greater proportions of time devoted to teaching activity, are nonetheless active players within the various categories of noninstructional activity. Indeed,

TABLE 1.6. MEAN NUMBER OF CLASSROOM HOURS AND STUDENT CONTACT HOURS FOR FULL-TIME INSTRUCTIONAL FACULTY AND STAFF AT FOUR-YEAR INSTITUTIONS, BY PROGRAM AREA (FALL 1987 AND FALL 1992).

Program Area and Year	Full-Time Instructional Faculty and Staff	Mean Classroom Hours	Mean Student Contact Hours[1]
1992			
All program areas in 4-year institutions[2]	405,783	9.4	303.4
Agriculture/Home Economics	9,698	8.5	229.2
Business	28,895	9.4	299.5
Education	30,127	10.0	270.4
Engineering	20,381	7.7	223.3
Fine Arts	26,874	11.9	252.2
Humanities	54,093	9.6	257.7
Natural Sciences	79,663	8.5	338.7
Social Sciences	48,030	8.6	309.2
All Other Fields	44,346	9.7	281.5
1987			
All program areas in 4-year institutions[2]	414,832	8.5	272.3
Agriculture/Home Economics	10,104	7.1	226.9
Business	28,630	9.0	300.6
Education	31,812	9.1	227.5
Engineering	20,915	7.8	249.5
Fine Arts	27,628	11.1	245.1
Humanities	60,781	9.3	248.6
Natural Sciences	74,852	7.9	311.9
Social Sciences	47,324	8.0	301.1
All Other Fields	29,042	9.4	267.0

Source: National Center for Education Statistics, 1997.

[1] Number of hours per week spent teaching classes, multiplied by the number of students in those classes.

[2] Health sciences faculty are included in the program area total but are not shown separately.

TABLE 1.7. MEAN NUMBER OF PUBLICATIONS AND PRESENTATIONS IN THE PAST TWO YEARS BY FULL-TIME INSTRUCTIONAL FACULTY AND STAFF, BY TYPE AND CONTROL OF INSTITUTION (FALL 1987 AND FALL 1992).

Type and Control of Institution and Year	Full-Time Instructional Faculty and Staff	Refereed or Juried Publications	Reviews and Non-Refereed Publications	Books and Book Chapters	Monographs and Technical Reports	Presentations and Exhibits	Patents, Copyrights, and Software
1992							
All Institutions[1]	528,261	1.9	1.4	0.5	0.9	4.4	0.1
Public Research	107,358	3.8	2.0	0.9	1.5	6.3	0.2
Private Research	32,164	4.5	2.1	1.2	1.3	6.5	0.3
Public Doctoral[2]	52,808	2.9	1.6	0.7	1.2	5.9	0.2
Private Doctoral[2]	28,684	2.3	1.6	0.7	0.9	4.1	0.1
Public Comprehensive	94,477	1.2	1.5	0.4	1.0	4.3	0.1
Private Comprehensive	38,561	0.9	1.1	0.4	0.8	3.9	0.1
Private Liberal Arts	38,052	0.9	1.3	0.3	0.6	3.8	0.1
Public 2-Year	109,957	0.2	0.5	0.1	0.4	1.8	0.1
Other[3]	26,200	0.8	1.4	0.3	0.7	3.8	0.1
1987							
All Institutions[1]	515,139	2.1	1.8	0.6	1.0	4.4	0.3
Public Research	102,115	4.1	2.0	1.0	1.6	5.8	0.2
Private Research	41,574	4.3	1.9	1.3	0.7	4.1	0.4
Public Doctoral[2]	56,294	2.9	2.1	0.7	1.1	5.1	0.2
Private Doctoral[2]	25,065	3.8	1.6	1.0	0.7	6.4	0.1
Public Comprehensive	97,131	1.2	2.0	0.4	1.1	4.8	0.3
Private Comprehensive	36,842	1.1	1.7	0.3	1.0	4.1	0.2
Private Liberal Arts	38,446	0.9	1.6	0.3	0.5	3.2	0.2
Public 2-Year	96,144	0.4	1.2	0.2	0.6	2.6	0.4
Other[3]	21,528	1.0	1.6	0.4	0.9	4.2	0.1

Source: National Center for Education Statistics, 1997.

[1] All accredited, nonproprietary U.S. postsecondary institutions that grant a two-year (A.A.) or higher degree and whose accreditation at the higher education level is recognized by the U.S. Department of Education.

[2] Includes institutions classified by The Carnegie Foundation as specialized medical schools.

[3] Public liberal arts, private two-year, and religious and other specialized institutions, except medical.

with the exception of refereed publications, the differences between comprehensive and liberal arts colleges and doctorate-granting universities is slight across all activity categories.

Table 1.8 demonstrates comparable noninstructional activity by full-time faculty across disciplines.

If faculty are productive outside the classroom, why all the fuss about irrelevant and exotic faculty research? Once again the question is, Are these the right measures? Looking back at Table 1.7, the American faculty member, on average, writes about two articles over a twenty-four month period, as well as a book review, perhaps a book chapter, and a monograph; he or she might make four presentations at professional meetings. The parent or legislator looking at these numbers will likely say, "So what?" "What does this mean to me?" "How does it improve the quality of education at American higher education institutions?" "How do these activities affect me and my child attending college?" Again, these are legitimate questions that call into question the responsiveness of the measures we currently use to discuss faculty productivity in noninstructional arenas.

The NSOPF data in Tables 1.1 through 1.8 demonstrate a high degree of stability from 1987 to 1992, suggesting that the depiction of how faculty allocate their time is reasonably accurate, as evidenced by two separate random samples. Similar descriptions of faculty activity over time are found in a national study titled "The American College Teacher," undertaken at regular intervals by the Higher Education Research Institute (HERI) at the University of California at Los Angeles (Sax, Astin, Arredondo, and Korn, 1996). The HERI Faculty Survey, like NSOPF, underscores the diverse nature of faculty activity and reinforces the fact that research is both an expectation and an area of primary interest to faculty at universities as well as four-year colleges.

However, as with NSOPF, the HERI Faculty Survey largely describes how faculty spend their time. There is no linkage between the time spent in teaching or research activity and specific outcomes measures from those activities. It is precisely that linkage that is needed to begin a discussion of faculty productivity.

Conclusion

This chapter has described the broad functional areas in which American faculty work. Faculty surveys such as those from the National Study of Postsecondary Faculty or UCLA's Higher Education Research Institute are extremely useful tools for understanding faculty quality-of-life issues. Time spent in various activities can be correlated with a number of variables, including but not limited to compensation levels, institutional support for faculty, and personal motivation and satisfaction.

TABLE 1.8. MEAN NUMBER OF PUBLICATIONS AND PRESENTATIONS IN THE PAST TWO YEARS BY FULL-TIME INSTRUCTIONAL FACULTY AND STAFF AT FOUR-YEAR INSTITUTIONS, BY PROGRAM AREA (FALL 1987 AND FALL 1992).

Program Area and Year	Full-Time Instructional Faculty and Staff	Refereed or Juried Publications	Reviews and Non-Refereed Publications	Books and Book Chapters	Monographs and Technical Reports	Presentations and Exhibits	Patents, Copyrights, and Software
1992							
All program areas in 4-year institutions*	405,783	2.4	1.6	0.6	1.1	5.1	0.2
Agriculture/ Home Economics	9,698	3.8	5.0	0.6	2.7	7.0	0.2
Business	28,895	1.9	1.3	0.5	1.3	2.9	0.2
Education	30,127	1.3	1.7	0.5	1.2	5.8	0.1
Engineering	20,381	3.7	1.9	0.5	2.8	5.3	0.4
Fine Arts	26,874	0.9	1.5	0.3	0.3	18.3	0.2
Humanities	54,093	1.4	1.8	0.8	0.4	3.1	0.1
Natural Sciences	79,663	3.7	1.1	0.5	1.1	3.5	0.2
Social Sciences	48,030	1.9	1.8	0.9	1.2	4.1	0.1
All Other Fields	44,346	1.2	2.1	0.6	1.2	3.8	0.1
1987							
All program areas in 4-year institutions*	414,832	2.5	1.9	0.7	1.1	4.9	0.2
Agriculture/ Home Economics	10,104	3.1	3.1	0.5	1.6	4.7	0.3
Business	28,630	1.4	1.1	0.4	0.9	2.0	0.2
Education	31,812	1.5	2.0	0.5	1.0	5.1	0.2
Engineering	20,915	2.7	1.7	0.5	2.1	3.2	0.7
Fine Arts	27,628	0.9	1.6	0.2	0.3	15.9	0.3
Humanities	60,781	1.6	2.7	0.8	0.3	3.2	0.1
Natural Sciences	74,852	3.3	1.2	0.5	1.6	3.0	0.4
Social Sciences	47,324	2.2	2.0	1.0	1.0	3.4	0.1
All Other Fields	29,042	1.2	3.1	0.4	1.4	4.0	0.1

Source: National Center for Education Statistics, 1997.

*Health sciences faculty are included in the program area total but are not shown separately.

These variables are important in attempting to provide an environment wherein faculty can optimize their various job functions and components. But they do *not* address productivity issues.

Now that we have a fair handle on how to measure *what* faculty do, the remainder of this book will focus on the issues of *how much* and *how well* they do it. These are the issues of concern to those outside the academy—issues that have not been adequately addressed.

CHAPTER TWO

RESPONDING TO PUBLIC PRESSURE FOR SYSTEMATIC ACOUNTABILITY

The first visible wave of national concern over productivity and accountability in higher education took the form of an ill-conceived mandate within the Higher Education Reauthorization Act of 1992. That bill authorized the creation of State Postsecondary Review Entities, commonly known as SPREs. SPRE oversight, originally intended for proprietary institutions that were defaulting on federal student loans at alarmingly high rates, was extended to all of postsecondary education.

The criteria on which a SPRE could evaluate a college or university extended well beyond financial information related to student loan defaults. Along with measures of institutional performance such as student persistence and postgraduation placement data, SPREs could examine the relationship between potential earning power in an occupation or profession and the tuition charged to obtain the appropriate credential for that occupation or profession. Other candidates for SPRE oversight were data on faculty credentials and activity, program length (as measured in clock hours or credit hours), recruiting and admissions practices, academic calendars, and grading practices. Catalogues, publications, and institutional advertising practice could also come under SPRE scrutiny, as could all records of student complaints. In short, SPREs were created in response to a range of public concerns related to the perception that colleges and universities were providing small returns on substantial tuition and public subsidy investments.

The general tone and tenor of the SPRE movement underscored government's distrust of the higher education accreditation process, which was rooted in institutional self-study and self-regulation. By and large, the measures that SPREs were prepared to impose on institutions had little to do with student loan defaults and even less to do with the productivity of institutions. The measures were created because, in the view of public officials, higher education could not be trusted to provide credible information that spoke to the outcomes of higher education. No such measures had historically emanated from higher education in any systematic fashion, and until they were forced to do so, colleges and universities would not have been likely to create such measures.

Fortunately, the SPRE regulations were rescinded after a storm of criticism from higher education institutions and associations. But the pressure for information on productivity and accountability did not disappear. Regional accrediting bodies emphasized outcomes assessment as a crucial component of institutional self-study but often resulted in measures that were confusing and obscure to those outside higher education. The distrust of the ability of the higher education community to report credible information on its activities and products persisted. In 1997 the State Higher Education Executive Officers (SHEEO) surveyed their constituents in each of the fifty states to determine the extent to which performance measures were being used to gauge productivity and accountability in higher education. The survey found that in 1997 more than half the states were using or planning to use performance measures *as components of their state budget processes.* In most instances these measures were in response to the public perception that full-time faculty, especially tenured and tenure-track faculty, were not teaching undergraduates and that baccalaureate education was less than first rate.

The performance measure movement is clearly a response to the failure of institutions to provide clear, verifiable productivity information. As noted earlier in this volume, the public perception is that faculty focus their energies largely on graduate education and on research and publishing. Although it is perfectly reasonable and fair for those who fund higher education to expect accountability with regard to what colleges and universities do, many of the state-mandated measures, like their SPRE predecessors, were poorly designed and yielded inaccurate or misleading information.

State-Mandated Performance Measures

Among the most widely publicized state-mandated performance standards are those in South Carolina. Although the state has promulgated thirty-seven so-called performance standards against which to base postsecondary funding decisions, for purposes of this discussion I am focusing on those relating to faculty and faculty activity. Exhibit 2.1 lists the performance indicators: (1) focus on institutional mission, (2) quality of faculty, (3) quality of instruction and collaboration, and (4) achievement of graduates.

Criticism of Measures

Interestingly enough, South Carolina is headed in the right conceptual direction with entirely the wrong set of measures. Institutional mission is very important, as it should provide the framework and context for everything that occurs at a college or university. And most certainly the quality of the faculty is related to the quality of their work. Instructional activity must be examined as a component of faculty productivity. And unlike the National Study of Post Secondary Faculty and the UCLA-HERI Faculty Survey, South Carolina is tying all of this to at least one output measure—the achievements of graduates. That said, they have gone after the easy measures—data elements that are readily accessible but that have little to do with what they purport to measure.

The mere expenditure of funds does not ensure that an institution's mission will be achieved. Adequate resources are certainly important, but how does simply measuring dollars spent on mission-generated activities provide information about institutional success? Similarly, the fact that curricula are in line with an institution's mission does not mean that they are being taught effectively or that students are learning. That a college or university has an approved mission statement and strategic plan says nothing about graduation rates, economic and social impact of faculty research and public service, and so on. The measures focus on the structural aspects of mission, which mean little unless the institution is generating a product that has value. In fact, these are not performance measures at all because nothing is being performed. They simply measure the "presence" of selected variables such as dollars, a mission statement, a curriculum, or a strategic plan.

The quality-of-faculty measures are no better. The fact that professors and instructors possess or lack terminal degrees does not measure the quality of work they do. Compensation of faculty is certainly a factor in the ability of an institution to attract gifted faculty, but it does not measure what they do. Similarly, the out-of-class availability of faculty to students does not assess whether faculty advice is good or bad, simply that it is being rendered. And the fact that community or public service is being performed for which no extra compensation is paid is a questionable measure at best. What difference does it make whether service activity is pro bono or performed on contract? What matters is whether the service has value to the institution or community and whether it is being carried out effectively. Again these are largely descriptor variables that have little to do with the performance they purport to measure.

EXHIBIT 2.1. SOUTH CAROLINA PERFORMANCE MEASURES FOR SELECTED COMPONENTS OF INSTITUTIONAL ACTIVITY.

Mission Focus

Expenditure of funds to achieve institutional mission

Curricula offered to achieve mission

Approval of a mission statement

Adoption of a strategic plan to support the mission statement

Attainment of goals of the strategic plan

Quality of Faculty

Academic and other credentials of professors and instructors

Performance review system for faculty to include student and peer evaluations

Post-tenure review for tenured faculty

Compensation of faculty

Availability of faculty to students outside the classroom

Community or public service activities of faculty for which no extra compensation is paid

Instructional Quality

Class sizes and student-faculty ratios

Number of credit hours taught by faculty

Ratio of full-time faculty to other full-time employees

Accreditation of degree-granting programs

Institutional emphasis on quality teacher education and reform

Achievements of Graduates

Graduation rate

Employment rate for graduates

Employer feedback on graduates who were employed or not employed

Scores of graduates on postgraduate professional, graduate, or employment-related examinations and certification tests

Number of graduates who continue their education

Credit hours earned by graduates

In fairness to South Carolina, two measures of faculty quality at least relate to an outcome or product. Student and peer evaluation of faculty and post-tenure review both imply that there is some assessment of faculty performance in the class-room and in scholarship. The measures are nebulous, however, and more precise measures will be described later in this volume.

Perhaps the most troubling of the South Carolina performance measures are those associated with instructional quality. Class size and student-faculty ratio do not measure performance. They are important indicators that help to suggest whether there is an environment conducive to learning, but they do not measure whether learning is taking place. The number of credit hours that faculty teach in no way indicates the quality or effectiveness of instruction and certainly does not speak to instructional outcomes. The ratio of faculty to other full-time employees is interesting as an issue in determining overhead and administrative costs but is not a direct measure of instructional quality. Two measures—institutional and programmatic accreditation and institutional emphasis on teaching effectiveness —are the only measures from the "instructional quality" list that can potentially show whether quality teaching is evident. But both of these are indirect measures that do not provide crucial information on whether students are learning.

Credible Measures

The only credible measures in the South Carolina list that deal with outcomes of faculty activity are those that relate to the achievement of graduates. No single measure tells the entire story, but multiple measures do yield useful information. Graduation rate is an indicator of student success, although by itself it simply in-dicates that students have achieved the required number of credits to earn a de-gree. But taken in combination with employment rates for graduates, feedback from employers relative to the adequacy of preparation of graduates, success on certification, licensure, and other professional credentialing, and the number of students pursuing postbaccalaureate education all speak to the effectiveness of faculty in the area of instruction. These performance measures do just that. They measure outcomes from the institution's instructional activity.

The South Carolina list is notably devoid of comparable outcome measures for noninstructional faculty activity. In thinking about the productivity of Amer-ica's faculty, it is important to have a comprehensive framework. As we know from both the National Study of Postsecondary Faculty and the UCLA-HERI Faculty Survey, faculty do not just teach, just do research, or dedicate themselves solely to public service. Higher education is a complex enterprise, and any discussion of ac-countability and productivity must take account of that complexity. The enter-prise, if it is to be held accountable and its productivity accurately assessed, must be described in its totality. This includes special emphasis on the outputs or products of higher education.

South Carolina's misadventures in performance measures are not isolated; they have simply received the most publicity. Unless institutions are completely forthcoming with appropriate measures that describe how productive they are, particularly with regard to faculty activity, then they are issuing an open invitation to those outside the academy to impose irrelevant and inappropriate measures. Keep in mind that funding is tied to performance measures in most states. Using the wrong measures has serious and profound implications.

Getting It Right

In 1996 the first steps were taken toward appropriately focusing the discussion on accountability and productivity in higher education. Having survived the SPRE scare and facing a growing performance measure movement in state legislatures, higher education associations in Washington, D.C., determined that a coordinated response to demands for information on productivity and accountability was needed. The Joint Commission on Accountability Reporting (JCAR) was created from constituents in three of the major higher education associations in Washington. Specifically, representative presidents from the National Association of State Universities and Land Grant Colleges (NASULGC), the American Association of State Colleges and Universities (AASCU), and the American Association of Community Colleges (AACC) became the governing commissioners for JCAR. These three organizations represent the full spectrum of state-assisted and state-related higher education institutions. The National Association of Independent Colleges and Universities (NAICU) was invited to participate but declined.

JCAR is a visible and tangible acknowledgment on the part of college and university officials of the need to respond to external constituencies seeking consistent, credible measures of accountability and productivity in higher education. The JCAR measures are by no means exhaustive, but they are comprehensive and do attempt to depict higher education in all of its complexities.

The nine commissioners who made up JCAR represented the diversity of American higher education. They came from institutions as small as Northwestern Connecticut Community and Technical College (just under 1,800 students and 100 faculty) to Pennsylvania State University (78,800 students throughout the Penn State System, and 4,100 faculty). The commission was geographically balanced and covered the Carnegie spectrum from community colleges through research universities.

The commission determined at the outset that it would focus its discussions and analyses on four areas:

- Placement rates and full-time employment in the field following completion of a higher education program or degree
- Graduation rates, persistence rates, withdrawal rates, licensure pass rates, and transfers of students
- Student charges and costs (JCAR commendably drew the distinction between the published tuition rates—the "sticker price"—for a college education and the true cost—institutional expenditures associated with delivering that education.)
- Faculty activity

These four areas are clearly interconnected. Faculty activity is related to persistence and graduation rates and to whether graduates obtain jobs, pass licensure exams, or go on to graduate school. JCAR did not suggest that there is a simple correlation between the quality of faculty activity and the aforementioned outcomes. Indeed, the JCAR documents underscored the complexity of the relationship between faculty activity and outcomes. But JCAR also acknowledged that it is fair to ask about the scope of activities in which faculty engage and the extent to which these activities contribute to institutional outcomes. For the first time, the crux of national discussions on faculty activity suggested a careful measurement of the relationship between that activity and institutional productivity.

In examining each of these issues, the commission set about creating consistent and credible standards against which discussion of accountability and productivity could be benchmarked. And in establishing the data definitions, calculation conventions, and data collection protocols for realizing these benchmarks, the commission created "technical work groups." These groups were made up of content experts, outstanding research methodologists, and communications experts from across the nation. Their charge was straightforward: produce a series of data-reporting formats that will provide consistent, comparable national information that is fully responsive to the most frequently asked accountability questions.

It is important to again note that the intended audience for JCAR reporting conventions were constituencies *outside* higher education. These were intended to be reporting tools for talking with legislators, parents, consumer groups, and other interested parties outside of colleges and universities. The reports were not intended as internal management tools. The remainder of this chapter will critically examine JCAR's pioneering effort to determine what higher education has accomplished and what still needs to be done.

The JCAR Issues

In their thinking about what a college does, JCAR has made a serious attempt to move the discussion away from so-called input measures. With regard to students, the discussion has moved away from measures such as enrollments, SAT and ACT scores, and demographic variables. Measures for faculty have gone beyond the percentage of time spent in teaching, research, and service activities. JCAR has attempted to achieve these shifts in direction by describing student and faculty activity at a college or university in terms of output measures.

Students attend a college or university to acquire knowledge, much of which will be used to pursue employment in a particular career field. A substantial portion of faculty instructional activity is directed at helping students learn what they need to know. Thus JCAR decided to look at the student outputs of instruction in terms of concrete success or productivity metrics. Specifically, for an entering cohort of students they examine persistence, transfer, and graduation rates. And beyond graduation they examine placement rates in fields related to the student's academic program or discipline and, where appropriate, licensure pass rates. These measures are very different from "percent of faculty time spent in the classroom" or "average SAT score of entering freshmen." The new measures provide baseline quantitative measures of the *outcomes* of educational activity. Do students graduate? Do they get jobs in fields related to what they studied? Do they have the requisite learning skills to pass a standard licensing exam? These are hardly exhaustive measures (we will look at a fuller inventory later in this volume). But they represent a marked departure from the previous confusing and, frankly, often obfuscating ways of talking about higher education.

JCAR was particularly concerned that the accountability measures they would ultimately recommend for national use would contain data definitions and calculation conventions that would have integrity and be consistent, thus facilitating inter-institutional comparisons. This too represented a marked departure from traditional thinking in higher education. Many institutions have feared invidious comparisons between and among institutions. But JCAR is taking a realistic approach to a contemporary environment in which an entire industry has sprung up outside higher education that is devoted to ranking colleges and universities along a number of variables, some of which are appropriate; others are not. If colleges and universities are to be compared, JCAR insists that it be on a consistent set of indicators.

The commission seeks to help a parent or a legislator answer questions such as

Is an institution's graduation rate as good as that for other colleges and universities?

What is the statewide or regional or national graduation rate?

Is an institution's graduation rate improving or declining over time?

The most significant features of the JCAR initiative are that they focus on the products or output measures of higher education and do so in a manner that uses consistent definitions and reporting formats. Consider the calculation of a graduation rate. The concept is not new. A college or university simply examines an entering cohort of new students from a given Fall semester and determines what proportion of that cohort have successfully acquired degrees within four years, five years, six years, and so on. The JCAR contribution to this metric is consistency in definitions. For example, some colleges had excluded students admitted under special circumstances ("at-risk" students), whereas other institutions excluded athletes admitted under nonacademic criteria. The JCAR definition of a first-time freshman cohort is straightforward: "Those students entering the reporting institution for the first time who have never attended any college, including students enrolled in the fall term who attended college for the first time in the prior summer term and students who entered with advanced standing (college credits earned before graduation from high school)."

No exclusions. No exceptions. Simply a straightforward characterization of the attributes of students who are to be included in an entering Fall cohort.

JCAR's New Language

In developing standard reporting definitions, JCAR has set a standard for discussing higher education activities with those outside the academy. It is very important to have a language that does not waver—a language that does not mean one thing in this instance but something altogether different in another. Consistency of meaning and consistency in language use are important principles that will be revisited throughout the remainder of this volume.

That is not to say that the JCAR conventions are insensitive to the idiosyncrasies of higher education. In looking at graduation rates, JCAR candidly admits to the following weaknesses in their reporting conventions:

• Students who begin study in a freshmen cohort at Institution A but who transfer after a period of time and complete their degree at Institution B are attrition statistics at Institution A and reduce the graduation rate at that institution. And although JCAR provides a reporting convention for "transfer out" students, these data are extremely difficult to collect and are generally not reported by most institutions, leaving an incomplete picture for that freshmen cohort.

• Students who enter as part of a freshmen cohort but who only wish to take three or four courses to prepare for a job, upgrade skills, or determine whether that college is right for them—and who subsequently leave the institution without graduating—are counted as attrition statistics. In fact, these students may have fully met their own educational goals and are successful in their own terms, but their "success" is not reported as part of the JCAR advancement statistics. Once again, JCAR provides mechanisms for data-rich institutions to deal with these exceptions. In fact, however, most institutions have neither the time nor the resources to do this sort of exceptional, extended student tracking.

• A simple graduation rate statistic does not, in and of itself, speak to the mission of a higher education institution. Public community colleges have very different missions—and graduation rates—from highly selective, private, four-year, liberal arts colleges. Urban universities and colleges that traditionally serve underrepresented populations have very different missions—and graduation rates—from flagship, state, land grant universities. These institutional missions must be used as "filters" when making any inter-institutional comparison of graduation rates.

Engaging those outside the academy in a discussion of institutional success, as measured in terms of graduation rates, can be useful and productive only if colleges and universities are free to acknowledge the limitations in reporting conventions and only if external publics acknowledge differences in missions between and among institutions. The JCAR conventions are an important first step in engaging the public in such discussions.

The JCAR reporting conventions are groundbreaking also in the sense that they provide a vehicle for institutions to report in a consistent fashion two other output measures: postgraduation placement and licensure pass rates. After four years or, more frequently, five to six years of baccalaureate study, it is perfectly reasonable for parents and students to ask about the likelihood that the graduate will be able to secure employment in a position related to the field of study. And if the graduate was educated in a professional field that uses an examination as a prerequisite to employment (for example, nursing, accountancy, or teaching), do graduating students possess the cognitive skills needed to pass the examination? The commission has provided the technical conventions to enable institutions to report placement rates and licensure pass rates in clear and consistent formats across institutions.

Once again JCAR is candid and forthright in identifying the limitations in their methodology. In the cases of placement and licensure pass rates, the JCAR conventions do not account for baccalaureate recipients who go on to graduate school and subsequently secure employment in their field of study or who become licensed in a profession related to their field of study.

The JCAR conventions for reporting institutional outputs are important because they are part of a "total reporting package" that looks at faculty activity at an institution and attempts to relate that activity to selected output and cost measures. Three JCAR publications—*A Need Answered, JCAR Technical Conventions Manual,* and *JCAR Faculty Assignment Reporting*—are fully referenced in the bibliography to this volume; interested readers should explore all three.

The remainder of this chapter examines the faculty activity portion of the JCAR reporting conventions, whereas the remainder of this volume will build on the momentum that the commission has established with respect to a candid discussion of faculty productivity.

The JCAR View of Faculty Productivity

As noted earlier, the JCAR commissioners assembled technical work groups to identify variables, create data definitions and calculation conventions, and describe reporting strategies for each of the content areas that JCAR intended to address. The work groups averaged a dozen individuals; they included faculty, senior administrators, and institutional researchers, all with national reputations for expertise in their field. When the JCAR groups were assembled in 1996, it was with the expectation that all four groups—the Post-Graduation Placement Rates, Graduation-Persistence Rates, Student Charges and Costs, and Faculty Activity Groups—would complete their work in twelve months and report the results concurrently. This did not happen. Because of the complexity in defining faculty activity reporting categories and associated calculation conventions, the Technical Work Group on Faculty Activity required an additional year to complete its tasks. The process involved extended discussion and debate and included a pilot testing of the recommended data definitions and calculation conventions to test their viability in the field.

The JCAR reporting calculations and conventions focus on what faculty are assigned to do and, within the area of instruction, which categories of faculty are teaching the students. The JCAR protocols are reasonable and appropriate for their intended audience—those outside the academy with little or no understanding of a faculty member's full range of responsibilities. For that audience, the protocols can provide a measure of understanding and appreciation for the complex nature of faculty activity. The JCAR conventions also enable, if not encourage, comparisons of assigned faculty activity between and among institutions and in academic departments within institutions. Such analyses underscore for those outside academe the fact that institutions vary by mission. For some, research and service are integral to their mission; for others, the focus is on teaching. The same variability occurs in departments within an institution. These comparisons are essential to a full understanding of the complexity and diversity of the universe of American higher education institutions. Those who work for those institutions take the complexity and diversity for granted. Many outside higher education still labor under the illusion that all colleges and universities have a single purpose: to teach.

If the JCAR faculty activity protocols have a fault, it is that they are too simple; they lack the richness and texture needed to be a useful management tool; the workload variables examined are limited in scope and number, and the analysis does not address individual faculty activity. However, that was not their intended use. Indeed, the inherent simplicities in the JCAR conventions and their lack of utility as management tools were underscored repeatedly in the deliberations of the technical work groups developing them. The limitations were further underscored during the pilot testing of the reporting conventions, as will be described later in this chapter.

I was a member of a technical work group, and I directed the national pilot study of the reporting conventions. The information I gleaned from both of those roles helped refine the framework for the development of other, different analytical frameworks with academic and institutional management emphases that will be discussed in the remaining chapters of this book.

My group—the JCAR Technical Work Group on Faculty Activity—acknowledged at the outset that any sort of retrospective, self-reported collection of data on faculty activity would lack the level of credibility that was the intended by-product of this exercise. As noted earlier, reports that contain faculty self-reported percentages of time spent in various categories of activity are simply not believed by legislators and parents who hear complaints that students cannot get the courses required for graduation or that their courses are staffed largely by inexperienced graduate teaching assistants. The task at hand, then, was to come up with a more credible set of measures.

The group decided to focus on what faculty *are assigned* to do. At most colleges and universities, faculty meet with deans or department chairs at the beginning of the academic year to map out a plan of activity for each faculty member for the next contractual year. In looking at faculty assignments, the work group was arguing for a prospective view of faculty activity rather than a retrospective one. Although faculty memories may be somewhat flawed in recalling activity during the preceding twelve months, the activity plan for the upcoming twelve months was a concept on which both faculty and the dean or department chair could agree. Implicit in the accountability thrust is the notion that academic managers (deans and department chairs) will actively enforce the workload agreements with faculty and that those faculty will, by and large, hold up their end of the bargain as well. How then can data be captured on what faculty are assigned to do?

The JCAR protocol for measuring faculty activity focuses on what faculty are expected to do as part of their base or contractual obligation. Overload activity that is done for supplemental payment is not to be included. The population of faculty under analysis is that defined by the American Association of University Professors (AAUP). This is an important underpinning in the discussion—it gives precision to the generic term *faculty,* which is all too often bandied about in productivity discussions without regard to who falls under that rubric. Here I mean by the term *faculty* the full-time and permanent part-time staff whose regular assignment is instruction, including those with released time for research. Faculty whose regular, full-time assignment is exclusively research are also counted, as are faculty on sabbatical leave. Replacements for faculty on leave *with* pay should not be reported, whereas replacements for those on leave *without* pay should be. Finally, department chairs with faculty rank and no other administrative title such as dean or provost should be included as well. These definitions are important, as the JCAR initiative is the first major national attempt at applying some precision and consistency to what we mean by the term *faculty* for analytical purposes.

JCAR attempted similar precision in defining the components of faculty work. Although the terms *teaching, research,* and *service* are freely used in higher education publications, what is really meant by *teaching?* Is it time spent in the classroom? Does it embrace lesson preparation and academic advising? The same ambiguity applies to research and service, in the absence of specifically defined parameters. It is useful to cite the JCAR definitions, as taken from *JCAR Faculty Assignment Reporting* (pp. 6–7), for the components of faculty activity, as they will be recurring themes throughout the remainder of this book:

Teaching—includes the direct delivery of instruction, as well as those activities supporting the teaching-learning process. Examples of direct delivery of instruction are lectures, seminars, directed study, laboratory session, clinical or student teaching supervision, and field-placement supervision. Activities directly supporting teaching include class preparation, evaluation of student work, curriculum development, supervision of graduate student research, including thesis or dissertation, academic and career advising, faculty training, and mentoring. Professional development geared to increasing faculty effectiveness in the foregoing activities would also be included.

Research or scholarship—includes an array of activities such as conducting experimental or scholarly research, developing creative works, preparing or reviewing articles or books, preparing and reviewing proposals for external funding, performing or exhibiting works in the fine and applied arts, and attending professional meetings or conferences essential to remaining current in one's field.

Service—draws on the professional or academic expertise of a faculty member and includes work within the campus community and outside the campus. Departmental and campus service includes work on various committees (for example, governance, recruitment) and department administration. Community or public service includes consulting, giving speeches, and working in organizations or on committees related to a faculty member's academic field.

Although the JCAR definitions are not exhaustive, and although some activities may not fall neatly into one of the three categories, the constructs of teaching, research, and service now have considerably more structure and definition. For further and more detailed descriptions of faculty activities, please see *An Introduction to Faculty Workloads*, published by the American Association of State Colleges and Universities.

A First Cut at Measuring Faculty Activity

The JCAR Technical Work Group on Faculty Activity determined that the most useful way to approach measurement of what faculty are assigned to do would be to express that activity in some tangible unit of measurement. Prior faculty studies have typically characterized faculty activity in terms of percentages of time spent in given functional areas. Units such as "50 percent" or "75 percent" may be accurate, but they lack relevance for someone outside higher education seeking an understanding of what—and how much—faculty are assigned to do. The JCAR protocols represent a first step in resolving that ambiguity.

The work group introduced the concept of the service month in describing what faculty are assigned to do. According to *JCAR Faculty Assignment Reporting*, a service month is

> a unit of work equivalent to one person working full time for one calendar
> month, and can be allocated by function, i.e., teaching, research, or service.
> For example, a full time 12-month employee with half time responsibility as a
> college's director of institutional research and half time responsibility as a member
> of the mathematics faculty, produces six administrative service months and
> six faculty service months in that year. In the case of those functioning solely

as faculty, service months can be distributed over the three categories of faculty work: teaching, research/scholarship, and service. Consider the full time 9-month faculty member whose *assigned* (not self-reported) responsibilities include 50 percent teaching, 30 percent research, and 20 percent service. The service months for that individual would be distributed as follows: 4.5 months in teaching (i.e., 9 months multiplied by 50 percent); 2.7 months in research (i.e., 9 months multiplied by 30 percent); and 1.8 months in service activity (i.e., 9 months multiplied by 20 percent). [p. 7]

The service month is not synonymous with a calendar month. Although a service month of service activity might well take place entirely within the calendar month of January, for example, it might just as easily reflect thirty days of research activity spread out over several calendar months. Reporting faculty activity in terms of service months, as opposed to the traditional percentage-of-time metric, provides a more tangible assessment of how faculty are expected to spend their time during the academic year. To say that a faculty member spends 50 percent of his or her time teaching does not convey a sense of how much time that represents. Is it 50 percent of an eight-hour day or 50 percent of a forty-hour week? If I know that a faculty member generates 4.5 service months from teaching, I can easily translate that into roughly 135 days out of the work year devoted exclusively to teaching activity.

The service month is the first nationally standardized *output* measure of faculty activity. Although it is purely quantitative and in no way speaks to the quality of what faculty do, it is nonetheless a step forward in that it provides a consistent, concrete measure of the volume of faculty activity at a given institution. That said, it is still a limited measure. It represents only how much time is to be spent in various functional activities as part of a faculty member's contractual assignment in terms that anyone can readily understand. It does not speak to outcomes, that is, *products* of those activities. It does, however, make clear to those outside the academy that there is a clear expectation on the part of both the faculty member *and* academic management that the scope of faculty duties will embrace more than instruction. Clarity on this point is important in helping parents, legislators, and others come to terms with the reality of faculty life, as opposed to the traditional perception of faculty members as simply teachers.

By adding three variables, the JCAR technical work group developed a useful way of expressing faculty activity to those outside higher education. Once again, citing from *JCAR Faculty Assignment Reporting:*

• *Contract month*—is the number of calendar months of an individual's appointment. A nine-month calendar "year" is typical for most faculty (although work may well continue through the summer, and this issue will be addressed), and this is equivalent to nine contract months. Although formal, written contracts are not unusual, use of the term *contract* in this and other key phrases in the JCAR protocols is not meant to require the existence of a written contract in order to adopt the methodology (p. 8).

• *Contract percent time*—is the proportion of faculty appointment (relative to full-time appointment) associated with a particular set of contract months. A faculty member funded 100 percent time for nine months, but holding a half-time administrative appointment working for the admissions office, would be 50 percent-time as a faculty member for nine months. Institutions will generally find the contract percent time included in their human resources database (p. 8).

• *Percent time allocated to teaching, research-scholarship, and service*—is the proportional assignment of faculty activity and will total 100 percent (p. 8). Note that this is the prospective allocation of faculty time that serves as the basis for the workload agreement between a faculty member and his or her chair or dean. It is not a hazy recollection of time spent but the framework on which an academic year's work is constructed.

How do these variables come together in an intelligible reporting format to those outside academe? Suppose we wished to report assigned faculty activity for the Biology Department and the Sociology Department at a small, research-oriented institution. Although the JCAR conventions are not intended for reporting the activities of *individual* faculty but for reporting faculty activity at various institutional levels of aggregation, the only way to get to those aggregations is to examine individual faculty records. JCAR notes that, formally or informally, faculty and department chairs achieve agreement at the beginning of the faculty year as to the distribution of the faculty member's efforts between and among teaching, research, and service in the coming academic year. Table 2.1 displays the agreed-on distributions for faculty members in our hypothetical departments.

The table contains the essential elements for reporting assigned faculty activity and is the template recommended by JCAR for collecting baseline data. The table includes contract months (Column C), contract percent time (Column D), and percent time allocated to each of the major activity functions (Columns E, F, and G). These are the critical data elements needed to calculate the work, in the form of service months, that an individual, department, or institution is dedicating to teaching, research, and service, respectively, during the forthcoming academic year.

To calculate the respective categories of service months for each faculty member, the number of contract months (Column C) is multiplied by the contract percent time (Column D) to determine the number of months that the individual is

TABLE 2.1. DEPARTMENTAL REPRESENTATIONS OF FACULTY ACTIVITY USING JCAR PROTOCOLS.

A	B	C	D	E	F	G	H	I	J	K
			Contract	Percent Time Allocated to			Service Months Generated in			Total
Department or Program	Faculty Name	Contract Months	Percent Time	Teaching	Research	Service	Teaching	Research	Service	Service Months
Biology	Smith	9	100%	50.0%	37.5%	12.5%	4.50	3.38	1.13	9.00
	Jones	9	100%	50.0%	25.0%	25.0%	4.50	2.25	2.25	9.00
	Brown	9	100%	62.5%	25.0%	12.5%	5.63	2.25	1.13	9.00
	White	9	100%	62.5%	25.0%	12.5%	5.63	2.25	1.13	9.00
	Black	9	60%	100.0%	0.0%	0.0%	5.40	0.00	0.00	5.40
	Johnson	9	100%	0.0%	100.0%	0.0%	0.00	9.00	0.00	9.00
	Adams	9	95%	70.0%	10.0%	20.0%	5.99	0.86	1.71	8.55
	Biology Subtotal						**31.64**	**19.98**	**7.34**	**58.95**
Sociology	Wilson	9	100%	50.0%	25.0%	24.0%	4.50	2.25	2.25	9.00
	McCabe	9	100%	62.5%	25.0%	12.5%	5.63	2.25	1.13	9.00
	Davis	12	100%	40.0%	20.0%	40.0%	4.80	2.40	4.80	12.00
	Sociology Subtotal						**14.93**	**6.90**	**8.18**	**30.00**

Source: JCAR Faculty Assignment Reporting, 1997, p. 10.

obligated to work. Then this figure is multiplied by the percent time allocated to teaching (Column E) to arrive at teaching service months; by the percent time allocated to research (Column F) to arrive at research service months; and percent time allocated to service (Column G) to arrive at public service service months.

Individual faculty members, even within the same department, work with different expectations during a given academic year. Some faculty have contracts or grants that legally obligate them to activities other than teaching. And although JCAR conventions caution against focusing on an individual faculty member, understanding what they are expected to do is critical to describing the overall faculty activity within an academic department or institution.

Specific examples are illustrated in Table 2.1. Looking first at the Biology Department, and specifically at Professor Smith, she is on a full-time (100 percent), nine-month contract. At most colleges and universities, the nine-month contract is the standard, although in many departments, typically in agriculture and other departments associated with research and extension activity, ten- or twelve-month contracts are not uncommon.

Professor Smith's assigned activity for the coming year is 50 percent time in teaching, 37.5 percent time in research, and 12.5 percent time in service activity. Using the protocol just described, Smith's 9 contract months is multiplied by contract percent time (100 percent) and by the percent time allocated to teaching, resulting in 4.5 teaching service months.

Repeating the protocol for research, Smith's 9 contract months are multiplied by 100 percent contract time and again multiplied by 37.5 percent time allocated to research, resulting in 3.38 research service months. Similarly, Smith's 9 contract months multiplied by 100 percent contract time, and again multiplied by 12.5 percent time allocation to service, results in 1.13 service months dedicated to service activity.

All other faculty in biology have similar calculations in generating service months, with the exceptions of Professors Black and Adams. Black's contract time is 60 percent, signaling that he is a part-time faculty member. Because most part-time faculty are not expected to do research, Black is 100 percent allocated to teaching activity. Thus the calculation for Black is as follows: 9 contract months multiplied by 60 percent contract time, multiplied by 100 percent time allocation to teaching, resulting in 5.4 teaching service months generated. Professor Adams has an arrangement with the department wherein he works less than full time; his contract percent time is 95 percent. As a de facto part-time faculty member, however, he carries time allocation assignments that are substantially different from Professor Black. Adams generates 5.99 teaching service months (9 contract months multiplied by 95 percent contract time multiplied by 70 percent time allocation to teaching). He generated 0.86 research service months (9 contract months multiplied by 95 percent contract time multiplied by 10 percent time allocation to research), and 1.71 service months in service activity (9 contract months multiplied by 95 percent contract time multiplied by 20 percent time allocation to service).

Faculty in the Sociology Department are similar to those in biology except for Professor Davis, who is on a twelve-month contract. The protocol operates in the same fashion as nine-month contracts. She generates 5.0 teaching service months (12 contract months multiplied by 100 percent contract time multiplied by 40 percent time allocation to teaching). She also generates 2.4 research service months (12 contract months multiplied by 100 percent contract time multiplied by 20 percent time allocation in research) and 4.8 service months of service activity (12 contract months multiplied by 100 percent contract time multiplied by 40 percent time allocated to service).

As noted earlier, the focus of the JCAR reporting protocols is not the individual faculty member but the appropriate levels of aggregation within the institution. For example, the summary data from Table 2.2 can be used to compare service months generated by departments at an institution with comparable departments at other institutions.

It is useful for colleges and universities discussing faculty activity and productivity to be able to talk with external constituencies in terms other than "percentage of time spent in various activities." It is a far more tangible and concrete metric to say that "our faculty in biology and sociology will collectively spend roughly forty-seven months in teaching, twenty-seven months in research activity, and fifteen months in service during the coming year." To say that faculty spend 50 percent of their time in teaching begs the question, 50 percent of what?, whereas the service month convention clearly illustrates 46.57 teaching service months out of a total of 88.97 service months of faculty activity generated.

TABLE 2.2. FACULTY WORKLOAD ASSIGNMENTS BY DEPARTMENT OR PROGRAM.

Department or Program	Service Months			Total
	Teaching	Research	Service	
Biology	31.64	19.98	7.34	58.96
Sociology	14.93	6.90	8.18	30.01
Total	46.57	26.88	15.52	88.97
Percent of Total	52.4%	30.2%	17.4%	100.0%

Source: JCAR Faculty Assignment Reporting, 1997, p. 13.

Rolled up to the institutional level of aggregation, the data can be graphically arrayed, as in Figure 2.1.

Using institutional summary data such as those depicted in the figure, it is possible to compare and contrast the missions of real colleges and universities in terms of the service months generated in teaching, research, and service. Baccalaureate and comprehensive institutions will show heavier faculty activity in teaching than in research or service. The research component will take on greater emphasis in doctorate-granting universities and will move toward maximum values in research universities. The service component will show its greatest emphasis among land grant universities.

Again clear communication of the fact that faculty are expected to engage in activity other than instruction is critical to helping those outside higher education to embrace the full scope of faculty *activity* as a prelude to understanding the full range of faculty *productivity*.

Who Is Teaching What to Whom?

In talking about communicating with external publics, it is essential to provide guidance on the controversial question of who is in the classroom. Within the area of instruction, the JCAR Technical Work Group on Faculty Activity looked at

FIGURE 2.1. FACULTY ACTIVITY ASSIGNMENTS: INSTITUTIONAL SUMMARY.

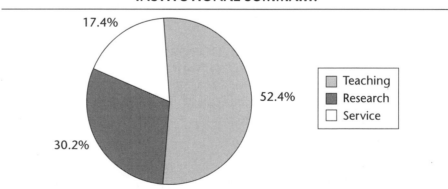

Source: JCAR Faculty Assignment Reporting, 1997, p. 13.

ways to respond to the contention that students—particularly freshmen and sophomores—are being taught by people other than regular faculty.

The group addressed the issue by assessing student credit hour generation by various categories of faculty. The first step was to clarify what is meant by *faculty*. In looking at faculty activity in the preceding sections, the standard AAUP definition was used: faculty are full-time and permanent part-time employees. It is obvious that this definition is not sufficient for examining who is teaching at a college or university. At most large, complex institutions, especially where graduate programs are present, it is common to have adjunct faculty and graduate students teaching classes, especially at the undergraduate level. Consequently, in addressing the question of who is teaching what to whom, the components of "faculty" need to be expanded. Specifically, the work group focused on the following categories: regular faculty, temporary faculty, and teaching assistants.

Regular faculty are classified, for purposes of analysis, as those in tenured or tenure-track positions and those in recurring, non-tenure-track positions. There has been a growing concern in recent years, particularly among faculty unions, that permanent, nontenured faculty are a growing "second class" of faculty, upon whom institutions increasingly rely for teaching due to lower personnel costs. It was important that the JCAR protocol provide a means for testing this hypothesis. The following definitions of the four categories of faculty are taken from *JCAR Faculty Assignment Reporting:*

• *Tenured and tenure-track faculty*—include tenured faculty and those eligible for tenure after a probationary period at the reporting institution. This category would also include administrators who hold tenured positions at the institution (for example, presidents, provosts, deans) and who also teach courses (p. 14).

• *Recurring non-tenure-track faculty*—may include instructors, lecturers, multiple-year, limited-term appointments, full-time one-year appointments such as visiting replacements for faculty on leave, which may or may not be renewed, or permanent part-time teaching personnel, so long as the criterion of recurring contract arrangement is met (p. 15).

• *Temporary faculty*—individuals with nonrecurring, limited-term appointments, or nontenured individuals whose primary institutional responsibility is other than teaching, research or scholarship, and service. These faculty usually include part-time, adjunct faculty, *nontenured* administrators who teach, and contributed service personnel (p.15).

• *Teaching assistants*—students at the institution who are listed as the instructor of record for a credit course. This reporting convention does not include graduate research assistants or teaching assistants who are not instructors of record (p.15).

Credit-bearing courses offered at a college or university are arrayed by level of instruction as follows, once again according to the *JCAR Technical Manual:*

- *Precollege instruction*—college or university courses usually referred to as developmental or remedial, which may be taken for credit but do not count toward graduation. These courses are intended to help students achieve an appropriate level of college preparedness, especially in the basic areas of reading, writing, and mathematics (p.15).
- *Lower-division instruction*—courses typically associated with the freshman and sophomore years of college study (p.15).
- *Upper-division courses*—courses typically associated with the junior and senior year of study (p.15).
- *Graduate-level instruction*—courses offered as part of postbaccalaureate programs of study (p.15).

The units of analysis in this reporting protocol are student credit hours generated by each category of faculty in courses at the various levels of instruction. After lengthy debate and discussion, the work group determined that the *student credit hour* is the most stable and consistent expression of teaching activity across institutions. The equivalent of a Carnegie course unit, the student credit hour represents a unit of achievement earned by a student for the successful completion of course requirements. Total student credit hour generation is a function of the credit value of the course multiplied by the enrollment.

In thinking about faculty accountability and productivity with regard to teaching activity, the group briefly considered the "student contact hour." It readily became apparent, however, that the notion of a contact hour has little stability and consistency across departments at a given institution, let alone across institutional boundaries. For example, a three-credit course in history generally implies three hours of instruction (contact hours) per week, or forty-five contact hours over the course of a fifteen-week term. But a three-credit course in clinical nursing or music performance, because of the individual supervision required, can easily approach twelve to fifteen contact hours per week. The group found this type of variation across the disciplines at virtually all institutions, from research universities to community colleges. However, the three-credit-hour course in history, with twelve students enrolled, generates the same thirty-six student credit hours as a three-credit-hour nursing course with twelve students, whether at a major land grant university or the local community college. Stability in metrics is critical to any analysis that involves comparisons across units or institutions.

Table 2.3 shows four views of student credit hour generation by a hypothetical academic department, using the JCAR reporting protocols. The first view simply

TABLE 2.3. FOUR VIEWS OF STUDENT CREDIT HOUR GENERATION USING JCAR PROTOCOLS.

Student Credit Hour Distribution

	Precollege	Lower Division	Upper Division	Graduate	Total
Permanent Faculty					
Regular tenured and tenure-track	0	750	900	825	2,475
Other regular faculty	0	1,250	525	150	1,925
Temporary faculty	250	500	50	0	800
Teaching assistants	300	450	0	0	750
Total	550	2950	1475	975	5950

Percent Distribution of Total Student Credit Hours Taught

	Precollege	Lower Division	Upper Division	Graduate	Total
Permanent Faculty					
Regular tenured and tenure-track	0.0%	12.6%	15.1%	13.9%	41.6%
Other regular faculty	0.0%	21.0%	8.8%	2.5%	32.4%
Temporary faculty	4.2%	8.4%	0.8%	0.0%	13.4%
Teaching assistants	5.0%	7.6%	0.0%	0.0%	12.6%
Total	9.2%	49.6%	24.8%	16.4%	100.0%

Percent Distribution of Total Student Credit Hours by Faculty Category

	Precollege	Lower Division	Upper Division	Graduate	Total
Permanent faculty					
Regular tenured and tenure-track	0.0%	30.3%	36.4%	33.3%	100.0%
Other regular faculty	0.0%	64.9%	27.3%	7.8%	100.0%
Temporary faculty	31.3%	62.5%	6.3%	0.0%	100.0%
Teaching assistants	40.0%	60.0%	0.0%	0.0%	100.0%
Total	9.2%	49.6%	24.8%	16.4%	100.0%

Percent Distribution of Total Student Credit Hours by Course Level

	Precollege	Lower Division	Upper Division	Graduate	Total
Permanent faculty					
Regular tenured and tenure-track	0.0%	25.4%	61.0%	84.6%	41.6%
Other regular faculty	0.0%	42.4%	35.6%	15.4%	32.4%
Temporary faculty	45.5%	16.9%	3.4%	0.0%	13.4%
Teaching assistants	54.5%	15.3%	0.0%	0.0%	12.6%
Total	100.0%	100.0%	100.0%	100.0%	100.0%

displays the volume of student credit hours generated by each category of faculty at each level of instruction. If we look at the numbers alone, it is evident that lower-division instruction is done largely by other than tenured or tenure-track faculty; tenured and tenure-track faculty generate the majority of upper-division and graduate student credit hours. This sort of view is useful for a quick sense of what a department is doing in the way of student credit hour generation, but the remaining three views provide a texture and context that the raw numbers alone cannot do.

For example, the second view, "Percent Distribution of Total Student Credit Hours Taught," examines each cell in the matrix as a numerator for the total 5,950 student credit hours taught in the department. Consequently, we know that of all the student credit hours generated by this academic unit, the largest proportion—21.0 percent—were generated by nontenured faculty teaching lower-division courses, followed by 15.1 percent generated by tenured and tenure-track faculty in upper-division courses, 13.9 percent by tenured and tenure-track faculty in graduate courses, and so on. If the concern is which faculty are teaching freshmen and sophomores, this display gives an instant answer.

The third view, "Percent Distribution of Total Student Credit Hours by Faculty Category," examines what each category of faculty teach. For example, of all the student credit hours taught by tenured and tenure-track faculty in this unit, 66.7% are taught at the undergraduate level—30.3 percent at lower division and 36.4 percent at upper division. Nontenured regular faculty, however, do virtually all (92.2 percent) of their teaching at the undergraduate level—64.9 percent at lower division and 27.3 percent at upper division.

The fourth and final view, "Percent Distribution of Total Student Credit Hours by Course Level," provides still more information. Of all the lower-division student credit hours generated by this academic unit, 42.4 percent are produced by nontenured, regular faculty. Tenured and tenure-track faculty, however, produce 61.0 percent of all upper-division student credit hours and 84.6 percent of all graduate student credit hours. Using student credit hours as the currency to measure instructional activity, the JCAR reporting protocols provide a useful response to the question, Who is teaching what to whom?

The most important facet of JCAR faculty activity reporting conventions, aside from their simplicity and straightforward presentation to those outside higher education, is that the measures will be tied to other outcomes defined within the overall JCAR framework. Assigned faculty activity, most especially instruction, should be viewed as it contributes to persistence and graduation rates at an institution. The same relationship with faculty activity holds true for postgraduation outcomes of students, whether being placed in a career-related field, passing a licensing exam, or moving on to graduate school. The JCAR framework provides a context for thinking about what faculty do, as it relates to what happened to the students who come into contact with them.

Shortcomings of the JCAR Conventions

The obvious shortcoming in the JCAR reporting conventions, as they relate to other portions of the JCAR framework, is that while JCAR talks about assigned faculty activity in research and public service, it is silent on any outcomes measures that might assess faculty productivity in that area. That does not preclude institutions from developing their own outcomes measures. However, because they are intended for non-higher-education consumers, such measures should have the same simplicity as the JCAR instructional outcomes. And real research and service outcomes measures can be used for internal management purposes. These will be fully described in Chapter Six.

With respect to the faculty activity reporting conventions, much was learned from the pilot testing that took place during the 1996–97 academic year, for which I served as director. The pilot study involved nine institutions ranging from a small, rural community college to a major, land grant research university. Virtually every Carnegie institution type was covered, and the operational settings of the institutions were diverse.

Not surprisingly, because the JCAR faculty activity reporting conventions are simple, they worked best in institutions that were the least complex. Community colleges found the protocols easiest to apply, although each and every one of the institutions successfully developed a reporting format firmly rooted in the JCAR methodology. Larger, more complex research institutions expressed serious concern over the JCAR format's capacity to accurately and realistically deal with faculty work during summer months. Although faculty are normally *assigned* activity over a nine-month academic year (consistent with the JCAR framework), these institutions argue that academic managers *expect* that faculty activity will occur over a full, twelve-month calendar year. That expected activity may or may not be compensated by the institution, but according to these pilot sites it nonetheless constitutes a portion of faculty activity and workload that would fall through the cracks using JCAR. Institutions facing this dilemma might consider modifying the JCAR conventions to include summer. However, they would lose comparability with institutions that do not have significant summer activity. In comparing faculty work among like institutions, this is not problematic; it is a major difficulty when analyzing across Carnegie institution types.

Similarly, there was genuine concern among unionized campuses that the JCAR methodology would be relatively meaningless at those institutions to the extent that JCAR conventions vary from the terms and definitions in contracts. Although the pilot study did not reveal overt manifestations of this concern, it would be irresponsible to suggest that such sentiments will not surface. Similarly, those institutions operating in public state systems with long-entrenched reporting methodologies indicated a general lack of enthusiasm for modifying those systems to accommodate JCAR, particularly when those systems underpin a reasonable level of state funding. It should again be underscored that JCAR is neither a tool for monitoring and enforcing a union contract nor a framework for formula funding. Rather it is a descriptive tool intended to provide an uncomplicated view of what faculty do and what some of the outcomes from that activity are, for persons not intimately familiar with the internal machinations of a college or university. It is a response to a demand for accountability, and institutions that appear to be unresponsive to those external demands, particularly as they emanate from parents and legislators, do so at their own peril.

With those concerns acknowledged, it is still important to highlight and underscore JCAR's significance. All four of the JCAR technical work groups attempted to arrive at consistent and credible definitions that dealt primarily with products and outcomes as opposed to inputs and processes. They attempted to develop measures of productivity, albeit simple in nature, that would provide some assessment of higher education accountability to those outside the academy, particularly parents and legislators. The State of Louisiana found the JCAR work sufficiently credible that they adopted it into their discussions of performance measures.

Summary

Public pressure for greater accountability in colleges and universities and better information on faculty productivity has not always resulted in useful reporting conventions. Indeed, many of the so-called performance measures do not measure faculty productivity—or any other sort of productivity in higher education.

Sensing the potential for a highly politicized round of college bashing under the rubric of "greater accountability," the major higher education associations in Washington created JCAR, which has been a refreshing and realistic departure from earlier attempts to explain what faculty do and how well they do it. JCAR combines measures for describing faculty assignments during an academic year, with baseline output measures of faculty activity—student credit hour production, student retention and graduation rates, postgraduation job placement, and professional licensure pass rates.

The JCAR measures are not perfect, but they do represent a significant departure from past practice. Although at long last it began dealing with output measures, JCAR also attempted to clarify discussions of faculty activity. The commission deliberately avoided policy statements involving discussions about full-time equivalent (FTE) students or FTE faculty. The concept of full-time equivalency, which will be discussed in detail in subsequent chapters, is a useful managerial construct, but it can appear to be a tool of obfuscation to someone outside higher education. If a nine-month contract is the norm, it is difficult to grasp the notion that the faculty member who works a summer overload is 1.33 FTE; that appears to be more than one full-time employee.

JCAR provides tangible measures for discussing the higher education enterprise. The service month construct may initially seem somewhat awkward and unfamiliar but once digested is a useful measure of how much work faculty can be expected to generate in teaching, research, and service during an academic year. It is fundamentally an input measure but when coupled with the other output measures in the full JCAR repertoire, it is a vital component in a strategy for explaining what colleges do to those outside higher education. The student credit hour generation matrix model for explaining who is teaching what to whom also represents a concrete and largely understandable measure for talking with external publics.

JCAR has opened the door for thinking about new paradigms for describing faculty productivity. It effectively uses basic output measures to describe higher education productivity to external publics. If it has limitations, however, they stem from its intended purpose, that is, to serve as a descriptive tool rather than a management tool. As a descriptive tool it satisfies certain basic requirements for describing faculty productivity. But it is not exhaustive. For example, it measures instructional activity solely in terms of student credit hour production. It overlooks instruction in zero-credit classes. It understates faculty consultation, both as dissertation and thesis supervisors and as academic advisers. Although the service month convention provides a useful quantitative measure of faculty work in teaching, research, and service, it does not describe the products of that work in any extensive way.

The JCAR Technical Work Group of Faculty Assignment Reporting was, however, quite candid in acknowledging the limitations of their reporting conventions. Indeed, in Appendix A of their technical manual, they reference another reporting tool—the National Study of Instructional Costs and Productivity— more commonly known as the Delaware Study, as providing the substance and detail for management purposes that the JCAR conventions lack. The Delaware Study is a useful starting point for thinking about comparative benchmarks for faculty productivity and is the focus of Chapter Five.

The next two chapters describe institutional strategies for building broadly accepted internal management databases with respect to faculty activity, as a prelude to the national inter-institutional comparisons that characterize the Delaware Study. Chapter Three examines a quantitative approach to measuring productivity; Chapter Four looks at qualitative dimensions.

CHAPTER THREE

A QUANTITATIVE PERSPECTIVE ON PRODUCTIVITY AND ACCOUNTABILITY

Two central issues have been established thus far: (1) there is a demand for accountability in higher education and (2) in order to gain accountability, particularly at a time when faculty roles are changing, better performance measures are needed.

In the Preface I cited Henry Rosovsky's words decrying the fact that deans have only the vaguest notion of what faculty do and that the make-up of the faculty workload has changed over the years without the active involvement of the deanery. Ernest Boyer, quoted in Chapter One, underscored the major place that research and service have in addition to (and sometimes in place of) teaching in a faculty member's work life.

If in fact the nature of faculty work has been in a state of flux over the past forty years, and senior academic management has either been unaware of it or incapable of directing it, there is a compelling need for better management information (data) to provide the essential direction. At the same time that an internal transformation in the nature and scope of faculty work was taking place within colleges and universities, external dissatisfaction with higher education became more vocal.

Chapter Two examined the initial public response to both issues. The reporting conventions developed by the Joint Commission on Accountability Reporting (JCAR) were designed to describe what faculty are assigned to do in a given academic year and to relate that activity to selected student outcomes. The JCAR conventions also prescribe a consistent framework for reporting mandatory tuition and fees, room and board, and other student expense data. Although these conventions describe the *price* paid to attend college, they do not address the *cost* of delivering that college education. In short, there is no clearly defined relationship between the activity that occurs at an institution and the expenditures associated with that activity.

That relationship has been at the core of criticism of higher education and in 1997 was the focus of a congressionally mandated examination of the cost of higher education. The Report of the National Commission on Higher Education will be described in detail later in this book. It is important to underscore here, however, that a framework is needed to tie instructional activity in some meaningful way to expenditure data. That framework is the focus of this chapter.

The JCAR Framework

The JCAR initiative was laudable in that it provided a concrete framework for responding to public concerns about accountability. It does a reasonable job of what it was intended to do, that is, communicate with those outside higher education. And it does attempt to talk in terms of productivity (student outcomes) rather than focus solely on input measures.

But JCAR is limited. In tying faculty activity in general and instructional activity in particular to student outcomes alone, JCAR paints a helpful but incomplete picture of faculty productivity. Certainly student retention and graduation, as well as postgraduation opportunities for employment or graduate school, are tied to the content knowledge acquired from a college or university education—in other words, to faculty instruction. But if faculty are also engaged in research and public service activity, what are the outcomes of those functions? Do they justify time spent away from the classroom? JCAR is silent on these questions that are integral to a full understanding of what faculty do.

Similarly, the JCAR student credit hour analysis of instructional activity—a helpful first effort to describe which types of faculty teach at which instructional levels—also produces an incomplete picture. Those who work in higher education know that a significant amount of teaching occurs in organized class sections that do not carry teaching credit. Many laboratory, recitation, and discussion sections that are required components of a course, along with the credit-bearing lecture section, are common features of course offerings at most colleges and universities. And because they do not generate student credit hours, they are omitted from the JCAR analysis. The same holds true for many forms of master's thesis and dissertation supervision.

A New Framework

The purpose of this chapter is to build a quantitative framework that (1) provides the information and data that deans and department chairs require to effectively manage instructional, personnel, and fiscal resources and (2) addresses the apparent gaps in the JCAR method in a fashion that allows the information to be used not only for internal management purposes but to portray a more complete picture of faculty productivity to those outside higher education.

The following pages examine strategies for measuring teaching, research, and service activity, first quantitatively and then qualitatively. The discussion of the analytical framework will address data issues, but one need not be an institutional research analyst to appreciate the information that the framework will yield. A thorough understanding of the data constructs in the framework ensures an awareness of the inherent strengths and limitations.

Measuring Teaching Activity

The fundamental question here is, Who is teaching what to whom? I have taught hundreds of workshops over the past decade on the subject of building a consistent and reliable teaching-workload database. Invariably, in talking with workshop participants, "staff" is the busiest faculty member on most campuses; staff teaches significant numbers of courses in virtually every discipline. It is one thing to open a term with "staff" as the instructor of record for a course. Sections are often added at the last moment, and regular or adjunct faculty have to be identified to teach them. It is an altogether different story when "staff" is still listed as instructor of record at the end of the term. Yet this is all too often the case at many institutions, underscoring Henry Rosovsky's claim that management does, in fact, have only the vaguest notion of what individual faculty members do. That claim has been reinforced to me in virtually every one of those aforementioned workshops. The simple fact is that higher education institutions, governed as they are in a collegial fashion, have not been pressed for management data that would hold them accountable for their use of personnel and fiscal resources or for data that would provide useful information on institutional productivity. The case has clearly been established in the first two chapters that those days of ambiguous, nonresponsive data are a thing of the past.

It should be a fairly straightforward proposition to populate Exhibit 3.1 for any department within an institution or for the institution in aggregate.

It is not unreasonable to ask a department chair how many student credit hours and class sections are taught by tenured and tenure-eligible faculty, that is,

EXHIBIT 3.1. STUDENT CREDIT HOURS AND
ORGANIZED CLASS SECTIONS TAUGHT, BY CATEGORY OF FACULTY.

	Student Credit Hours			Organized Class Sections		
Taught by	Lower Division	Upper Division	Graduate	Lower Division	Upper Division	Graduate
Tenured or tenure-track faculty FTE _____						
Permanent nontenurable faculty FTE _____						
Supplemental faculty FTE _____						
Graduate teaching assistants FTE _____						

those in whom the institution has the greatest long-term investment. How many student credit hours and class sections are taught by permanent faculty who are not eligible for tenure? How many are taught by adjunct faculty or administrators and professional staff with primary job obligations other than teaching? How many are taught by graduate students functioning as teaching assistants? The same questions might be further refined to ask how much of the undergraduate teaching activity was directed primarily at freshmen and sophomores (lower-division instruction), how much at juniors and seniors (upper-division instruction), and how much of the teaching was graduate instruction? That higher education has not answered these questions is evidenced by the avalanche of criticism in recent years. As noted earlier, common practice at many colleges and universities suggests that Exhibit 3.1 should have a fifth row for "staff," and that row would be heavily populated.

How can Exhibit 3.1 be populated with data that accurately reflect teaching activity in a department or program? As I suggested in the Preface, the prime motivation for obtaining accurate data is that the information be used in policy decisions, especially decisions related to resource allocation and reallocation. The framework proposed in this chapter for describing teaching activity must then satisfy those motivations by yielding information that describes instructional productivity but that also addresses costs and other considerations that flow into personnel and fiscal resource allocation and reallocation decisions.

In order to report accurate data on teaching activity—data that truly reflect how much faculty teach and whom they are teaching, as well as provide information that can be used for academic planning and management—a framework for developing those data is needed. That framework must be assembled from the level of the academic department or program. It is there that the department chair or program director has the most reliable information on who is teaching what to whom. From the department or program level, data can then be aggregated up to the larger units (schools, colleges) and to the institutionwide (college or university) level.

Defining *Faculty*

Construction of the framework begins with definitions. The terms used in this book, although familiar to those in higher education, must be sufficiently clear that they can be understood and used easily by those outside higher education. Because the focus of the book is faculty, the definitions should start there. Who are the faculty? They fall into four basic categories. (Note that these definitions depart from those specified by JCAR in Chapter Two.)

Regular faculty are those individuals who are hired to teach and who may also do research or service. They are characterized by a recurring contractual relationship in which the individual and the institution both assume a continuing appointment. These faculty typically fall into two categories: (1) tenured and tenure-eligible and (2) non-tenure-track.

Tenured and Tenure-Eligible Faculty. These are individuals who either hold tenure or for whom tenure is an expected outcome. At most institutions, these are full, associate, and assistant professors. The JCAR conventions included in this category presidents, provosts, deans, and others who hold tenure at an institution and who teach courses but whose primary function is other than teaching. They did this to display the largest possible number of student credit hours within the tenured faculty category, which was the focus of much of the external criticism.

Within this framework, however, a narrower definition is applied. Specifically, the category includes those individuals whose specific job assignments are made for the principal purpose of conducting instruction, research, and public service and who meet the definition of faculty as stipulated by the National Center for Education Statistics for the Integrated Postsecondary Educational Data System (IPEDS). Although that sounds like technical jargon, when reduced to its basic terms this defines the people usually thought of as faculty—those whose primary job function is teaching, research, and service. If the purpose here is to focus on *faculty* productivity and to generate credible information, it makes little sense to include presidents, provosts, deans, and others—regardless of their tenure status —whose primary function is administration or some other noninstructional activity. Department chairs, whose administrative duties are in support of the instruction function, would be included. The teaching activity of noninstructional personnel who teach are taken into account in this framework but not by including them as tenured faculty.

Non-Tenure-Track Faculty. These individuals teach on a recurring contractual basis, but their academic title or the budget line renders them ineligible for academic tenure. At most institutions, these titles include instructors, lecturers, visiting faculty, and so on. National faculty groups such as the American Association of University Professors (AAUP) and the National Education Association (NEA) argue that these faculty are a growing "second class" in higher education, teaching far greater loads than tenured and tenure-track faculty, with none of the job security or privileges. A worthwhile analytical framework will enable the testing of this hypothesis.

In addition, in two categories of nonrecurring faculty, teaching activity has increasingly become the focus of media and other critics who argue that an institution's regular faculty have become unproductive or nonproductive: (1) supplemental faculty and (2) teaching assistants.

Supplemental Faculty. These faculty are characteristically paid to teach out of a pool of temporary funds. Their appointment is nonrecurring, although the same individual might receive a temporary appointment in successive terms. The key point is that the funding is, by nature, temporary, and there is no expectation of continuing appointment. The category includes adjuncts, administrators, or professional personnel at the institution who teach but whose primary job responsibility is nonfaculty, and contributed service personnel.

Teaching Assistants. Teaching assistants are students at an institution who receive a stipend strictly for teaching activity. The category includes teaching assistants who are instructors of record but may include teaching assistants who function as discussion section leaders, laboratory section leaders, and other types of organized class sections in which instruction takes place but may not carry credit and for which there is no formal instructor of record. Graduate research assistants are *not* included here.

Defining Teaching Activity

What are the appropriate metrics for assessing faculty teaching activity? How are courses best defined and measured? Certainly, the JCAR convention of looking at student credit hour generation is important. But it is not sufficient, for as noted, instruction occurs in many types of classes that carry no credit, hence do not generate student credit hours. To exclude these is to significantly understate teaching activity and associated faculty productivity. Additional definitions are needed for constructing the framework for measuring and describing teaching activity.

First let us be clear about what a *course* is. A course is an instructional activity, identified by academic discipline and number (for example, ENG 110 might be an introductory English course), in which students enroll, typically to earn academic credit applicable to a degree objective. Excluded are noncredit courses such as personal development courses offered through a division of continuing education, but "zero-credit course sections" that are requirements of or prerequisites to degree programs are included; these courses are scheduled, and consume institutional or departmental resources in the same manner as "credit courses." Zero-credit course sections are typically supplements to the credit-bearing lecture portion of a course. Zero-credit sections are frequently listed as laboratory, discussion, or recitation sections in conjunction with the credit-bearing lecture portion of a course.

Other useful definitions are as follows:

Organized class course: A course that is provided principally by means of regularly scheduled classes meeting in classrooms or similar facilities at stated times

Individual instruction course: A course in which instruction is not conducted in regularly scheduled class meetings; includes "readings" or "special topics" courses, "problems" or "research" courses, including dissertation or thesis research, and "individual lesson" courses (typically in music and fine arts)

Course section: A unique group of students that meet at regularly scheduled times with one or more instructors

Course credit: The academic credit value of a course; the value recorded for a student who successfully completes the course

Lower-division instruction: Courses typically associated with the first and second year of college study

Upper-division instruction: Courses typically associated with the third and fourth year of college study

Graduate-level instruction: Courses typically associated with postbaccalaureate study

Student credit hours: The credit value of a course (typically three or four credits) multiplied by the enrollment in the course

Reporting Productivity Data

As noted earlier, construction of the framework for accurately reporting teaching information begins at the department or program level. Table 3.1, which is a portion of an actual departmental teaching roster with fictitious faculty names, illustrates the practical utility of these definitions.

TABLE 3.1. SAMPLE DEPARTMENTAL TEACHING ROSTER FOR SOCIOLOGY.

1	2	3	4	5	6	7	8
Name	Rank and Course(s)	Number of Organized Sections	Tenure/ Credits	Home Department/ Course Type	% Load	Students Enrolled	Student Credit Hours
Thomas Jones	Chairperson		Tenured	Sociology			
	SOC 454	1	3 hours	Lecture	50	9	27
	SOC 964	0	3–12 hours	Supervised study	100	1	3
	Total	1			Total	10	30
Mary Smith	Professor		Tenured	Sociology			
	SOC 201-01	1	3	Lecture	100	246	738
	SOC 201-02	1	0	Recitation	100	35	0
	ANT 203	1	3	Lecture	50	50	150
	Total	3			Total	331	888
William Davis	Professor		Tenured	Sociology			
	CSC 311 Cross-listed with SOC 311		3 hours	Lecture	100	8	24
	SOC 311 Cross-listed with CSC 311	1	3 hours	Lecture	100	38	114
	SOC 327	1	3 hours	Lecture	100	13	39
	SOC 366	0	1–3 hours	Supervised study	100	1	1
	SOC 866	0	1–6 hours	Supervised study	100	1	3
	Total	2			Total	61	181

Name	Rank		Course	Count	Department	Type	Tenure	Hours	%		
Pauline Lee	Associate Professor				Sociology		Tenured				
			PSY601			Lecture		3 hours	100	12	36
			Cross-listed with SOC 601								
			SOC 341	1		Lecture		3 hours	100	37	111
			SOC 401	1		Lecture		3 hours	100	23	69
			SOC 601	1		Lecture		3 hours	100	5	15
			Cross-listed with PSY 601								
			Total	**3**					Total	77	231
Roger Brown	Assistant professor				Sociology		Non-tenure-track				
			SOC 454	1		Lecture		3 hours	50	9	27
			SOC 467	1		Lecture		3 hours	100	7	21
			400 level meets with 600 level								
			SOC 667			Lecture		3 hours	100	1	3
			600 level meets with 400 level								
			SOC 213	1		Lecture		3 hours	100	77	231
			Cross-listed with WOMS 213								
			WOMS 213			Lecture		3 hours	100	21	63
			Cross-listed with SOC 213								
			Total	**2**					Total	115	345
Harry Jefferson	Adjunct				Sociology		Non-tenure-track				
			SOC 201-03	1		Recitation		0 hours	100	40	0
			Total						**Total**	**40**	**0**

The column headings require some clarification. Column numbers have been inserted into the table for ease in reading. Column 2 provides the faculty member's academic rank, where appropriate, and identifies the courses taught, by departmental call letters (for example, SOC) and course number (for example, 454). Column 3 lists the number of organized sections taught. Column 4 provides two pieces of information for each faculty: tenure status, where appropriate, and the credit value of each of the courses taught. Column 5 identifies the home department, that is, the department to which the faculty member's salary is budgeted and also identifies the type of course or section being taught—lecture, laboratory, recitation, discussion, supervised study, and so on. Column 6 reflects what is termed "% load," and this identifies the number of faculty teaching the course. If % load is 100, there is a single faculty teaching. If % load is 50, the course is being team taught by two faculty; if % load is 33, there are three faculty, and so on. These are important data when discussing productivity. If a course is team taught, workload credit must be appropriately apportioned.

Column 7 indicates the number of students enrolled; Column 8 indicates the student credit hours generated, that is, enrollment (Column 7) multiplied by credit value of the course (Column 4). The importance of accurately measuring and reporting teaching load data will become evident in the examples that follow.

A number of nuances in the table are important to accurate reporting of faculty productivity data. Note first that Thomas Jones is chair of the Sociology Department. Because his administrative duties are directed in support of the instruction function, he is included among the tenured faculty in sociology, consistent with the definition and as evidenced in Column 4. Jones is teaching SOC 454, a lecture section, which actually has eighteen students enrolled and generates fifty-four student credit hours. In Jones's case, the value in the "% load" field is 50, which indicates that he is team teaching the course with another faculty member, in this instance, Roger Brown. Consequently, Jones receives half the workload credit—nine students enrolled and twenty-seven student credit hours generated—with Brown receiving the other half. This apportioning of workload credit is especially important when the faculty members who are team teaching are not from the same department. It is important that each department receive an accurate accounting for work done by the faculty they financially support. This will be clear when Mary Smith's teaching load is discussed.

Note that Jones teaches SOC 964, which is dissertation supervision. Because dissertation supervision is essentially directed, independent study that meets at mutually convenient times for the faculty and students, as opposed to a scheduled time, it does not meet the definition of an organized class section and appears in Column 3. One student has registered in this variable credit course (Column 4), in this instance for three credits, and is reflected as three student credit hours generated in Column 8.

Mary Smith's teaching load merits comment. She teaches Sociology 201, Section 01, which is a three-credit, organized class *lecture* section with 246 students enrolled, generating 738 student credit hours. She also teaches Sociology 201, Section 02, which is one of the zero-credit *recitation* sections associated with the credit-bearing portion of the course. It is clearly identified as such, and although it has thirty-five students enrolled who meet at regularly scheduled times, because it carries zero credit it generates no student credit hours. This teaching activity would be lost under the JCAR reporting conventions.

Finally, Professor Smith also team teaches (note that the % load is 50) a course for the Anthropology Department, ANT 203, in which one hundred students are actually enrolled and generating three hundred student credit hours. However, Professor Smith's salary is entirely budgeted to sociology, with no compensation received from anthropology for this course. In order to accurately report faculty productivity, it is important to view teaching activity through an *origin of instructor* lens. Origin of instructor means that all teaching activity is credited to the department to whom the instructor's salary is budgeted, regardless of whether the teaching is being done in the instructor's home department or another. As colleges and universities attempt to encourage more interdisciplinary study and interdepartmental cooperation, it is imperative that workload be apportioned in a fashion consistent with fiscal resource allocation. In the instance of Professor Smith, her salary is clearly budgeted to sociology (Column 5), hence the teaching activity associated with anthropology migrates to sociology. It is doubtful that Professor Smith would have been released from the department paying her salary to teach in another were the workload not appropriately credited.

As important as it is to appropriately credit workload to the correct department, it is equally important not to overstate it. William Davis's teaching illustrates a common practice in higher education—cross-listing courses across two or more departments. In this instance SOC 311, a lecture section staffed and paid for by the Sociology Department, can also be registered for under the Cultural Studies call letters (CSC) and is displayed as CSC 311. Eight students registered for the course as CSC 311, and thirty-eight registered as SOC 311; therefore it meets as a single section and is a single organized class, not two. Because the Sociology Department is paying the instructor's salary, SOC 311 reflects the organized class section under Column 3. Pauline Lee's teaching load also illustrates cross-listing with SOC 601 and PSY 601.

Roger Brown's teaching load shows not only cross-listing (SOC 213 and WOMS 213) but dual listing, that is, the organized class sections wherein upper-division undergraduates and beginning graduate students are taught simultaneously, but they register for the course at their respective instructional level. In this instance, the undergraduates are registering for the course titled "Introduction to Sociological Research Methods" as SOC 467; graduate students register for the same course as SOC 667. Because it is a single course section and the majority of students registered are undergraduates, it is listed as an undergraduate, organized section in Column 3 under Brown's workload. Brown's team teaching of SOC 454 with Thomas Jones is also reflected (% load is 50).

Finally, Harry Jefferson, an adjunct faculty with no tenure status (Column 2), is teaching a recitation section, SOC 201–03, which is associated with the credit-bearing portion of the course (SOC 201–01) being taught by Mary Smith. It is a required component of that course and meets with forty undergraduates at regularly scheduled times. However, because it is zero-credit it generates no student credit hours. As with Smith's recitation section, this teaching activity would be lost under the JCAR conventions.

The nuances and subtleties in correctly apportioning and reporting teaching load data are not trivial. It is easy to see how, if there were no consequences for doing so, it would be easy to let "staff" be the default instructor for many of the courses in Table 3.1 that require manipulation in order to be correctly reported. In conversations over the past ten years with institutional researchers and registrars at colleges and universities across the country, I have found that the "staff" default option was virtually standard practice with zero-credit laboratory, recitation, and discussion sections and was frequently used in the more complicated dual- and cross-listed courses. Clearly, "staff" makes it virtually impossible to accurately report the volume of teaching done by respective faculty categories. This is a particularly serious flaw in the instance of tenured and tenure-track faculty who, as noted earlier, are the most visible targets for critics of higher education.

The level of detail evident in Table 3.1 concerning teaching activity at the departmental level makes it more than feasible to complete a simple summary such as Table 3.1 without ever referring to "staff." In fact, Table 3.1 enables an academic manager to provide a comprehensive and auditable response to the question, Who is teaching what to whom?

Tying the Data to Costs

How can academic departments ensure that the teaching-load data in Table 3.1 are accurate? There clearly must be an incentive for doing so, as well as a set of consequences for inaccurate information. The general opinion, as reflected in comments in earlier chapters by Zemsky and Massy (1990) and the Boyer Commission (1998), that undergraduates are paying more to attend college where they receive less for their money than in years past, provides a context for developing incentives and consequences. If the data can be tied to the issue of instructional costs and costs can be contained (although not at the expense of quality), then opportunities exist for resource allocation and reallocation decisions. With that opportunity in mind, the framework under development will move toward tying teaching load data to cost-expenditure data.

Verifying the Data

The data depicted in Table 3.1 constitute a departmental teaching roster. The first step in ensuring the accuracy of the data is multiple verifications by the department chair or program director. My experience in working with institutions across the country suggests that two times during any academic term are ideal for verification purposes. The first is the "official" census date on which colleges and universities freeze data files for internal and external reporting purposes. This typically occurs after the "free" period in which students can add or drop courses without financial or academic consequences.

At many institutions, the census date occurs after the tenth day of classes in a term. The census data capture all courses in the registration file and have either a faculty name or "staff" as instructor of record. The chair or director will verify that the faculty name is correct and will replace "staff" with a faculty name when the instructor has been identified. The chair or director also verifies other descriptive information associated with the course, for example, credit value, course type, whether it is team taught, and so on.

The second verification point is at the end of the academic term. It is conceivable that for course sections added during the opening of a term as the result of extraordinary demand, instructor names may not have been identified by the census date. It is not acceptable, however, to have "staff" as the instructor of record when the books are closed at the end of an academic term. The second verification should be viewed as a final audit, that is, a sign-off by the academic manager that the course registration files do, in fact, reflect reality.

I have worked for the past fifteen years with the framework I am describing. My institution offers between 3,800 and 4,000 courses, depending on the term, many with multiple organized class sections such as lectures, labs, recitations, and discussion sections. During the first iteration of data verification in 1986, "staff" was the end-of-term instructor of record on just under 10 percent of the sections listed in the course record file. In the most recently completed term (Fall 1999), "staff" was instructor of record in fewer than two dozen courses, all of which were appropriate, for example, courses where credit was given by examination. Similar progress has been reported by other institutions with whom I have worked over the years using this framework. Teaching load verification, where incentives and consequences are broadly understood, works.

The departmental teaching load verification rosters, as exemplified by Table 3.1, contain a summary table for the department at the end of the roster.

TABLE 3.2. INSTRUCTIONAL WORKLOAD SUMMARY, BY COURSE TYPE AND BY FACULTY TYPE.

All Faculty	Course Level	Students		Teaching	
		Enrolled	Credits	Credits	Sections
Regularly Scheduled Classes	Lower Division	2,378	7,048	52	18
	Upper Division	942	2,907	97	31
	Graduate	35	89	13	5
	Total	3,355	10,080	162	54
Supervised Study	Lower Division	1	3	1	
	Upper Division	37	106	37	
	Graduate	19	69	19	
	Total	57	178	57	
Regular and Supervised	Lower Division	2,379	7,087	53	18
	Upper Division	979	3,013	134	18
	Graduate	54	158	32	5
	Total	3,412	6,381	219	54
Tenured and Tenure-Track Faculty					
Regularly Scheduled Classes	Lower Division	2,127	6,381	45	15
	Upper Division	760	2,361	79	25
	Graduate	34	86	13	5
	Total	2,921	8,828	137	45
Supervised Study	Lower Division	1	3	1	
	Upper Division	32	93	32	
	Graduate	18	63	18	
	Total	51	159	51	
Regular and Supervised	Lower Division	2,128	6,384	46	15
	Upper Division	792	2,454	111	25
	Graduate	52	149	31	5
	Total	2,972	8,987	188	45

The summary table is displayed in Table 3.2. The data in the table are important because, as will be demonstrated shortly, once verified, it is not the last time that a chair, dean, or provost will see the numbers.

The summary information is straightforward—number of students enrolled and student credit hours generated, number of organized sections taught and associated teaching credits. Teaching credits are simply the credit value of the courses(s) taught, as previously seen in Column 4 of Table 3.2. The summary teaching data are broken out by course type—regularly scheduled and supervised study—and by level of instruction—undergraduate (lower division and upper division) and graduate. Note that meeting times for supervised study are, by definition, arranged as opposed to regularly scheduled, so there are no entries under this course type for organized sections taught. The data are further displayed for all faculty and separated out for tenured and tenure-track faculty.

Tying Productivity to Planning

The quantitative framework we have been constructing begins to come together in a reporting structure that will be referred to as "budget support data" (see Table 3.3). The purpose in constructing the framework is to get an assessment of teaching productivity and to tie it in some meaningful way to academic budget and resource planning.

Colleges and universities with whom I have worked have adopted some variation on a Budget Support Notebook, which provides a productivity-cost profile for each department or program at an institution. Table 3.3 represents a typical department profile, which brings together traditional and nontraditional measures of productivity and effectively links them with expenditure data. A review of the profile components will prove useful.

FTE Majors. Many institutions have gauged the teaching productivity of a department, in part, by the number of students majoring in the discipline(s) in which the department specializes. It is not a terribly useful measure. It reports headcount (the FTE formula calls for dividing the number of part-time students by 3 and adding the quotient to the number of full-time students) and in no way reflects teaching activity. It is displayed largely for informational purposes and for context in resource allocation decisions, as will be discussed shortly.

Number of Degrees Granted. Degrees granted is a useful output measure of departmental productivity but does not reflect the entire picture of teaching productivity. Clearly, a department such as the example in Table 3.3, with relatively few majors, will generate relatively few degrees each year. But as will be seen momentarily, taken by itself degrees granted can be a very misleading measure.

Student Credit Hours Taught. The department pictured in Table 3.3 is generating, on average, 6,000 to 8,000 student credit hours per term over the course of the six terms (Fall and Spring) displayed. Forty majors, each carrying a full-time load of 15 credits, would account for only 600 student credit hours—less than 10 percent of the hours being taught. Clearly a lot of teaching occurs that affects non-majors. This is precisely why headcount majors are an inappropriate measure of teaching productivity. The Student Credit Hours Taught data in Table 3.3, arrayed by Lower Division, Upper Division, Graduate, and Total, are taken directly

TABLE 3.3. BUDGET SUPPORT DATA, 1995–1996 THROUGH 1997–1998, UNDERGRADUATE DEPARTMENT IN THE HUMANITIES.

A. TEACHING WORKLOAD DATA

	Fall 1995	Fall 1996	Fall 1997	Spring 1996	Spring 1997	Spring 1998
FTE Majors						
Undergraduate	32	38	31	40	38	40
Graduate	0	0	0	0	0	0
Total	32	38	31	40	38	40
Degrees Granted						
Bachelor's				20	19	19
Master's				0	0	0
Doctorate				0	0	0
TOTAL				20	19	19
Student Credit Hours Taught						
Lower Division	7,554	6,246	5,472	6,399	4,518	6,156
Upper Division	719	826	638	946	1,159	951
Graduate	195	183	153	192	195	276
Total	8,468	7,155	6,263	7,537	5,872	7,383
% Credit Hours Taught by Tenured or Tenure-Track Faculty	77%	77%	81%	75%	82%	91%
% Credit Hours Taught by Other Faculty	23%	23%	19%	25%	18%	9%
% Credit Hours Consumed by Nonmajors	98%	97%	98%	96%	98%	97%
FTE Students Taught						
Lower Division	504	416	365	427	301	410
Upper Division	48	48	43	63	77	63
Graduate	22	20	17	21	22	31
Total	574	484	425	511	400	504
FTE Faculty						
Department Chair	1.0	1.0	1.0	1.0	1.0	1.0
Faculty on Appointment	15.0	15.0	16.0	14.0	15.0	15.0
Supplemental Faculty	1.8	1.5	1.0	1.8	1.0	0.8
Total	17.8	17.5	18.0	16.8	17.0	16.8
Workload Ratios						
Student Credit Hours/FTE Faculty	477.1	408.9	347.9	450	345.4	440.8
FTE Students Taught/FTE Faculty	32.3	27.7	23.6	30.5	23.5	30.1

TABLE 3.3. *(Continued)*

B. FISCAL DATA

	FY 1996 ($)	FY 1997 ($)	FY 1998 ($)
Research and Service			
Research Expenditures	0	0	5,151
Public Service Expenditures	0	0	0
Total Sponsored Research/Service	0	0	5,151
Sponsored Funds/FTE Faculty On Appointment	0	0	312
Cost of Instruction			
Direct Instructional Expenditures	1,068,946	1,060,975	1,141,927
Direct Expense/Student Credit Hours	67	81	84
Direct Expense/FTE Students Taught	986	1198	1229
Revenue Measures			
Earned Income from Instruction	4,561,245	3,960,208	4,366,720
Earned Income/Direct Instructional Expense	4.27	3.73	3.82

from the summary data section similar to that seen in Table 3.2 and are used in the calculations that will be discussed in the following paragraphs. Consequently, over time, deans, department chairs, and program directors, seeing that the data from departmental workload files are, in fact, being used, are reinforced in the importance of verifying those data.

In addition to displaying the total volume of student credit hours generated through teaching activity within the department, two additional pieces of information are provided. The percentage of student credit hours taught by tenured and tenure-track faculty is an important measure, and it too is taken directly from the summary data that were displayed in Table 3.2. Tenured and tenure-track faculty, because of the permanent nature of their employment status, are the faculty group in whom the institution has the greatest investment. And it is fair to ask, What is the return on investment? In the case of the departmental example in Table 3.3, a fairly large volume of student credit hours, 6,000 to 8,000 per term, are being taught largely by tenured and tenure-track faculty—nearly four out of every five student credit hours, as reflected by the percentages in the table. In departments where the percentages are substantially lower than those depicted, say in the 50 to 60 percent range on average over multiple terms, it makes good management sense to investigate the nonteaching nature of faculty activity in those units.

A second useful piece of data is the percentage of student credit hours consumed by nonmajors. In the case of the department in Table 3.3, 96 to 98 percent of the student credit hours taught are generated by nonmajors. This clearly is a service department, and any decisions made with regard to resource allocations have potential implications for students from other departments. The department in the table is in the humanities, and it is evident from the data that nonmajors make extensive use of it to satisfy general education requirements. The service nature of this teaching department must come into play in any resource allocation or reallocation decisions. A fuller discussion of this issue will be presented later in this chapter.

FTE Students Taught. Considering the volume of full-time students taught by a department, it makes far more sense to use a measure that is derived from the teaching activity itself, as opposed to an irrelevant headcount construct such as that used in creating the FTE major metric discussed earlier. It is a commonly accepted convention across the country that a full-time undergraduate course load is fifteen credits per term, whereas that for graduate students is nine. The typical load is somewhat higher in two-year colleges. By dividing the total undergraduate student credit hours taught (lower division plus upper division) by 15, and the total graduate student hours taught by 9, a FTE student count is generated from the teaching workload. That number is a far more appropriate metric to use in a student-faculty ratio or a cost-per-student-taught calculation than a simple headcount FTE. It represents the quantitative outcome of teaching activity, as measured by volume of students taught. The "FTE Students Taught" fields in Table 3.3 were derived from student credit hours taught using the aforementioned calculation and will be used in subsequent productivity and cost ratios.

FTE Faculty. These data are taken from the institution's personnel database, where appropriate, and are imputed, where needed. Department chairs and faculty on appointment are found in a college or university's personnel file. Faculty on appointment refers to all full-time and permanent part-time individuals on budgeted lines. They typically include tenured and tenure-track faculty and nontenurable faculty on recurring contract with the institution.

Supplemental faculty, however, include adjuncts—professional staff who teach but whose primary function is noninstructional, graduate teaching assistants, and so on. The FTE for this group can be imputed. At four-year institutions, it is a generally accepted convention that if a faculty member did nothing but teach, the standard term teaching load is twelve teaching credits. That translates into four three-credit courses or three four-credit courses. The FTE for supplemental faculty is derived by summing the teaching credits, that is, the credit value for all courses taught by supplemental faculty and dividing that total by 12. By adding the FTE for faculty on appointment to that for supplemental faculty, a total faculty FTE is arrived at that can be used in productivity calculations.

Because a central objective of this framework is credibility, not only for external audiences but internal constituencies as well, institutions across the country that have adopted the framework adhere to the following rule: *The FTE for any single faculty member cannot exceed 1.0.* This is simply common sense. A full-time faculty member has an administered, agreed-upon teaching workload during any given term. If that individual elects to do additional teaching on an overload compensation basis, that overload should be viewed as supplemental activity, and any additional FTE derived as the result of that overload activity should be reported under supplemental faculty. Teaching overload courses does not make a faculty member more "full time" than others who do not. Few things are more confusing or self-defeating than trying to explain to a legislator or agency head how a full-time faculty member can be 1.25 or 1.33 FTE.

Workload Ratios. In looking at teaching productivity, two related quantitative measures are useful: student credit hours taught per FTE faculty and FTE students taught per FTE faculty. Because faculty do more than teach, it is important to look at both of these ratios in a larger context. If these ratios are steadily declining over time, and there is no qualitative issue (for example, intentionally planned, smaller class sizes) or offsetting research and service activity, then it is fair to explore the underlying reasons for the decline and, where appropriate, make resource allocation-reallocation decisions in light of those declines.

Obtaining Consistent Financial Information

In marrying productivity data to cost data, institutional financial databases come into play. It is important to underscore the fact that it does not require an MBA or a degree in accounting to understand and use the information in these files. Most colleges and universities subscribe to what are referred to as generally accepted accounting principles. The intrinsic value in these principles is that accounting books are kept in essentially the same fashion, whether at a major research university or at the local community college. With respect to cost information, these generally accepted principles require that each time institutional funds are spent, a transaction code must be assigned to the expenditure.

Imbedded in that transaction code are two crucial pieces of information: an object code and a function code. The object code identifies the category on which the funds were spent, for example, on salaries, benefits, scholarships, and support costs such as travel and supplies. The function code identifies the institutional purpose for which the funds were spent. Examples are instruction, sponsored research, and public service.

Table 3.4 displays fiscal year expenditures, by object and by function, for the example department in the humanities that was the focus of the teaching-load analysis in Table 3.3.

The table displays precisely how much was expended on professional, faculty, and staff salaries and how much within various support funds categories such as travel and supplies. The data can be disaggregated to any organizational unit (academic department or program) within a college or university. In fact, Table 3.4 can easily be reconstructed at any institution by using a basic statistical software package and cross-tabulating a department's expenditure data by object code and function code. The data in these financial files have generally been audited, and they provide a solid base of fiscal information to which productivity data can be married. They also provide verifiable evidence that the fiscal metrics used in this productivity framework are, indeed, accurate. It is imperative, however, that the institutional research office, or other office at the college or university that is conducting these analyses, work closely with the budget office to ensure proper use of the fiscal data elements. As the data become more widely accepted and used across campus, it may also make sense to involve the campus computing center in development of production reports that yield the same information as the statistical software package's cross-tabulation. Production reports are far more economical and efficient to generate, especially in terms of personnel time.

With reference to Table 3.3, and in particular to Part B, Fiscal Data, the link between faculty activity and expenditure data begins to be evident. This section draws on three expenditure data elements: (1) *direct* expenditures for instruction, (2) *direct* expenditures for research, and (3) *direct* expenditures for public service. Definitions will follow.

To ensure data consistency, the definitions given in the following section were developed by the National Association of Collegiate and University Business Officers (NACUBO) and are used in the Integrated Postsecondary Educational Data System (IPEDS) reporting system. IPEDS was developed by the National Center for Education Statistics within the U.S. Department of Education, and collects data from virtually every college and university in the United States receiving any form of federal financial aid. The data definitions, therefore, have an integrity and consistency that is applicable to nearly every postsecondary institution's accounting system.

It is important to underscore that for each of the expenditure categories only *direct costs* are measured. In creating a framework for productivity analysis, it is

TABLE 3.4. DEPARTMENTAL EXPENDITURES, BY OBJECT AND BY FUNCTION: FISCAL YEAR 1998, UNDERGRADUATE DEPARTMENT IN THE HUMANITIES.

	Instruction (01–08)	Departmental Research (09)	Organized Activity Education Departments (10)	Research (21–39)	Public Service (41–43)	Academic Support (51–56)
Expenditures						
Salaries						
Professionals	26,509	0	0	0	0	0
Faculty						
Full-Time (including department chair)	977,775	0	0	0	0	0
Part-Time (including overload)	33,968	0	0	0	0	0
Graduate students	0	0	0	0	0	0
Postdoctoral fellows	0	0	0	2,591	0	0
Tuition/Scholarship	0	0	0	0	0	0
Salaried/Hourly staff	62,224	0	0	0	0	0
Fringe benefits	0	0	0	0	0	0
Subtotal	1,100,476	0	0	2,591	0	0
Support						
Miscellaneous wages	3,721	160	0	0	0	0
Travel	9,045	6,645	0	0	0	0
Supplies and expenses	18,315	6,860	0	2,560	0	0
Occupancy and maintenance	1,287	0	0	0	0	0
Equipment	0	0	0	0	0	0
Other expenses	9,083	0	0	0	0	0
Credits and transfers	0	0	0	0	0	0
Subtotal	41,451	13,665	0	2,560	0	0
TOTAL	1,141,927	13,665	0	5,151	0	0

important that the data be credible and verifiable. The standard definitions are clear and precise for identifying direct expense by institutional functional category. Measuring indirect costs, that is, administrative costs, utilities costs, capital costs, and so on, is far less uniform and precise. Indeed, on any given campus there are multiple calculations for indirect costs based on the academic discipline for which costs are being recovered. For the sake of clarity, simplicity, and credibility, the discussion of costs that follows in this chapter and throughout the book will in no way attempt to measure full costs, only direct expenses.

Direct Expenditures for Instruction. These would include all expenditures directly charged to the instruction function, including general academic instruction, occupational and vocational education, community education, preparatory and adult basic education, and remedial and tutorial instruction conducted by the teaching faculty for the institution's students. Departmental research and service that are not *separately budgeted* are included under instruction. In other words, externally funded research and service should be *excluded* from instructional expenditures, as should any departmental funds expended for the purpose of matching external funds as part of a contractual or grant obligation. Direct instructional expenses exclude expenditures for academic administration where the primary function is administration. For example, deans and provosts would be excluded from instructional expenditures, but department chairs whose function is primarily the coordination of instructional activity would be included.

Direct Expenditures for Research. This category includes all expenditures for activities specifically organized to produce research outcomes and commissioned by an agency external to the institution or separately budgeted by an organizational unit within the institution, such as a research center.

Direct Expenditures for Public Service. Similar to direct research expenditures, this category embraces all funds expended through contracts or grants, or *separately budgeted* for public service and expended for activities established primarily to provide noninstructional services beneficial to groups external to the institution. Examples include extension activity and community outreach projects.

Table 3.3 brings these expenditure data together with data elements previously defined in Part A of the same table, Teaching Workload Data. Specifically, research and service expenditure data are divided by FTE faculty on appointment to produce a ratio: sponsored funds to FTE faculty on appointment. Faculty on appointment, that is, tenured and tenure-track faculty, as opposed to total faculty, are used in this ratio because that category of faculty is expected to generate research outcomes. That is not generally an expectation for supplemental faculty or graduate students. The cost of instruction is reflected in two additional ratios wherein direct instructional expenditures are divided by student credit hours taught and FTE students taught to arrive at direct expense per student credit hour and direct expense per FTE student taught. The utility of these various ratios can be seen in the example in Table 3.3.

Again with reference to Part B of Table 3.3 under Research and Service, no expenditures are listed for two of the three fiscal years. The third year, FY 1998, shows limited activity. (Note that these data are taken directly from the appropriate categories in Table 3.4.) This is not surprising for a department in the humanities; external funding for research and public service in these disciplines is limited at best. Where there is limited buy-out of a faculty member's time (for example, contract or grant activity that carries a legal obligation to do something other than teach), it is reasonable to expect robust teaching activity. The department in Table 3.3 meets that expectation in the workload ratios in Part A. Student credit hour per FTE faculty ratios approaching 400 are indicative of heavier teaching loads, as are FTE students taught per FTE faculty ratios in the high 20s and low 30s.

In biological and physical science departments and engineering departments, where external funds are more readily available, it is not uncommon to see total direct research and service expenditures well into the millions of dollars, with "sponsored funds / FTE faculty on appointment" ratios running well into the tens to hundreds of thousands of dollars. Conversely, in departments with heavy external research and service expenditures, it is also common to see teaching workload ratios well below those indicated for the humanities department in Table 3.3. More often than not, academic departments, generally in the sciences and engineering with heavy sponsored research and service expenditures, have significant graduate education components. Graduate instruction in these disciplines cannot be measured exclusively in student credit hours taught. The most valuable educational experiences often come in the interaction between a faculty member who is engaged in substantial research and his or her research assistants.

Increasingly, research universities are extending this interaction to undergraduate research scholars as well. The funds generated through research and service contract and grant activity support the research and service but support educational opportunities for students working with the researchers as well. This form of faculty productivity is rarely measured and is usually lost on those outside the academy; it may even be lost to those in other departments in the same institution. The fiscal measures just described give this framework for describing faculty activity a context for looking at relationships between and among teaching, research, and service activity.

Although they are useful and often enlightening, it would be totally erroneous to suggest that separately budgeted research and expenditure data are either the only or the best measures of research and service activity. Disciplines in the fine arts and humanities rarely receive significant external funding, yet faculty are expected to produce works for juried art exhibits, compose and perform original musical works, create and publish fiction and poetry, and so on. For disciplines that do not have external funding as a proxy for research and service activity, there still must be a vehicle for reporting what faculty do. That will be the subject of the next chapter.

The cost of instruction is a key point in the construction of this quantitative framework for faculty productivity. It clearly ties expenditure data to the volume of teaching being done. Direct instructional expenditures, as they appear in Table 3.4, are taken directly from the audited expenditures, by function, that are displayed in Table 3.3. The two ratios are straightforward. Total direct instructional expenditures for an academic department or program within a given fiscal year are divided by the total number of student credit hours taught and FTE students taught within terms (semesters, quarters) supported by those instructional expenditures. In other words, all teaching activity supported by the departmental instructional budget is reflected in these ratios. Excluded is teaching activity supported by other than the instructional budget. For example, many colleges and universities operate winter and summer terms that are supported by an Office of Special Sessions or some similar administrative unit. Faculty from a given department may teach during the winter or summer term, but if their winter or summer stipend is supported by the Office of Special Sessions as opposed to the departmental budget, then the workload cannot be attributed to the department. Similarly, if a faculty member from the History Department teaches a course on overload in the Political Science Department, and the overload stipend is funded by the Political Science Department, then the student credit hours and FTE students taught are credited to Political Science—the unit that paid for the instructional activity.

This may at first seem like "overaccounting" in tying teaching activity to expenditure data. But if colleges and universities are to be responsive to external (and often, internal) criticism with regard to productivity and cost, then the analytical framework for assessing those issues must be precise. What is being required in this analysis is an accurate measurement of what faculty are teaching, as measured by student credit hours and FTE students taught, and tying that teaching to the instructional expenditures within the department or program paying for it.

The cost of instruction ratios in Table 3.3 reflect a department with a heavy teaching mission. The direct expense per student credit hour and FTE student taught ratios depicted are low compared with those from other disciplines. The value of these ratios, as well as the research and service expense ratios previously described, is that they provide a comparative benchmark for comparing productivity and cost between and among similar disciplines within a college or university.

And as will be seen in later chapters, the benchmarks take on more explanatory power and utility when they can be compared across groups of peer departments within peer institutions.

In Table 3.3 the cost, research, and service ratios are depicted over a three-year period. It is important to examine any data of this nature on a trend-line basis. Any single year of data can be idiosyncratic. A sabbatical leave or leaves will result in salaries included in instructional expenses but loss of teaching productivity for the period of the leave. The purpose of ratios of this sort is not to cast a department within the context of "empirical absolutes" but rather to be used as tools of inquiry for framing policy questions. For example:

> If teaching load ratios (student credit hours and FTE students taught per FTE faculty) are low, are research and service ratios (direct expenditures per FTE faculty on appointment) sufficiently high to provide additional contextual information as to how faculty are productively spending their time?

> The reverse question is also appropriate: If research and service expenditure ratios are declining over time, are teaching workloads increasing as an offset?

> If teaching load ratios are declining over time and instructional expenditure ratios are increasing, are there qualitative issues that can explain these trends (for example, smaller class size, additional faculty, shift in curricular emphases)?

In working with colleges and universities who have adopted this analytical framework over the past decade, I have urged senior administrators to refrain from using these data as a basis for either rewarding or penalizing a department or program. The data should be viewed over a trend line as quantitative barometers for framing larger policy questions as to how faculty in the unit are spending their time, whether they have achieved a balance between teaching, research, and service that is appropriate to the mission of that department, and whether they are, in fact, as productive as they can be.

The final pieces of information in Table 3.3 provide the basis for a broader understanding of how colleges and universities actually operate, that is, whether there is a true balance between teaching-oriented departments and research- or service-oriented departments. The "Revenue Measures" are interesting but are also potentially misunderstood and misused. Institutions adopting them should be aware that they have limitations. "Earned Income from Instruction" is a derived measure. It is calculated by looking at an institution's total tuition revenue (available in the audited financial statement for a given fiscal year or in the institution's IPEDS Survey of Finances, which is submitted annually to the National Center for Education Statistics), and dividing that total tuition revenue by the total number of student credit hours taught at the institution during the academic terms covered under that fiscal year. The result is a "tuition revenue per student credit hour taught" unit, which can then be multiplied by the number of student credit hours taught by a department during the same fiscal year. The result is "earned income from instruction," or revenue generated from teaching activity. The earned income from instruction can then be divided by total direct instructional expenditures to arrive at an "earned income/direct instructional expense" ratio.

The obvious limitation in the ratio is that it accounts only for direct expenses. Many academic units, on seeing this calculation, assume that an income-to-expense ratio of 1.0 means that they are a self-sufficient unit—a "tub on their own bottom." It must be remembered that direct instructional expenses do not include the costs associated with admitting students to an institution, registering them in courses, providing libraries, academic advising and other student services, and lights and heat. Tuition revenue is often expected to cover those costs. Once again, this analytical framework is not intended to be a full-cost model but simply a way to describe the relationship between selected measures of productivity and direct expenses for teaching, research, and service.

Having said that, looking at income-to-expense ratios across disciplines is an interesting exercise. It is common to find low (less than 1.0) income-to-expense ratios in the sciences and engineering, with high ratios (greater than 2.0) in some humanities, social sciences, and business departments. Rather than focus on the hackneyed perception that certain departments are "cash cows" and others are "cash drains," it is far more instructive to look at the pedagogical differences that often underpin the ratios. Science and engineering classes are typically equipment-intensive, require smaller class sections, especially for laboratories, and with the exception of a few courses, are not ordinarily service departments. Humanities, social sciences, and business departments can more frequently employ large lecture sections, which are far more cost-effective than laboratory instruction. And although the humanities, social sciences, and business programs may generate larger volumes of tuition revenue than science and engineering units, the latter are more frequently engaged in high-volume research and service contract and grant activity that generates income from indirect cost recovery that is nowhere accounted for in the income-to-expense ratio but from which all departments at an institution benefit.

Conclusion

Over the past ten years I have both engaged in and facilitated discussions of the full range of quantitative measures that have been developed for the framework outlined in this chapter. Those discussions are particularly useful because they underscore both the strengths and weaknesses of quantitative productivity analyses. Although the measures described are clearly richer in context and superior in analytical capabilities to the simplistic measures described in Chapter Two for the State of South Carolina, they nonetheless yield an incomplete picture. They do not address the qualitative aspects and measures of productivity that will be discussed in the next chapter. Yet the underpinning constructs that lead to the budget support data in Table 3.3—the faculty management rosters in Table 3.1, and the detailed expenditure data in Table 3.4—provide a dean or department chair with basic information concerning deployment of both faculty and fiscal resources. And the metrics in Table 3.3 itself provide units of analysis for both productivity and cost that enable cross-departmental comparisons, or basic benchmarking of data. Intra-institutional comparisons are, in fact, the first level of benchmarking for productivity and cost measures. It is both instructive and helpful to academic managers at a college or university to see how similar departments within appropriate disciplinary groupings compare with each other along the ratios that were developed in Table 3.3. But as useful as comparisons may be between and among departments at a given college or university, those comparisons take on even more significance when they can be made between and among the same departments at different institutions within appropriate peer groupings. That level of benchmarking will be the focus of Chapter Five. In the meantime, Chapter Four will address the qualitative dimensions of productivity that provide the still-missing pieces of a full analytical and benchmarking capability.

CHAPTER FOUR

MEASURING PRODUCTIVITY

What About Quality?

Chapter Three provided a framework for developing a comprehensive and detailed—and quantitative—response to the question, Who is teaching what to whom and at what cost? The framework enables the tracking of both credit-bearing and zero-credit teaching activity, by faculty category, and links that instructional activity to expenditure data.

However, the framework will not always provide complete answers to the question: How are research and service measured in disciplines where external contracts and grants are not readily available? The discussion in Chapter One that described data from the National Study of Postsecondary Faculty clearly demonstrates that research is an expectation across the disciplines. When it takes the form of externally funded laboratory activity in the sciences or engineering, it is easily measured in terms of the framework. But how is creative capital measured? How can a productivity and accountability framework capture the creative energy generated by an art department or a music performance department? How can the creativity that gives birth to a volume of fiction or poetry be assessed?

Adding the Qualitative Dimension

My colleagues and I have been sensitive to these issues. As the framework described in Chapter Three was evolving, we were discussing ways to identify additional variables that would more fully describe faculty activity across all disciplines and at the same time provide a qualitative dimension to the analysis. Our objective was to expand the question asked earlier—Who is teaching what to whom?—to include the dimension, How well? All parties to the discussion had heard the hackneyed excuses: "Quality can't be measured"; "Our department is unique and doesn't lend itself to comparison," and so on. The simple fact confronting higher education in general and institutional researchers in particular was that excuses could no longer be tolerated. There was a clear demand, inside and outside academe, for information about what faculty do and how well they do it. Consequently, in addition to the quantitative framework for evaluating faculty activity, an assessment of quality was needed. And the variables, in order to be credible and useful, had to be measurable and benchmarkable.

Our early discussions were fruitful; a list of consistent, qualitative variables emerged. And with a list of consistent variables from which to choose, qualitative as well as quantitative benchmarking, both within a single institution and across institutions, became possible. The qualitative dimension of faculty productivity is in fact characterized by specific, measurable activities.

Qualitative Variables

The initial variables on the list are comparable to those found in Chapter One, which characterized responses to the National Survey of Postsecondary Faculty. They include the following, which should be measured over a fixed period of time:

- Refereed publications (for example, in the past thirty-six months) produced
- Textbooks, reference books, novels, volumes of collected works edited or written
- Edited volumes produced
- Juried shows mounted or performances given
- Editorial positions held
- Externally funded contracts or grants received

These variables are attractive in that they not only describe measurable outputs from faculty activity but they reveal information about the quality of those activities. For example, in the first variable the data indicate quality work when a publication has a panel of editorial referees who accept and reject manuscripts based on the merit of their content. The same is true for juried exhibitions for artists and invited or commissioned performances for musicians, actors, and dancers. Both academic and commercial presses employ editorial criteria and standards in producing textbooks and other volumes of creative work.

A qualitative filter is applied to the output number being reported. An editorial position, be it for a single volume or a regularly published journal, implies that the incumbent has special expertise that qualifies him or her to hold that position. It is a statement about the quality of the person and the work he or she has produced over the years. And finally, contracts and grants are generally awarded on a competitive basis; successful proposals are superior in quality to those that are not funded.

It is important to measure these outputs over a fixed period; the creation of intellectual capital requires time. The time elapsing from the inception of creative thoughts leading to a journal article, book, or creative work to final delivery of the product can vary. Most institutions agree that it is appropriate and generous to allow a faculty member thirty-six months to produce a piece of work.

Not every faculty output, however, has to pass muster with editors, juried panels, or contract and grant commissioners. Presenting papers at regional and national meetings, writing white papers for local, regional, state, and national policy development issues, writing articles for the editorial pages of regional and national newspapers, and providing noncontractual public service are also characteristic of what faculty do. In addition, faculty spend extraordinary amounts of time developing curriculum materials and teaching strategies, and engaging in other faculty development activities. Indeed, on my campus and on campuses across the country, faculty are hard at work modernizing teaching techniques to take advantage of current technology. That technology allows virtually asynchronous learning through the use of Internet-based teaching modules, twenty-four-hour e-mail communication with students, and creation of learning assessment tools to measure the impact of technology on the quantity and quality of what is being learned.

Variables Related to Change

A paradigm shift is occurring in higher education, wherein the emphasis in developing curricular materials is to focus on *learning* as opposed to *teaching*. Consistent with other forms of assessment, it is the product that is important; the process is less so. Foundations such as the Pew Charitable Trusts are funding faculty initiatives to develop curricula and train colleagues in new pedagogical strategies such as "problem-based learning," wherein students work in teams to research and resolve complex intellectual problems, and the faculty member serves as mentor and guide in the process.

Any serious examination of the qualitative dimension of faculty productivity must acknowledge that faculty are increasingly being required to spend time coming to terms with and internalizing these teaching-learning paradigm shifts. Consequently, the variable list should be expanded to include the following (again the outputs should be produced over a fixed period of time):

- The number of professional conference papers and presentations given
- The number of nonrefereed publications produced
- The number of *active* memberships in professional associations or honor societies
- The nature and scope of faculty or curriculum development activities

Persistence and Graduation Rates

The pioneering work of the Joint Commission on Accountability (JCAR) described in Chapter Two also yields qualitative variables that speak to the issue of quality in faculty activity. These include

- Undergraduate persistence and graduation rates
- Opportunities to assess student satisfaction with the quantity and quality of academic advisement from faculty, out-of-class availability of faculty, and the overall quality of interaction with faculty
- The proportion of graduating students finding curriculum-related employment within twelve months of graduation
- The proportion of students passing licensing, certification, or accreditation examinations related to their chosen profession
- The proportion of graduating students going on for further graduate or professional education

Although undergraduate persistence and graduation rates are complex measures that include a host of variables other than faculty activity, it is nonetheless fair to ask to what extent students who matriculate at a given institution actually receive a degree from the program to which they sought admission. If the offer of admission and its subsequent acceptance is viewed as an implicit promise of a credential on completion of degree requirements, it is perfectly legitimate to look at the activities of all parties to that contract—faculty as well as students. Although students leave college without graduating for a variety of reasons, the quality of teaching and other experiences with faculty can be reasons for student attrition. The criticisms of undergraduate education in Chapters One and Two related in no small way to the assertion that faculty do not teach undergraduates and that the quality of interaction with faculty is significantly inferior to what it was thirty years ago.

Consequently, persistence and graduation rates, coupled with an assessment of student satisfaction with interaction with faculty, can yield useful information with regard to the quality of instructional activity. Many data-collection instruments can capture student satisfaction data. In working with colleges and universities across the nation, I most frequently encounter the American College Testing Program's *Student Opinion Survey*, Indiana University's *College Student Experiences Questionnaire*, and the Pew Charitable Trust's new initiative, *The National Survey of Student Engagement*. Each of these provides useful, benchmarkable information for better understanding persistence and graduation rates at a given institution, as well as the quality of student experiences with faculty.

Postgraduate Employment Rates

For those students who do graduate, JCAR has identified three outcomes that reflect the quality of instruction at an institution: (1) graduates obtain jobs in the fields for which their college or university experiences prepared them; (2) graduates routinely pass licensure, certification, accreditation, or other competency-based tests that provide quality control for entry into an occupational field; and (3) students electing to pursue further education are admitted to good-quality graduate or professional schools.

Quality of Interaction with Faculty

Variables measuring the quality of interaction with faculty should be expanded beyond instruction. Variables taking on increasing importance in higher education and reflecting indirectly on the quality of faculty activity include the following:

- Opportunities to work with faculty on substantive projects of undergraduate research
- Opportunities for internships and practica that provide work-related experience prior to graduation
- The proportion of graduating students who author or coauthor an article or chapter with a faculty mentor
- The proportion of graduating students presenting or copresenting a paper at a professional meeting with a faculty mentor

The data from the National Study of Postsecondary Faculty in Chapter One clearly underscore the importance of research in the life of a faculty member. What is not evident in those data but is nonetheless becoming an increasingly commonplace phenomenon is the involvement of undergraduate students in faculty research. Student outcomes clearly can be attributed to collaboration with faculty on research projects, and they merit some discussion here. The University of Michigan, with support from the Fund for Improvement of Post Secondary Education (FIPSE), has created a model program—the Undergraduate Research Opportunity Program (UROP)—that brings together first- and second-year undergraduates with faculty to collaborate on original and substantive research. Along with the opportunity to work with faculty and gain hands-on experience in research design and methodology, the University of Michigan students participating in this program also have access to peer advisers throughout the research experience. An added outcome from the project is enhanced student retention. The attrition rate for students participating in the Undergraduate Research Opportunity Program is half that for nonparticipants. The pattern holds true for underrepresented minority students.

The University of Delaware, under the aegis of a grant from the NSF, is conducting an extensive assessment of the relationship between participation in undergraduate research activity with a faculty mentor and enhancement of cognitive skills. Faculty and students both report that the undergraduate research experience contributes in substantial ways to the development of skills such as enhanced intellectual curiosity, better understanding of scientific findings, and an expanded capability to think logically about complex materials and to synthesize information from diverse sources. The assessment data show significant skills gains for students who participate in undergraduate research activity, compared with students who do not.

Because both research and teaching are at the center of faculty activity, it makes sense to examine the qualitative dimension of research in ways that integrate it with teaching. Certainly, improved retention and graduation rates, accompanied by measurable gains in cognitive and affective skills, are characteristics of a qualitatively better academic program. The University of Michigan and the University of Delaware models for incorporating an undergraduate research experience into the curriculum are the most frequently cited and provide a useful context for assessing quality from the student perspective.

Variables at the Department Level

In attempting to collect data on the qualitative dimensions of faculty productivity, as was the case with the quantitative framework, it makes sense to begin at the departmental level (see Exhibit 4.1). As noted earlier in this discussion, not all of the variables enumerated thus far are appropriate for each and every department or program at an institution.

Exhibit 4.1 shows a departmental checklist of qualitative variables; the list has grown out of my discussions with colleagues across the country who are attempting to measure faculty productivity. The variables, when applied to departments and programs, lend themselves to grouping. Those that are appropriate for fine arts are different from those for physical sciences and engineering, which in turn are different from the social sciences. Such groupings enable appropriate interdepartmental comparisons within a single institution and are absolutely critical to inter-institutional comparisons, as I will discuss later in this volume.

Research and Service

Although some people would like for colleges and universities to do nothing but teach, the simple fact is that faculty life has evolved to the point that research and, to a lesser extent, public service are core functions along with teaching. The central role of research in faculty life is especially evident in the following highlights from National Science Board's (1998) web-based *Science and Engineering Indicators—1998:*

- In 1997 approximately $23.8 billion was spent in research and development activity at academic institutions in the United States.
- The academic sector performs over 50 percent of basic research, continuing to be the largest source for basic research in the United States.
- The fact that research is intimately integrated with graduate education is evident in that two of every three full-time graduate students in the United States are funded through a research assistantship.
- Over 101,000 scientific and technical articles were published by the academic community in 1995 (the most recent year for which complete data are available) in journals included in the *Science Citation Index.*
- The number of academic patents rose more than sevenfold in just over two decades, from 250 annually in the early 1970s to more than 1,800 in 1995. Academic patenting is increasing faster than any other category of U.S. patents; among institutions with patents are growing number of universities and colleges not traditionally counted among research universities (http://www.nsf.gov).

The foregoing highlights reflect only research activity in the science and engineering disciplines. There alone, academic research activity has profoundly changed medicine and pharmaceuticals. Research has made technology part of everyday life, especially in the area of personal computing and information

EXHIBIT 4.1. DEPARTMENTAL CHECKLIST: QUALITATIVE MEASURES OF FACULTY ACTIVITY.

Number of refereed publications within past 36 months _____

Number of textbooks, reference books, novels, or volumes
of collected works within past 36 months _____

Number of edited volumes within past 36 months _____

Number of juried shows or performances within past 36 months _____

Number of editorial positions held within past 36 months _____

Number of externally funded contracts and grants received
within past 36 months _____

Number of professional conference papers and presentations
within past 36 months _____

Number of nonrefereed publications within past 36 months _____

Number of active memberships in professional associations
and/or honor societies within past 36 months _____

Number of faculty engaged in faculty development or curriculum
development activity as part of their assigned workload _____

Five-year undergraduate persistence and graduation rates for
most recent cohort _____

Most recent average student satisfaction scores for
  • Quality of faculty academic advisement _____
  • Out-of-class availability of faculty _____
  • Overall quality of interaction with faculty _____

Proportion of most recent graduating class finding curriculum-
related employment within 12 months of commencement _____

Proportion of students passing licensing, certification, or
accreditation examinations related to academic major _____

Proportion of most recent graduating class continuing to
pursue further graduate or professional education _____

Number of students engaged in undergraduate research
with faculty mentor within past 12 months _____

Number of students engaged in internships or practica under
direct supervision of faculty over past 12 months _____

Number of students who author or coauthor with a faculty mentor
an article or chapter over past 36 months _____

Number of students presenting or copresenting with a faculty
mentor a paper at a professional meeting _____

transmission. However, the preceding data do not speak to creative research in the fine arts and humanities that result in new musical compositions, theatrical productions, and innovative art forms, all of which provoke thought and enrich the human spirit.

Public service is even more difficult to document. Cooperative Extension and Agricultural Extension are the two largest public services, and their nature and scope are well documented by the members of the National Association of State Universities and Land Grant Colleges (NASULGC). Outreach activity originating in an academic department (for example, a political science department placing undergraduate interns and graduate fellows in a state legislature or a nursing department placing student nurses in community health organizations) can only be documented at the institutional level.

An approach adopted by many colleges and universities in describing the impact of their teaching, research, and service activities is to do so in economic terms. Since the early 1970s, pure and applied research and service activities have been the target of criticism from a variety of audiences. From those outside higher education who wonder why faculty are doing research and service when they should be teaching to Senator William Proxmire's (former senator from Wisconsin) infamous Golden Fleece Awards for perceived waste in federal research funding, higher education is not always pictured in the most flattering light. This, once again, is due to the poor job that higher education has done to describe the economic importance of research and service convincingly.

Many colleges and universities have moved away from philosophical arguments about the public good derived from research and service activities. Instead they have opted to supplement those arguments with a language that speaks to both taxpayers and legislators: economic impact studies. Such studies examine revenues generated from tuition and from externally sponsored research or service contracts and grants as components of faculty activity. These revenues are then translated into spending by higher education employees and students in the state and region and are further translated into jobs created and tax revenues derived therefrom.

I work at a university in a small state, where a significant number of out-of-state students are enrolled. For years, state and local legislators complained about the growing number of nonresident students. The Office of Institutional Research and Planning at that institution, working with faculty economists and graduate students, developed an economic impact model that pointed out the following facts:

- Of the $600-plus million in total resources available to the institution annually, only 20 percent was in the form of state subsidies.
- The university spends over $60 million a year in sponsored activity, much of this owing to contracts and grants for research and public service. Wherever appropriate, the funds are spent in the local economy.

- The university returns in excess of $10 million in employee withholding taxes every year to state and municipal coffers.
- The university acts as a good corporate citizen, using $20 million of its current expenditures for public service and extension activity.
- Total spending by university employees exceeds $110 million annually, supporting over 3,000 jobs outside the university and $55 million in associated wages.
- The university's employee benefits package supports an additional 700-plus jobs outside the university every year, along with $14 million in associated wages.
- Over and above tuition, fees, and room and board, university students annually spend in excess of $80 million off campus, supporting over 1,500 jobs and $32 million in associated wages. Of the $32 million, $21 million is attributable to nonresident students.
- The total economic impact of university employees and students on the state economy is in excess of $83 million in taxable salaries and wages generated.

Economic Impact

Although the foregoing data are clearly quantitative, they have a qualitative dimension as well. In addition to making the philosophical argument that research and service activity lead to the sorts of biomedical, technological, and other sorts of gains previously described, it is also possible to argue that the infusion of monies from employees and students, which would not happen were teaching, research, and service not taking place, creates jobs and tax revenues that ultimately improve the quality of life in the state and region. These sorts of economic impact studies are now fairly commonplace among major research universities; Ohio State University, the University of North Carolina, and Pennsylvania State University are three particularly good examples.

But smaller regional institutions are also making economic impact arguments to underpin institutional activity. The Office of Institutional Research and Planning at Southeastern Louisiana University in Hammond, Louisiana, has developed a straightforward, easily replicated economic impact model that lends itself particularly well to smaller institutions with a primary teaching mission.

Conclusion

When I customized the general quantitative and qualitative frameworks outlined in Chapter Three and in this chapter for my institution, interdepartmental benchmarking within the institution quickly became an accepted practice. A change in senior leadership in the early 1990s brought a president, a provost, and an executive vice president who were comfortable with and committed to the benchmarking concept as a way of better understanding an academic department's or program's productivity and management practices.

As useful as interdepartmental comparisons were, senior management felt that the data would be more meaningful if the History Department or the Physics Department at my institution were compared with history departments and physics departments at other peer institutions. This simple request for better comparative data triggered a series of events that has resulted in a major national study of the productivity of America's faculty. That study has resulted in consistent and reliable benchmarking data that have been used in diverse and creative ways to better explain what faculty do, while providing better information for managing faculty resources and containing costs. The remainder of this book will extend the frameworks and methodologies described thus far and will describe the evolution of the National Study of Instructional Costs and Productivity, better known as the Delaware Study, and will detail the results of years of benchmarking activity at the institutional, state, and national levels.

CHAPTER FIVE

LAYING THE GROUNDWORK FOR DEPENDABLE PRODUCTIVITY BENCHMARKS

Chapter Three provided a framework for developing consistent and reliable measures of instructional productivity and costs, as well as contextual measures of externally sponsored research and service activity. By using this framework at any institution, it is possible to compare, between and among academic departments and programs, variables such as lower-division undergraduate student credit hours taught per FTE tenured and tenure-track faculty (or any other faculty category), direct expense per student credit hour taught, research and service expenditures per FTE faculty on appointment, and so on.

Suppose, however, that the focus could be on cost per student credit hour taught in physics at Research University A compared with the average cost per credit hour in physics at a large sample of research universities. Or suppose it were possible to compare the FTE students taught to FTE faculty ratio in foreign languages at Institution A with the average ratio at institutions offering only the baccalaureate in foreign languages. Clearly the next step in comparative data analysis of teaching productivity and cost information is to establish national benchmarks at the academic discipline level.

As noted at the end of Chapter Four, in the early 1990s senior management at the University of Delaware determined that there was a real need at the institution for comparative benchmarking data that would enable inter-institutional comparisons, at the academic department level, of variables that measured faculty instructional productivity, costs, and externally sponsored faculty activity. The

Office of Institutional Research and Planning was given responsibility for collecting such data. The institution was so committed to this benchmarking activity that it agreed to underwrite the costs for a national data collection.

At the time, this data collection, which would turn out to be my task, seemed daunting. Shortly after I arrived at the University of Delaware as director of institutional research in 1985, I tried to secure some simple, basic data on teaching loads and instructional costs (for example, total student credit hours taught, student-faculty ratios, cost per credit hour) at the department level from five flagship institutions in states similar in size and mission to Delaware: Vermont, New Hampshire, Maine, Rhode Island, and Connecticut. To my chagrin it might have proven easier and more productive to ask for gold bullion from Fort Knox than to ask for teaching-load and cost data from academic departments at other institutions. Such data were jealously guarded and generally unavailable to outsiders. So when I was charged with responsibility for a national data collection, I was willing to pursue the task, but I was not optimistic.

The early 1990s brought a different set of circumstances to higher education than those prevailing in 1985. Critics of higher education were beginning their chorus of complaints that tenured faculty were not teaching and that undergraduate students were being shortchanged on their tuition dollars. Indeed, the seminal article referenced in Chapter One by Zemsky and Massy titled "Cost Containment: Committing to a New Economic Reality" appeared in *Change Magazine* in 1990 and called for better management of both faculty teaching loads and instructional costs. The so-called accountability movement was gaining steam, and discussion of performance measures was becoming the vogue in statehouses across the nation. Much of the nation was mired in an economic recession, and public and private financial support for higher education was stagnant. If ever there was a time for exchange of information that could lead to better management of both faculty and fiscal resources, this was it.

Initial Data Collection

The National Study of Instructional Costs and Productivity (NSICP) was launched at the University of Delaware in 1992. The initial data collection was primitive at best. A data collection form was developed and pilot tested at four institutions that spanned the Carnegie taxonomy from comprehensive college to research university. A total of 360 institutions were invited to participate; 16 research universities, 22 doctoral universities, and 58 comprehensive colleges ultimately provided data during the 1992 cycle. The data were analyzed, and five basic productivity and cost ratios were developed:

- Student credit hours taught per FTE faculty
- FTE students taught per FTE faculty
- Instructional cost per student credit hour
- Instructional cost per FTE students taught
- Sponsored research and service expenditures per FTE faculty

The operating hypothesis was that faculty at comprehensive institutions would teach more at lower cost than faculty at doctoral universities who, in turn, would teach more at lower cost than faculty at research universities. The reverse pattern was expected for research and service, with the highest levels expected at research universities and the lowest levels at comprehensive institutions.

Things do not always work out as expected; the 1992 data analysis was a case in point. The data suggested that across the disciplines, doctoral universities taught heavier loads than either comprehensive institutions or research universities, whereas research and service at doctoral and comprehensive institutions were essentially on a par. These findings were counterintuitive but nonetheless merited reporting. I prepared papers for presentation at the 1994 annual meeting of the Association for Institutional Research (AIR) (Middaugh, 1994a) and the Society for College and University Planning (SCUP) (Middaugh, 1994b). The papers presented the data analyses in great detail and offered explanations for why the results might be misleading.

Difficulties with Collection

Potential error rested primarily in two sources: idiosyncratic anomalies growing out of sample dependency within the data, particularly among the relatively small number of research and doctoral universities reporting, and an overly simplistic and incomplete data collection format. Exhibit 5.1 displays the data collection form that was used in that initial 1992 data cycle. I show it not so much for what it asks as for what it *does not* ask.

In requesting data at the academic discipline level of analysis, respondents were asked to identify academic departments or programs using the Classification of Instructional Programs (CIP) code taxonomy developed by the National Center for Education Statistics (NCES). NCES uses this taxonomy in national data collections related to Fall enrollments, degree completions, retention and graduation rates, and so on, to ensure integrity and consistency across institutions when reporting data by discipline. It is a tried and true taxonomy that is well understood by colleges and universities across the country. And it is just about the only data element from this initial data collection form that has survived over the years.

EXHIBIT 5.1. 1992 NSICP DATA COLLECTION INSTRUMENT.

DISCIPLINE _____ (CIP CODE = _____)

1. Total Full-Time Equivalent Enrollment
   a. Fall 1991 Semester
      Undergraduate _____
      Graduate   _____
   b. Spring 1992 Semester
      Undergraduate _____
      Graduate   _____
2. Student credit hours generated in courses originating in this
   department during 1991–92 academic year
      Undergraduate _____
      Graduate   _____
3. Total headcount enrollment in courses originating in this department
   during 1991–92 academic year.

      _____

4. Full-time equivalent faculty as of November 1, 1991
      Chair   _____
      Regular Faculty on Appointment _____
      Supplemental Faculty   _____
5. Percent of regular faculty who hold tenure _____
6. Total expenditures for instruction during fiscal year 1992

      _____

   Total expenditures for separately budgeted research and service
   activity during Fiscal Year 1994

      _____

The difficulties with the data collection instrument are best summarized as follows:

• The form collected detailed data on enrollment. But, as I noted in Chapter Three, there is not necessarily a correlation between the number of majors in a department and the volume of teaching activity. Service departments such as philosophy or anthropology may have few majors but do extensive teaching, as nonmajors use departmental courses to satisfy general education requirements.

• The form collected data on student credit hours taught at the undergraduate and graduate levels but did not enable distinction between lower-division instruction (freshmen and sophomores) and upper-division instruction (juniors and seniors), nor did it distinguish between general graduate-level instruction and individual instruction such as thesis and dissertation supervision. The form was silent on any non-credit-bearing instruction.

• Although data on student credit hour generation were collected, there was no request for information on highest degree offered within a program. The cost of delivering instruction in a baccalaureate-only program is different from those in which doctoral study is a significant component. The relative emphasis on graduate education also has a significant effect on average teaching loads.

• The form consistently asked for data on a semester time frame, ignoring the roughly one-third of institutions that were on quarter calendars. Term workloads are very different in semester-based and quarter-based institutions. No corrective algorithm was built into the analysis.

• The form asked for data on the number of regular and supplemental faculty but did not permit easy distinction between tenured and tenure-track faculty and other nontenurable faculty on recurring contracts. Nor did it enable the easy disaggregation of graduate teaching assistants from supplemental faculty, despite the fact that much of the criticism directed at higher education centered on the use of graduate teaching assistants in place of regular faculty. Without this level of detail, the teaching workload ratios are less than instructive.

• Although the form asked for expenditure data for instruction, it did not allow for identification of specific cost drivers such as salaries, benefits, and other-than-personnel-expenses. The missing detail helps to provide explanatory information for any extreme variations in the data.

The AIR and SCUP presentations in 1994 were heavily attended, and the discussion focused on many of the methodological issues that relate data collection and data definition. The comments were decidedly constructive. When I presented those papers at AIR and SCUP, I believed I was reporting data from a one-time collection. The participants at those two national meetings were both pleased and excited that institutions were, at long last, prepared to share teaching-workload and cost data at the academic discipline level of analysis. I was urged to replicate the study with enhancements and modifications that addressed the concerns raised at the meetings.

TIAA-CREF/FIPSE Support for New Data Collection

This was not a trivial request. The University of Delaware had funded the initial data collection, and expenses ran well into the thousands of dollars. If the study were to be replicated, external funding would be essential. So in early 1995 I approached the Teachers Insurance Annuity Association–College Retirement Equities Fund (TIAA-CREF) at their New York City corporate headquarters to determine whether there was interest in funding a second data collection under the TIAA-CREF Cooperative Research Grant Program. The response was both positive and enthusiastic. The NSICP was viewed as a potential tool for helping academic managers plan and contain costs. A funding arrangement was achieved within weeks. The speed with which TIAA-CREF underwrote the project and their level of support was clear indication that the issues being addressed were of immediate and pressing interest not only to colleges and universities but to the agencies and organizations that are associated with higher education.

With support from TIAA-CREF, a data collection was planned for Fall 1995 that was decidedly different from the initial 1992 cycle. The grant enabled two strategic initiatives in defining the course of the 1995 data collection. It provided sufficient funds to cover promotional costs that were aimed at greater visibility for and institutional participation in the NSICP. It also funded the creation and implementation of an advisory panel to the project director. The panel was made up of acknowledged experts from across the nation in the areas of measuring faculty work, instructional teaching loads, and instructional, research, and service costs. Among the key individuals who have served on the advisory panel are

- Paul Brinkman, University of Utah; author of numerous books, chapters, articles on higher education costs
- Robert Kuhn, Louisiana State University; a leader in identifying definitional and practical problems associated with collecting and interpreting expenditure data
- Mary Sapp, University of Miami; acknowledged national expert on productivity indicators (Sapp and Tamares, 1992); key resource person on data needs of private and independently chartered institutions
- Deborah Teeter, University of Kansas; consultant to the National Center for Higher Education Management Systems (NCHEMS) on their *Handbook on Human Resources: Record Keeping and Analysis*; Chair, JCAR Technical Work Group on Faculty Activity Reporting

The advisory panel concept has been retained since the initial 1995 meeting. The panel has, on an annual basis, systematically reviewed and revamped the data definitions, methodology, calculation conventions, and reporting structures to arrive at the broadly accepted practices that are currently in place and that will be described in detail in Chapter Six. The TIAA-CREF funding that underwrote the 1995 data cycle resulted in significant gains: the number of participating research universities increased from 16 to 36; doctoral universities increased from 22 to 45; comprehensive colleges and universities increased from 58 to 115. Because the TIAA-CREF grant was a one-time, single-year grant, the project director immediately moved to secure additional funding and was successful in securing a three-year grant from the Fund for Improvement of Post Secondary Education (FIPSE) within the U.S. Department of Education. The successive TIAA-CREF-FIPSE grants enabled a protracted period in which the National Study of Instructional Costs and Productivity—the Delaware Study, as it had come to be known—could be actively and aggressively promoted, while the advisory panel continued to review and build on successful methodological enhancements.

Maturation of the Delaware Study

If the Delaware Study has developed a defining characteristic during its maturation from 1992 to the present, it is that, despite its name, the University of Delaware does not own the study. Although that institution is host to the project, the methodology and analytical conventions have been defined by the institutions that have participated in it over the years. In addition to an ongoing advisory panel, participants in the study are encouraged to comment on all aspects of the project throughout any given data collection cycle. As a result of this openness and receptivity to suggestions, the Delaware Study represents the collective wisdom of faculty, academic deans and department chairs, institutional researchers, and budget officers across the United States. There is a sense of investment in and return on investment from all of the data collection and analytical activities associated with the study. It is appropriate, then, to examine the current data collection process and to examine basic analytical strategies before moving into a fuller discussion of national benchmarks in Chapter Six.

The Data Collection Form

The data collection form for the Delaware Study has become substantially more comprehensive and complex than the initial 1992 version. Exhibit 5.2 displays the first portion of data currently being collected. Included are general institutional data, as well as specific information on instructional teaching loads.

Note that earlier oversights with respect to highest degree offered and type of academic calendar have been corrected. The data collection now seeks not only the highest degree offered but the three-year average number of degrees awarded at the baccalaureate, master's, doctoral, and professional levels as well. This has proved to be an excellent proxy measure for determining the relative emphasis that a department places on undergraduate and graduate-level education. It is important when comparing benchmark data that predominantly undergraduate departments be compared with like units, whereas predominantly graduate units are compared with other graduate departments. With respect to academic calendar, quarter calendar institutions offer three academic terms within a fiscal year, compared with two at semester calendar campuses. It is therefore essential that data be adjusted for comparability, given the different workloads that result

EXHIBIT 5.2. THE DELAWARE STUDY OF INSTRUCTIONAL COSTS AND PRODUCTIVITY, PART A: INSTRUCTIONAL COURSELOAD.

Institution: _____

Department/Discipline: _____

Associated CIP Identifier: _____

Please indicate the average number of degrees awarded in this discipline at each degree level over the 3-year period from 1994–95 through 1996–97.

Bachelor's: _____
Master's: _____
Doctorate: _____
Professional: _____

Place an "X" in the box below if this discipline is non-degree granting.

_____

A. INSTRUCTIONAL COURSELOAD: FALL SEMESTER, 1997

Please complete the following matrix, displaying student credit hours and organized class sections taught, by type of faculty, and by level of instruction. Be sure to consult definitions before proceeding. Do not input data in shaded cells except for those mention in the important note below that pertains to (G) and (J).

	Faculty			Student Credit Hou			
	FTE Faculty			(D) Lower Div OC*	(E) Upper Div OC*	(F) Undergrad Indv Instruct	(G) Total Undergra SCH
Classification	**(A) Total**	**(B) Separately Budgeted**	**(C) Instruc- tional**				
Regular faculty Tenured/Tenure Eligible							
Other Regular Faculty							
Supplemental Faculty		NA					
Teaching Assistants Credit Bearing Courses		NA					
Non-Credit- Bearing Activity		NA		NA	NA	NA	NA
TOTAL							

*oc=organized class

In the box to the right, indicate the number of Gradua Individualized Instruction Student Credit Hours from th Total that are devoted to supervised doctoral dissertatio

Place an "X" in the box below that
describes your academic calendar:

| | Semester |
| | Quarter |

(H) Grad OC*	(I) Graduate Indv Instruct	(J) Total Graduate SCH	(K) Total Student Credit Hours	(L) Lab/Dsc/ Rec Sections	Organized Class Sections			(P) Total
					Other Section Types (Lecture, Seminar, etc.)			
					(M) Lower Div	(N) Upper Div	(O) Graduate	
NA	NA	NA	NA					

from calendar differences. The advisory panel has developed an algorithm that converts quarter calendar data to semester data for analytical purposes, ensuring apples-with-apples comparisons.

The first point to be underscored is the timing of data collection. Exhibits 5.2 and 5.3 on page 103 display the two data collection components of the study. As a conceptual overview statement, the Delaware Study collects general data on academic year student credit hour production and fiscal year expenditures with respect to instruction, research, and service activity. It also collects detailed teaching-load data for the Fall term within the academic year under examination. In all instances, it is important that institutions have sufficient time to verify and audit data prior to submission.

To illustrate the process, Exhibits 5.2 and 5.3 reflect a data collection cycle that took place during the summer of 1999. The data collected were verified and audited for academic and fiscal year 1997–98 and, in that academic year, the Fall 1997 teaching-load data. A data collection occurring in summer of 1999 would not have allowed for appropriate verification of either 1998–99 instructional or fiscal year data. Chapter Three underscored the importance of involving academic deans and department chairs in verifying teaching-load data, as well as institutional budget personnel to verify and audit expenditure data. To be done correctly, this is a painstaking process that requires time. The Delaware Study acknowledges the importance of accurate data and provides sufficient time within its data collection cycles for complete and accurate verification and audit processes. This is crucial to developing and reporting benchmark data that are both reliable and credible.

Part A in Exhibit 5.2 displays the instructional course-load matrix currently being used by the Delaware Study to capture data on faculty teaching activity. The conceptual definitions for the data elements in the matrix were developed and discussed in Chapter Three. For readers with an interest in the specific definitions used in the Delaware Study, Appendix A to this volume contains the data element dictionary and basic calculation conventions for each of the items in the data collection. The discussion here is restricted to important conceptual issues.

The instructional course-load matrix examines three factors: faculty, student credit hours taught, and organized class sections taught. Keep in mind throughout these discussions that the purpose of the data collection is to create benchmarks against which a given institution can compare itself with respect to teaching loads, instructional costs, and research-service productivity. In refining the data collection activity to the instructional course-load matrix in Part A, the advisory panel sought information that is both complete and accurate. With reference to the faculty portion of the matrix, faculty are disaggregated into the four core groups identified and defined in Chapter Three: tenured and tenure-track faculty, other regular nontenurable faculty, supplemental and adjunct faculty, and graduate teaching assistants.

Note that for purposes of developing accurate teaching-load benchmarks, it is important to focus on an instructional FTE for faculty. Consequently, the first three columns in the matrix, under FTE Faculty, facilitate identification of an FTE instructional faculty. Specifically, institutions are asked to begin with the FTE Faculty for a given department, as it appears in their personnel database (Column A), then to identify on a case-by-case basis those faculty who are contractually obligated to do something other than teach; they are then to back out the FTE that is associated with that nonteaching activity (Column B) to arrive at Instructional FTE (Column C).

A specific example will help clarify this procedure. Suppose Mary Smith is a full-time, tenured chemist who has an NSF grant that supports one-third of her salary for research. Her FTE is 1.0, and that would appear in the Tenured/ Tenure-Eligible row under Column A. However, the grant contractually obligates her to spend one-third of her time in research (0.33 under column B), with one-third of her salary being paid by NSF to support that activity. This time cannot be spent teaching; hence it must be subtracted from the 1.0 FTE in Column A to arrive at an instructional FTE of 0.67 in Column C. It is important to make these adjustments to arrive at an accurate instructional FTE.

For each of the faculty categories, benchmarks will be created that ratio teaching-load data elements against FTE instructional faculty, for example:

- Lower-division student credit hours taught per FTE faculty
- Total undergraduate student credit hours taught per FTE faculty
- Organized class sections taught per FTE faculty

Unless FTE adjustments are made to back out portions of a faculty member's time that are legally unavailable for teaching, the magnitude of instructional workload will be understated, that is, the faculty divisor in any ratio will be too large. This is particularly crucial in the instance of tenured and tenure-eligible faculty who have long been criticized for teaching excessively light loads while nontenurable faculty do the bulk of undergraduate teaching.

Student credit hour generation data are disaggregated in useful ways. Undergraduate student credit hours (SCH) can be captured in total (Column G) or as they are generated in lower-division organized class (OC) sections (Column D), upper-division OC class sections (Column E), and undergraduate individualized instruction (Column F), for example, in directed readings and independent study. Similarly, graduate student credit hours can be captured in total (Column J) or as they are generated in OC section (Column H) and individualized instruction

(Column I). Note that the data collection matrix further asks that individualized instruction devoted to doctoral dissertations be reported at the bottom of Column I.

Organized class sections taught are reported out as Lower Division, Upper Division, and Graduate lecture-seminar sections (Columns M, N, and O), with laboratory, discussion, and recitation (Lab-Dsc-Rec) sections reported separately. Thus if a tenured faculty member were teaching a three-credit introductory chemistry lecture section but also met with a zero-credit laboratory section and a zero-credit recitation section (Column L), both required in addition to the lecture, one section would be reported in the Tenured/Tenure-Eligible row under Column M (lower-division organized class) and two under Column L (laboratory, recitation, discussion).

Thus the course-load matrix enables the production of the following benchmark ratios for *each* of the four core faculty types:

- Lower-division student credit hours taught per FTE instructional faculty
- Upper-division student credit hours taught per FTE instructional faculty
- Individualized undergraduate student credit hours taught per FTE instructional faculty
- Total undergraduate student credit hours taught per FTE instructional faculty
- Graduate organized class section student credit hours taught per FTE instructional faculty
- Graduate individualized instruction student credit hours taught per FTE instructional faculty
- Total student credit hours taught per instructional FTE faculty
- Lower-division organized class sections taught per FTE instructional faculty
- Upper-division organized class sections taught per FTE instructional faculty
- Graduate organized class sections taught per FTE instructional faculty
- Laboratory, recitation, or discussion sections taught per FTE instructional faculty

These ratios can be calculated for faculty within a single institution and will provide answers to questions such as, Do nontenurable faculty teach more undergraduates than tenured faculty? or Do graduate teaching assistants and adjunct faculty teach the majority of lower-division undergraduate student credit hours? These are precisely the sorts of assertions that have taken on an air of fact, despite the absence of any careful quantification of teaching-load data. And as valuable as these ratios are in describing teaching patterns within a single institution, the Delaware Study, with its range of benchmarking capabilities, provides even richer information. The questions can be expanded to include, Are undergraduate and graduate teaching patterns at my institution similar to or different from those in appropriate peer groups? The chair of the History Department at the University of North Carolina can look at the teaching loads of that department's faculty by category and, using the ratios given, determine whether North Carolina's ratios are comparable to benchmarks for research universities throughout the country. Or the chair can select a dozen or so institutions from the pool of universities participating in the study and do a customized peer analysis. The same is true for virtually any chair in any discipline at any four-year institution whether it is a research university, doctoral university, comprehensive college, or baccalaureate college. Specific examples will be illustrated in Chapter Six.

Exhibit 5.3 displays Part B of the data collection form, which focuses on academic year instructional productivity and fiscal year expenditures for instruction, research, and service.

EXHIBIT 5.3. THE DELAWARE STUDY OF INSTRUCTIONAL COSTS AND PRODUCTIVITY, PART B: COST DATA.

B. COST DATA: ACADEMIC AND FISCAL YEAR 1997–98

1. In the boxes below, enter the total number of student credit hours that were generated in AY 1997–98 during terms that were supported by the department's instructional budget. (*Note:* Semester calendar institutions will typically report Fall and Spring student credit hours; quarter calendar institutions will usually report Fall, Winter, and Spring student credit hours.)

A. Undergraduate

B. Graduate

2. In the boxes below, enter total direct expenditures for instruction in FY 1997–98.

A. Salaries — Are the benefits included in the number reported for salaries (Y/N)?

B. Benefits — If the dollar value is not available, what percent of salary do benefits constitute at your institution?

C. Other than personnel expenditures

D. Total

3. In the box below, enter total *direct* expenditures for separately budgeted research activity in FY 1997–98.

4. In the box below, enter total *direct* expenditures for separately budgeted public service activity in FY 1997–98.

The undergraduate and graduate student credit hours reported for the academic year in Exhibit 5.3 are used to calculate FTE students taught, as was done in Chapter Three using the same assumptions about average annual credit loads for undergraduate and graduate students, respectively. The data from Exhibit 5.3, coupled with the imputed FTE students taught and with the tenured and tenure-track total FTE from Exhibit 5.2, enable calculation of the following ratios:

- Direct instructional expense per student credit hour taught
- Direct instructional expense per FTE student taught
- Personnel costs as a percent of total direct instructional expense
- Direct research expenditures per tenured and tenure-track FTE faculty on appointment
- Direct service expenditures per tenured and tenure-track faculty on appointment

Once again, each of these ratios is interesting and helps an institution understand productivity and cost issues between and among its own departments. But when used with Delaware Study national benchmarks for departments at comparable Carnegie institution types or within a customized peer group, the institution has a better sense of where it stands comparatively on quantitative dimensions and can frame appropriate policy questions. Scenarios of this sort will be discussed in Chapter Six.

The National Data

Since the 1995 data collection, 55 research universities, 50 doctoral universities, 125 comprehensive colleges and universities, and 25 baccalaureate colleges have participated in the Delaware Study. Two-thirds of these institutions are state-supported or state-related; one-third are private or independently chartered. Most institutions participate on an annual basis; others elect to step out for a period and re-enter at a later date. Most institutions submit data for both Part A (Fall teaching-load data) and Part B (academic and fiscal year productivity and expenditure data) on the data collection form as displayed in Exhibits 5.2 and 5.3, although institutions do have the option of submitting Part A only or Part B only.

Development of National Benchmarks

The principal purpose for creating the Delaware Study was to develop a set of credible benchmarks that would inform users about teaching workload, instructional cost, and productivity measures, by discipline, from a rich pool of national data. These benchmarks would then be used to make comparisons with institutional data in order to more fully understand how a college or university is using its resources and with what degree of economy and efficiency.

The Delaware Study benchmarks were developed using a fairly conservative methodology. For each variable for which data are submitted in the collection form, as displayed in Exhibits 5.2 and 5.3, a benchmark is developed. For example, suppose the variable in question was "undergraduate student credit hours taught per FTE tenured/tenure-track faculty" or "direct instructional expenditures per student credit hour taught." Institutional responses to these two variables (and any others) are grouped by academic discipline, using one of three analytical lenses: (1) Carnegie classification of the institution, (2) highest degree offered by the institution in the discipline under examination, and (3) the relative emphasis on undergraduate education in the discipline. The last is determined by looking at the proportion of total degrees awarded in the discipline that are undergraduate and placing the institution in the appropriate quintile.

The benchmark is calculated as follows. All institutional responses for a given variable are summed, and an "initial mean" is calculated. In order to prevent an idiosyncratic piece of institutional data from exerting undue influence on the data set, discrete institutional responses are then examined to identify those that are more than two standard deviations above or below the initial mean. These responses are flagged as outliers and are excluded from further calculations. The remaining responses are then re-summed and a "refined mean" is computed. This refined mean then becomes the national benchmark.

The benchmarks are powerful information tools. The Delaware Study presents them in a variety of ways. Tables 5.1, 5.2, and 5.3 provide sample benchmarks for Fall term teaching loads, as calculated from data provided in Part A of the Delaware Study data collection form (shown in Exhibit 5.2). Table 5.4, to be shown later in the chapter, displays benchmarks calculated from the academic and fiscal year data provided in Part B of the Delaware Study data collection form (see Exhibit 5.3).

The benchmarks are presented in different analytical arrays. Institutions tend to rely most heavily on the benchmarks arrayed by Carnegie institutional classification. Research universities prefer to compare their departmental teaching loads, instructional costs, and externally funded activity with those at other research universities. Doctoral universities and comprehensive and baccalaureate institutions are no different. The examples in the following pages reflect that Carnegie classification array. Other arrays include highest degree offered and proportion of total degrees awarded that are baccalaureate.

Table 5.1 contains representative examples of the first of the four basic tables of Delaware Study benchmarks, in this instance reflecting Fall 1997 teaching loads. The table focuses on three disciplines within the social sciences—history, political science, and sociology—although the presentation format would be identical for any discipline included in the study.

Table 5.1 shows the percentage of student credit hours and organized class sections taught by each of the four faculty categories examined in the Delaware Study. Section A reflects tenured and tenure-track faculty; Section B reflects other permanent nontenurable faculty; Section C reflects supplemental faculty; Section D reflects graduate teaching assistants. Put another way, whereas Part A of the collection form (see Exhibit 5.2) examines the rows, Table 5.1 analyzes the columns.

For example, of all the lower-division student credit hours produced in organized classes, what proportion are taught by tenured and tenure-track faculty? By other nontenurable permanent faculty? By supplemental or adjunct faculty? By graduate teaching assistants? Table 5.1 provides quantitative information that enables institutions to respond in detail to the question, Who is teaching what to whom?

Each of the sections of Table 5.1 identifies the discipline and its associated CIP identifier. This reflects the fact that each participating institution has identified this discrete CIP code for the data being submitted for history, political science, and sociology. Within each discipline the data are arrayed for research, doctoral, comprehensive, and baccalaureate institutions. The number of institutions responding within each Carnegie class is displayed, as are data for the following variables, moving left to right across the table:

Student Credit Hours

- Percent of all student credit hours generated in lower-division organized classes that are taught by the respective faculty category (% LD OC)
- Percent of all student credit hours generated in upper-division organized classes that are taught by the respective faculty category (% UD OC)
- Percent of all undergraduate student credit hours generated in organized class sections *and* individualized instruction that are taught by the respective faculty category (% UG OC+II)
- Percent of all graduate student credit hours generated in organized class sections *and* individualized instruction that are taught by the respective faculty category (% UG OC+II)

TABLE 5.1. 1998 NSICP NORMS BY CARNEGIE CLASSIFICATION: PERCENT STUDENT CREDIT HOURS AND ORGANIZED CLASS SECTIONS TAUGHT BY FACULTY CATEGORY WITHIN COURSE LEVEL.

Section A: Percent Student Credit Hours and Organized Class Sections Taught by Faculty Category Within Course Level, Tenured and Tenure-Track Faculty: Fall 1997

CIP	Discipline/ Carnegie Class	N	Student Credit Hours				Organized Class Sections				
			% LD OC	% UD OC	% UG OC+II	% GR OC+II	% Lab/Disc	% LD OC	% UD OC	% UG OC	% GR OC
45.08	History										
	Research	51	66	85	72	93	25	60	84	71	90
	Doctoral	24	77	87	78	94	21	70	85	75	90
	Comprehensive	50	73	91	76	96	0	74	91	77	94
	Baccalaureate	9	72	91	75	na	22	70	92	77	na
45.10	Political Science and Government										
	Research	50	65	74	68	94	4	64	73	67	93
	Doctoral	22	68	81	70	93	28	62	80	72	92
	Comprehensive	42	74	81	76	87	0	74	80	77	87
	Baccalaureate	7	86	83	84	na	0	85	82	82	na
45.11	Sociology										
	Research	49	64	76	68	98	7	59	74	65	94
	Doctoral	21	51	73	60	94	28	50	73	62	96
	Comprehensive	43	73	81	76	67	0	71	84	77	63
	Baccalaureate	8	85	77	84	67	25	75	81	78	67

TABLE 5.1. (continued)

Section B: Percent Student Credit Hours and Organized Class Sections Taught by Faculty Category Within Course Level, Other Nontenurable Permanent Track Faculty: Fall 1997

CIP	Discipline/ Carnegie Class	Student Credit Hours					Organized Class Sections				
		N	% LD OC	% UD OC	% UG OC+II	% GR OC+II	% Lab/Disc	% LD OC	% UD OC	% UG OC	% GR OC
45.08	History										
	Research	51	7	5	6	1	0	7	5	6	2
	Doctoral	24	4	1	4	1	0	4	2	3	2
	Comprehensive	50	3	4	3	1	0	3	2	3	1
	Baccalaureate	9	7	5	6	na	0	7	5	5	na
45.10	Political Science and Government										
	Research	50	6	8	8	1	0	7	7	8	1
	Doctoral	22	7	2	4	0	0	5	3	3	1
	Comprehensive	42	9	4	7	2	0	7	3	5	1
	Baccalaureate	7	0	4	1	na	0	0	11	3	na
45.11	Sociology										
	Research	49	8	7	10	1	0	6	5	8	1
	Doctoral	21	12	7	9	1	0	12	8	9	2
	Comprehensive	43	6	4	6	4	0	5	3	4	4
	Baccalaureate	8	3	3	3	33	0	2	2	2	33

Section C: Percent Student Credit Hours and Organized Class Sections Taught by Faculty Category Within Course Level, Supplemental/Adjunct Faculty: Fall 1997

CIP	Discipline/ Carnegie Class	N	Student Credit Hours				Organized Class Sections				
			% LD OC	% UD OC	% UG OC+II	% GR OC+II	% Lab/Disc	% LD OC	% UD OC	% UG OC	% GR OC
45.08	History										
	Research	51	9	7	7	5	1	9	7	8	6
	Doctoral	24	12	9	12	4	0	12	9	12	4
	Comprehensive	50	18	5	18	2	0	18	5	16	4
	Baccalaureate	9	17	2	16	na	0	17	1	14	na
45.10	Political Science and Government										
	Research	50	11	11	11	4	1	12	11	12	3
	Doctoral	22	14	13	15	5	0	14	13	13	4
	Comprehensive	42	12	7	12	8	0	17	7	13	8
	Baccalaureate	7	3	0	3	na	0	11	0	4	na
45.11	Sociology										
	Research	49	7	9	9	1	0	10	10	11	2
	Doctoral	21	30	16	22	3	2	29	15	20	2
	Comprehensive	43	15	10	15	21	0	17	10	16	23
	Baccalaureate	8	7	4	7	0	0	8	3	7	0

TABLE 5.1. (continued)

Section D: Percent Student Credit Hours and Organized Class Sections Taught by Faculty Category Within Course Level, Graduate Teaching Assistants: Fall 1997

CIP	Discipline/ Carnegie Class	N	Student Credit Hours				Organized Class Sections				
			% LD OC	% UD OC	% UG OC+II	% GR OC+II	% Lab/Disc	% LD OC	% UD OC	% UG OC	% GR OC
45.08	History										
	Research	51	12	1	9	0	0	16	0	9	0
	Doctoral	24	5	0	3	0	0	5	0	5	0
	Comprehensive	50	0	0	0	0	0	0	0	0	0
	Baccalaureate	9	0	0	0	na	0	0	0	0	na
45.10	Political Science and Government										
	Research	50	11	3	8	0	2	11	3	8	0
	Doctoral	22	9	1	6	0	0	8	1	4	0
	Comprehensive	42	0	0	0	0	0	0	0	0	0
	Baccalaureate	7	0	0	0	na	0	0	0	0	na
45.11	Sociology										
	Research	49	12	3	10	0	2	16	4	12	0
	Doctoral	21	4	2	4	0	0	4	2	4	0
	Comprehensive	43	0	0	0	0	0	0	0	0	0
	Baccalaureate	8	0	0	0	0	0	0	0	0	0

Organized Class Sections

- Percent of all organized laboratory, discussion, and recitation sections that are taught by the respective faculty category (% Lab/Dsc)
- Percent of all lower-division organized class sections that are taught by the respective faculty category (% LD OC)
- Percent of upper-division organized class sections that are taught by the respective faculty category (% UD OC)
- Percent of all undergraduate organized class sections that are taught by the respective faculty category (% UG OC)
- Percent of all graduate organized class sections that are taught by the respective faculty category (% GR OC)

Whereas Table 5.1 analyzed the columns in Part A of the collection form, Table 5.2 analyzes the rows. Of all of the student credit hours taught by tenured and tenure-track faculty in a given discipline, what percent are lower division? Upper division? Graduate? Because by using this analytical lens, institutions focus almost exclusively on tenured and tenure-track and permanent nontenurable faculty (both recurring expense categories), the Delaware Study presents national benchmarks only for those two groups of faculty.

Table 5.2 displays data for tenured and tenure-track faculty in Section A, whereas Section B displays comparable information for permanent nontenurable faculty. Once again, the data are broken out by the Carnegie classification of the participating institutions.

Feedback from institutions participating in the Delaware Study over the years indicates that, when looking at issues dealing with faculty teaching loads, Table 5.3 is the one that provosts and deans rely on most. It displays productivity ratios (for example, student credit hours taught per FTE faculty, class sections taught per FTE faculty, and FTE students taught per FTE faculty). It is straightforward and clear and contains benchmarks that are easy for busy executives to understand.

Table 5.3 is divided into Sections A through D, each related to one of the four respective faculty categories, and again with the data arrayed by the Carnegie classification of the participating institution. The variables analyzed include the following:

- Undergraduate student credit hours (UG SCH) taught per FTE instructional faculty, by category
- Undergraduate organized class sections (UG OC), excluding laboratories, recitations, and discussions, taught per FTE instructional faculty, by category

TABLE 5.2 1998 NSICP NORMS BY CARNEGIE CLASSIFICATION: PERCENT STUDENT CREDIT HOURS AND ORGANIZED CLASS SECTIONS BY COURSE LEVEL WITHIN FACULTY CATEGORY.

Section A: Percent Student Credit Hours and Organized Class Sections by Course Level Within Faculty Category, Tenured and Tenure-Track Faculty: Fall 1997

CIP	Discipline/ Carnegie Class	N	Student Credit Hours				Organized Class Sections				
			% LD OC	% UD OC	% UG OC+II	% GR OC+II	% Lab/Disc	% LD OC	% UD OC	% UG OC	% GR OC
45.08	History										
	Research	51	56	33	92	8	4	30	42	74	18
	Doctoral	24	58	32	92	8	1	35	39	79	21
	Comprehensive	50	71	27	99	4	1	56	36	94	14
	Baccalaureate	9	71	22	100	na	1	57	40	97	na
45.10	Political Science and Government										
	Research	50	49	40	89	11	2	22	45	68	28
	Doctoral	22	50	35	89	13	1	26	42	71	30
	Comprehensive	42	63	33	98	6	0	49	42	93	15
	Baccalaureate	7	67	32	100	na	0	49	44	98	na
45.11	Sociology										
	Research	49	51	39	93	7	2	25	45	73	26
	Doctoral	21	38	51	92	9	1	22	53	76	25
	Comprehensive	43	61	37	100	3	0	45	51	97	10
	Baccalaureate	8	66	31	100	2	1	55	40	97	4

Section B: Percent Student Credit Hours and Organized Class Sections by Course Level Within Faculty Category, Other Non-tenurable, Permanent Faculty: Fall 1997

CIP	Discipline/ Carnegie Class	N	Student Credit Hours				Organized Class Sections				
			% LD OC	% UD OC	% UG OC+II	% GR OC+II	% Lab/Disc	% LD OC	% UD OC	% UG OC	% GR OC
45.08	History										
	Research	51	60	36	99	1	0	50	42	93	7
	Doctoral	24	65	24	99	1	0	67	20	87	6
	Comprehensive	50	65	29	99	2	0	56	37	96	10
	Baccalaureate	9	70	29	100	na	0	69	31	100	na
45.10	Political Science and Government										
	Research	50	50	46	99	2	2	40	52	94	4
	Doctoral	22	56	23	99	1	0	39	42	92	11
	Comprehensive	42	68	30	100	1	0	59	35	95	3
	Baccalaureate	7	20	77	100	na	17	17	67	83	na
45.11	Sociology										
	Research	49	52	39	99	1	0	42	48	95	3
	Doctoral	21	52	44	99	3	0	41	48	93	13
	Comprehensive	43	59	37	99	6	0	52	43	98	11
	Baccalaureate	8	52	30	82	18	0	47	42	89	11

TABLE 5.3. 1998 NSICP NORMS BY CARNEGIE CLASSIFICATION: NUMBER OF STUDENT CREDIT HOURS, ORGANIZED CLASS SECTIONS, AND FTE STUDENTS TAUGHT PER FTE INSTRUCTIONAL FACULTY.

Section A: Number of Student Credit Hours, Organized Class Sections, and FTE Students Taught per FTE Instructional Faculty: Tenured and Tenure-Track, Fall 1997

CIP	Discipline/Carnegie Class	N	UG SCH	UG OC Sections (Exc. Lab)	GR SCH	GR OC Sections (Exc. Lab)	Total SCH	Total OC Sections (Exc. Lab)	Total OC Sections (Inc. Lab)	FTE Students Taught
45.08	History									
	Research	51	234	1.7	21	0.4	258	2.2	2.3	18.1
	Doctoral	24	223	2.1	19	0.7	242	2.7	2.7	16.9
	Comprehensive	50	258	3.2	11	0.4	263	3.4	3.5	17.7
	Baccalaureate	9	185	3.2	na	na	187	3.2	3.3	12.5
45.10	Political Science and Government									
	Research	50	191	1.4	22	0.6	214	2.0	2.1	15.3
	Doctoral	22	162	1.8	25	0.7	187	2.5	2.5	13.5
	Comprehensive	42	224	3.2	15	0.5	232	3.4	3.4	16.3
	Baccalaureate	7	194	2.9	na	na	196	2.9	3.0	13.1
45.11	Sociology									
	Research	49	282	1.6	22	0.5	298	2.2	2.4	20.8
	Doctoral	21	245	2.0	21	0.6	255	2.5	2.6	17.8
	Comprehensive	43	297	3.3	11	0.4	300	3.4	3.4	20.1
	Baccalaureate	8	242	3.2	3	0.1	243	3.3	3.4	16.3

Section B: Number of Student Credit Hours, Organized Class Sections, and FTE Students Taught per FTE Instructional Faculty: Other Nontenurable, Permanent, Fall 1997

CIP	Discipline/Carnegie Class	N	UG SCH	UG OC Sections (Exc. Lab)	GR SCH	GR OC Sections (Exc. Lab)	Total SCH	Total OC Sections (Exc. Lab)	Total OC Sections (Inc. Lab)	FTE Students Taught
45.08	History									
	Research	51	372	2.4	4	0.1	379	2.5	2.6	25.6
	Doctoral	24	349	3.0	4	0.2	359	3.2	3.3	27.7
	Comprehensive	50	302	3.2	6	0.3	305	3.3	3.3	20.5
	Baccalaureate	9	235	3.5	na	na	235	3.5	3.5	15.6
45.10	Political Science and Government									
	Research	50	377	2.7	4	0.1	384	2.8	2.8	25.9
	Doctoral	22	215	2.6	6	0.2	234	3.0	3.0	16.4
	Comprehensive	42	347	3.6	1	0.1	352	3.7	3.8	23.7
	Baccalaureate	7	234	5.6	na	na	234	5.6	7.6	15.6
45.11	Sociology									
	Research	49	505	2.7	3	0.1	516	2.7	2.8	34.8
	Doctoral	21	436	3.6	6	0.2	444	3.6	3.6	30.0
	Comprehensive	43	381	3.2	6	0.4	388	3.4	3.4	26.1
	Baccalaureate	8	239	3.4	32	0.4	272	3.8	3.8	19.6

TABLE 5.3. (*continued*)

Section C: Number of Student Credit Hours, Organized Class Sections, and FTE Students Taught per FTE Instructional Faculty: Supplemental/Adjunct, Fall 1997

CIP	Discipline/ Carnegie Class	N	UG SCH	UG OC Sections (Exc. Lab)	GR SCH	GR OC Sections (Exc. Lab)	Total SCH	Total OC Sections (Exc. Lab)	Total OC Sections (Inc. Lab)	FTE Students Taught
45.08	History									
	Research	51	319	3.1	14	0.5	340	3.6	4.0	23.6
	Doctoral	24	314	3.4	6	0.4	327	3.8	3.8	22.4
	Comprehensive	50	344	3.5	4	0.3	347	3.6	3.7	23.2
	Baccalaureate	9	325	3.0	na	na	326	3.0	3.1	21.8
45.10	Political Science and Government									
	Research	50	372	3.0	9	0.2	384	3.4	3.6	26.2
	Doctoral	22	304	3.0	13	0.7	318	3.6	3.6	21.9
	Comprehensive	42	236	3.1	12	0.5	244	3.5	3.5	16.6
	Baccalaureate	7	183	3.0	na	na	183	3.0	3.0	12.2
45.11	Sociology									
	Research	49	387	3.2	4	0.2	392	3.7	3.7	26.4
	Doctoral	21	422	3.6	4	0.1	427	3.8	3.9	28.7
	Comprehensive	43	281	3.7	3	0.5	283	3.8	3.9	19.0
	Baccalaureate	8	244	3.3	0	0.0	244	3.3	3.3	16.3

Section D: Number of Student Credit Hours, Organized Class Sections, and FTE Students Taught per FTE Instructional Faculty: Graduate Teaching Assistants, Fall 1997

CIP	Discipline/ Carnegie Class	N	UG SCH	UG OC Sections (Exc. Lab)	GR SCH	GR OC Sections (Exc. Lab)	Total SCH	Total OC Sections (Exc. Lab)	Total OC Sections (Inc. Lab)	FTE Students Taught
45.08	History									
	Research	51	414	3.1	0	0.0	414	3.1	4.5	27.6
	Doctoral	24	473	3.5	0	0.0	473	3.5	3.5	31.5
	Comprehensive	50	357	2.8	0	0.0	357	2.8	2.8	23.8
	Baccalaureate	9	na	na	na	na	na	na	na	na
45.10	Political Science and Government									
	Research	50	363	3.0	0	0.0	364	3.0	3.8	24.3
	Doctoral	22	350	2.6	0	0.0	350	2.6	2.6	23.4
	Comprehensive	42	na	na	na	na	na	na	na	na
	Baccalaureate	7	na	na	na	na	na	na	na	na
45.11	Sociology									
	Research	49	462	2.8	0	0.0	462	2.9	3.9	30.9
	Doctoral	21	477	3.3	0	0.0	477	3.3	3.3	31.8
	Comprehensive	43	500	3.5	0	0.0	500	3.5	3.5	33.3
	Baccalaureate	8	na	na	na	na	na	na	na	na

- Graduate student credit hours (GR SCH) taught per FTE instructional faculty, by category
- Undergraduate organized class sections (UG OC), excluding laboratories, recitations, and discussions, taught per FTE instructional faculty, by category
- Total student credit hours (Total SCH) taught per FTE instructional faculty, by category
- Total organized class sections (Total OC), *excluding* laboratories, recitations, and discussions, taught per FTE instructional faculty, by category
- Total organized class sections (Total OC), *including* laboratories, recitations, and discussions, taught per FTE instructional faculty, by category
- FTE students taught per FTE instructional faculty, by category

Why exclude laboratories, recitation, and discussion sections from several of the organized class section ratios? The Delaware Study is rooted in reality and credibility. And the reality is that despite institutions' best attempts to cleanse data before submitting it, tenured and tenure-track faculty or "staff" often persist as instructors of record for zero-credit labs, recitation, and discussion sections. Consequently, the Delaware Study Advisory Panel recommends that the "organized class sections per FTE faculty" benchmark exclude those ambiguous sections when analysis is done by instructional level, that is, by undergraduate and graduate sections. They further recommended providing two "total organized class section" benchmarks, one excluding and one including labs, recitations, and discussions and the other including them.

Table 5.3 reflects that advice. Section A of Table 5.3 reflects instructional productivity ratios for tenured and tenure-track faculty; Section B for other permanent nontenurable faculty; Section C for supplemental and adjunct faculty; and Section D for graduate teaching assistants.

Table 5.4 displays the data found in the academic year and fiscal year productivity and expenditure benchmarks, which are calculated from data provided in Part B (as displayed in Exhibit 5.3) of the data collection form.

Benchmarks are displayed for each of the following variables:

- Direct instructional expenditures per student credit hour taught
- Direct instructional expenditures per FTE student taught
- Personnel expenditures as a percent of total instructional expenditures
- Separately budgeted research expenditures per FTE tenured and tenure-track faculty (the faculty category that is expected to generate contracts and grants)
- Separately budgeted public service expenditures per FTE tenured and tenure-track faculty

TABLE 5.4. 1998 NSICP NORMS BY CARNEGIE CLASSIFICATION: INSTRUCTIONAL COST RATIOS, RESEARCH, AND PUBLIC SERVICE.

Section A: Instructional Cost Ratios, Research and Public Service Expenditure Ratios, Academic and Fiscal Year 1997–98

CIP	Discipline/ Carnegie Class	N	Direct Exp. per SCH	Direct Exp. per FTE Student	Personnel of Direct Instr. Exp.	Research FTE T/TT Faculty	Service FTE T/TT Faculty	Research and Service FTE T/TT Faculty
45.08	History							
	Research	38	129	3,964	96	1,285	250	1,624
	Doctoral	22	139	3,922	96	1,638	312	2,309
	Comprehensive	45	106	3,121	98	221	3	280
	Baccalaureate	8	108	3,236	97	na	na	na
45.10	Political Science and Government							
	Research	37	160	4,777	94	3,686	699	5,274
	Doctoral	20	172	4,849	95	2,766	448	5,651
	Comprehensive	37	121	3,582	97	23	0	142
	Baccalaureate	6	160	4,795	97	na	na	na
45.11	Sociology							
	Research	36	108	3,254	95	13,123	830	15,621
	Doctoral	19	122	3,598	95	5,716	354	6,374
	Comprehensive	39	96	2,751	97	233	0	77
	Baccalaureate	7	130	3,773	98	na	na	na

- Total separately budgeted expenditures for research and public service combined per FTE tenured and tenure-track faculty

The data in Table 5.4 reflect full academic and fiscal year activity and provide a consistently measured and straightforward presentation of benchmarks assessing direct instructional costs and separately funded scholarly activity.

The examples of Delaware Study data presented thus far have focused on arraying the data by Carnegie classification of participating institutions. Table 5.5 shows two other arrays for the data, that is, by highest degree offered in the discipline and by undergraduate-graduate program mix. The latter is assessed by examining undergraduate degrees awarded as a percent of total degrees in each discipline and assigning the institution to the appropriate quartile for that discipline.

Clearly the Delaware Study provides a richly textured array of data on teaching loads, instructional costs, and externally funded research and service. The next chapter focuses on both national and institutional uses of these benchmarks. It will quickly become evident that the Delaware Study data represent a significant breakthrough, both in terms of explaining what faculty do and as a basis for academic planning decisions at the institutional level. The Delaware Study is the product of extended national conversations between and among colleges and universities with expressed needs for these sorts of data. But it is also the product of a carefully conceived and highly refined methodology that attempts to ensure the integrity and consistency of the data being collected. It is the only study that examines data at the level of the academic discipline, and the foregoing pages provide ample evidence that the Delaware Study yields a treasure trove of information.

Conclusion

The utility of quantitative measures of teaching loads, instructional costs, and research-service productivity was clearly established in Chapter Three. However, restricting comparisons that use these measures solely to interdepartmental comparisons within a single institution is limiting. The national need for consistent and reliable inter-institutional comparisons at the academic discipline level became evident from the initial iteration of the NSICP and its growth and maturation, both in terms of data content and volume of participants, into what is now referred to as the Delaware Study. This chapter has detailed the development of a broad range of data variables for describing teaching loads, instructional costs, and externally sponsored research and service productivity. The

TABLE 5.5. 1998 NSICP NORMS BY HIGHEST DEGREE OFFERED: PERCENT STUDENT CREDIT HOURS AND ORGANIZED CLASS SECTIONS TAUGHT BY FACULTY CATEGORY WITHIN COURSE LEVEL.

Section A: Percent Student Credit Hours and Organized Class Sections Taught by Faculty Category Within Course Level for Tenured and Tenure-Track Faculty: Fall 1997

CIP	Discipline/ Carnegie Class	N	Student Credit Hours				Organized Class Sections				
			% LD OC	% UD OC	% UG OC+II	% GR OC+II	% Lab/Disc	% LD OC	% UD OC	% UG OC	% GR OC
45.08	History										
	Doctorate/ Professional	45	68	86	72	95	30	64	85	72	92
	Master's	46	72	86	74	91	3	65	86	73	89
	Bachelor's	42	75	91	77	96	0	75	91	77	98
45.10	Political Science and Government										
	Doctorate/ Professional	40	63	73	66	95	7	58	72	64	93
	Master's	38	68	82	73	88	8	69	79	74	87
	Bachelor's	39	75	81	79	95	0	76	82	79	94
45.11	Sociology										
	Doctorate/ Professional	42	59	74	64	98	9	53	73	62	94
	Master's	28	57	76	65	95	30	57	77	68	95
	Bachelor's	48	76	82	77	59	0	74	83	75	57

TABLE 5.5. (*continued*)

Section A: Normative Percent Student Credit Hours and Organized Class Sections by Faculty Category within Course Level for Tenured and Tenure-Track Faculty, Fall 1997

			Student Credit Hours				Organized Class Sections				
CIP	Discipline/ Carnegie Class	N	% LD OC	% UD OC	% UG OC+II	% GR OC+II	% Lab/Disc	% LD OC	% UD OC	% UG OC	% GR OC
45.07	Geography										
	UG degree: 75–100%	38	69	77	70	91	10	69	75	71	88
	UG degree: 50–75%	18	71	82	72	98	30	67	85	73	100
45.08	History										
	UG degree: 75–100%	107	72	87	75	94	2	69	87	75	90
	UG degree: 50–75%	26	66	89	71	93	38	62	89	71	93
45.10	Political Science and Government										
	UG degree: 75–100%	98	70	78	72	92	2	67	78	72	91
	UG degree: 50–75%	17	71	78	74	88	9	73	77	73	87

chapter has provided a strategy for developing reliable and usable benchmarks against which a given institution's data can be measured.

The proof of the utility of a benchmark is the extent to which it factors into institutional planning and decision making. The remainder of this book will focus on how Delaware Study data are currently being used and on planned enhancements in the range and scope of information being benchmarked. Chapter Six examines how the well-established quantitative measures from the Delaware Study are being used. The planned enhancements address an earlier theme in this book: that although quantitative measures of productivity and costs are both useful and instructive, they do not present a complete picture. The qualitative dimension of faculty and departmental activity must also be addressed, and that presents the next frontier for the Delaware Study, as will be seen in Chapter Seven.

CHAPTER SIX

USING QUANTITATIVE BENCHMARKING DATA

Chapter Five described the inception and maturation of the Delaware Study as a vehicle for benchmarking institutional measures of faculty teaching activity, instructional productivity, and expenditure data for instruction and externally sponsored research and service activity. Although these benchmarks appear promising, their value can be fully realized only if they are used for academic planning and policy analysis.

This chapter explores ways in which Delaware Study data are being used to describe instructional productivity and costs at both the national and institutional level. The discussion will begin with a clear response to the question, How much do faculty really teach? Having established the utility of national benchmarking data for mega-level analysis, the focus will then shift to how institutions use benchmark data for self-improvement and academic planning.

Productivity and Cost Benchmarks: A National Perspective

As I mentioned in Chapter Five, the initial Delaware Study data collection in 1992 was fairly primitive and yielded little of value other than a willingness on the part of institutions to share data on teaching productivity and costs that had heretofore been jealously guarded. However, beginning with the 1995 data collection—the first under the auspices of an advisory committee—the data have revealed an integrity and consistency that demonstrate the maturity and stability of the Delaware Study.

To illustrate this stability, an analysis of the national data has been performed annually at the University of Delaware since the 1995 data collection. The intent of the analysis is to regularly examine a broad spectrum of curricula that would typically be offered at any four-year institution in the United States. Those curricula would then be examined with respect to the question, Who is teaching what to whom and at what cost?

In the analysis, the national benchmarks are examined for twenty-four academic disciplines that are generally offered at most colleges or universities, regardless of Carnegie classification or funding control. Those disciplines include the following:

Communications	Psychology
Computer and Information Sciences	Anthropology
Education	Economics
Engineering	Geography
Foreign Languages and Literature	History
English	Political Science
Biological Sciences	Sociology
Mathematics	Visual and Performing Arts
Philosophy	Nursing
Chemistry	Business Administration
Geology	Accounting
Physics	Financial Management

Data were collected from forty-eight research universities, forty doctorate-granting universities, eighty comprehensive colleges and universities, and eighteen baccalaureate colleges. (The exact number varies by discipline and year of data collection.) The University of Delaware analyzed the data and developed national benchmarks each year within each academic discipline and sorted the benchmarks based on Carnegie institution type within the discipline.

The analysis focuses largely on teaching-workload benchmarks that are associated with tenured and tenure-track faculty. The focus is on this category of faculty because they represent fixed costs, that is, once tenure is granted, these faculty are with the institution until they retire or resign. And because 85 to 90 percent of direct instructional costs are associated with salaries, it is all the more compelling to focus on the category of faculty that typically are better paid than others. And finally, tenured and tenure-track faculty are the most visible and have been the most common targets for criticism in the popular media.

Delaware Study benchmarks were examined for the following variables:

- Proportion of lower-division student credit hours taught by tenured and tenure-track faculty
- Proportion of lower-division organized class sections taught by tenured and tenure-track faculty
- Proportion of undergraduate student credit hours taught by tenured and tenure-track faculty
- Proportion of undergraduate class sections taught by tenured and tenure-track faculty
- Undergraduate student credit hours per FTE tenured and tenure-track faculty
- Undergraduate organized class sections per FTE tenured and tenure-track faculty
- Total student credit hours per FTE tenured and tenure-track faculty
- Total organized class sections per FTE tenured and tenure-track faculty
- Direct instructional expense per student credit hour taught
- Direct separately budgeted research and service expenditures combined, per FTE tenured and tenure-track faculty

The benchmarks within each discipline were examined to arrive at an average (mean of the means) for the twenty-four disciplines. For example, in Fall 1997 on average across the twenty-four disciplines, tenured and tenure-track faculty taught 52.5 percent of all lower-division student credit hours at research universities and 48.6 percent of organized class sections.

It is important to be clear about what this statement does and does not say. It says that when the proportion of lower-division student credit hours and organized class sections taught by tenured and tenure-track faculty is examined for each discipline, the *average proportion* of lower-division student credit hours taught by tenured and tenure-track faculty for those disciplines is 52.5 percent, whereas the *average proportion* for organized class sections is 48.6 percent. The statement does *not* say that tenured and tenure-track faculty generate 52.8 percent of all lower-division student credit hours and 48.6 of all organized class sections that are taught at research universities.

It is important that this analytical perspective be used in looking at teaching-workload issues. Critics of higher education argue that undergraduate students, most especially freshmen and sophomores, rarely encounter tenured and tenure-track faculty in the classroom, particularly at research and doctoral institutions. Rather, they argue that these students are taught predominantly by part-time faculty and graduate students. If one looks only at the overall proportion of lower-division student credit hours or organized class sections taught at an institution by tenured and tenure-track faculty, large departments like English or foreign languages, which generate a large volume of workload numbers and make extensive use of adjuncts and teaching assistants, would exert undue influence on the institutionwide proportion. But students do not take courses exclusively in English or foreign languages; hence the proportion based on an institutional total of student credit hours or organized class section may well be misleading. The *average proportion* across disciplines is a better representation of the likelihood of a student encountering a tenured or tenure-track faculty member in classes taken within the full spectrum of his or her program of courses.

At this writing, there are four cycles of stable data from the Delaware Study in hand. The data reflect teaching loads from Fall 1993, 1994, 1996, and 1997, as well as instructional cost and externally funded research and service data from academic and fiscal years 1993–94, 1994–95, 1996–97, and 1997–98.

Table 6.1 displays information from the four data cycles for each of ten teaching-workload and expenditure variables. (For readers interested in the detail that underpins the information in Table 6.1, Appendix B at the end of this volume contains the complete data set for all twenty-four disciplines.) In each instance, the high, low, and mean values are displayed from the four cycles. (In the instance of baccalaureate institutions, there are only three cycles; there were not enough institutions of that type in 1993–94 to report their data separately.) The data are striking:

- One in two student credit hours generated in lower-division courses at research and doctoral universities, on average across the disciplines, are generated by tenured and tenure-track faculty. The proportion climbs to two of three student credit hours at comprehensive institutions and three of four student credit hours at baccalaureate colleges.
- Just under half of the lower-division organized class sections, on average across disciplines, are taught by tenured and tenure-track faculty at research universities, whereas the proportion is just over half at doctoral universities, two-thirds at comprehensive institutions, and nearly three-fourths at baccalaureate colleges.
- Nearly two-thirds of all undergraduate student credit hours and organized class sections, on average across the disciplines, at research and doctoral universities are taught by tenured and tenure-track faculty, whereas the proportion is three-fourths at comprehensive and baccalaureate institutions.

TABLE 6.1. MAXIMUM, MINIMUM, AND MEAN VALUES FOR SELECTED TEACHING WORKLOAD AND EXPENDITURE VARIABLES IN TWENTY-FOUR SELECTED DISCIPLINES IN FOUR DELAWARE STUDY DATA COLLECTION CYCLES SPANNING ACADEMIC AND FISCAL YEARS 1993–94 THROUGH 1997–98.

		Research Universities	Doctoral Universities	Comprehensive Institutions	Baccalaureate Institutions
Average proportion of lower-division student credit hours taught by tenured/tenure-track faculty	High	53.4	55.5	73.8	76.4
	Low	51.8	52.0	65.2	73.6
	Mean	52.7	54.1	68.2	74.9
Average proportion of lower-division organized class sections taught by tenured/tenure-track faculty	High	49.6	54.1	71.8	73.8
	Low	39.4	47.2	65.0	70.7
	Mean	46.7	51.4	67.3	72.6
Average proportion of undergraduate student credit hours taught by tenured/tenure-track faculty	High	63.0	65.0	79.3	85.8
	Low	61.9	59.8	71.9	78.6
	Mean	62.4	63.4	74.8	79.6
Average proportion of undergraduate organized class sections taught by tenured/tenure-track faculty	High	63.3	66.1	78.2	79.1
	Low	54.6	60.2	72.8	72.8
	Mean	60.3	63.4	75.1	76.8

		Col 1	Col 2	Col 3	Col 4
Average number of undergraduate student credit hours taught per FTE tenured/tenure-track faculty	High	190.4	208.0	243.8	194.5
	Low	188.1	183.3	221.9	193.3
	Mean	189.5	199.6	233.7	193.9
Average number of undergraduate organized class sections taught per FTE tenured/tenure-track faculty	High	1.7	2.1	3.2	3.2
	Low	1.4	1.8	2.9	2.9
	Mean	1.5	2.0	3.0	3.0
Average number of total student credit hours taught per FTE tenured/tenure-track faculty	High	227.7	243.7	254.0	197.4
	Low	220.3	207.6	232.5	195.1
	Mean	223.2	226.5	244.9	196.2
Average number of total organized class sections taught per FTE tenured/tenure-track faculty	High	2.3	2.8	3.4	3.2
	Low	2.0	2.4	3.2	2.9
	Mean	2.1	2.7	3.3	3.0
Average direct instructional expense per student credit hour taught	High	182	159	137	179
	Low	152	129	125	157
	Mean	164	147	129	171
Average total direct separately budgeted research and service expenditures per FTE tenured/tenure-track faculty	High	29,634	16,958	3,249	na
	Low	21,202	9,025	920	na
	Mean	26,337	13,932	2,001	na

What makes these data striking is the fact that they support a much greater instructional presence for tenured and tenure-track faculty than has been characterized by critics. The odds are one in two that a freshman or sophomore will encounter a tenured or tenure-track faculty member in the credit-bearing portion of a course, across the twenty-four disciplines routinely analyzed using Delaware Study data, at doctoral and research universities—the primary targets of criticism. The odds are two in three for undergraduates. These data suggest that when parents and students purchase a student credit hour of instruction, it is likely that it will be delivered by the faculty group in whom the institution has the greatest investment, that is, tenured and tenure-track faculty.

This is not a trivial observation; the "student credit hour" is the instructional coin-of-the-realm in higher education. It is the unit by which we distinguish between full-time and part-time students. It is the unit whose accumulation determines progress toward a degree. And it is the unit that is most frequently delivered to undergraduate students by tenured and tenure-track faculty. Are undergraduates ever taught by part-time faculty or graduate students? Of course. And this happens more often in disciplines such as English, foreign languages, and mathematics than in others.

As shown in Table 6.1, the average proportion of lower-division student credit hours taught by tenured and tenure-track faculty at research universities is 52.7 percent. That proportion drops to 46.7 percent for organized class sections. The phenomenon is still present but less emphatic at doctoral universities and comprehensive and baccalaureate institutions. That is because organized class sections include zero-credit recitation, discussion, and laboratory sections, which are most frequently met by graduate teaching assistants or adjunct faculty.

There is no body of research showing that instruction from graduate teaching assistants and adjunct faculty is pedagogically unsound or inferior to that from tenured and tenure-track faculty. Indeed, higher education institutions might benefit from a more proactive posture with regard to this type of instruction, suggesting that these zero-credit organized class sections are, in fact, designed to enhance prospects for student success in a given course.

That said, it is interesting to return to Table 6.1 and examine the teaching loads carried by tenured and tenure-track faculty at the respective Carnegie institution types. Not surprisingly, both in terms of student credit hours and organized class sections taught per FTE faculty, the lightest loads are at research universities. The workloads become progressively heavier with moves to research universities to doctoral universities to comprehensive institutions. The teaching loads at baccalaureate institutions more closely resemble those at research universities than other institution types. This may be a function of the specific baccalaureate colleges that participate in the Delaware Study; they tend to be small, private, highly selective liberal arts colleges that stake their academic reputations on small class sizes. The doctoral and comprehensive institutions in the study, however, tend to be large public institutions that have large class sections.

Instructional costs are consistent with the foregoing observation. Research universities are more expensive per student credit hour taught than are doctoral universities, which in turn are more expensive than comprehensive institutions. Baccalaureate colleges are more expensive per student credit hour taught than research universities. Again, this is likely a function of the specific baccalaureate institutions in the Delaware Study, with their emphasis on small class sizes.

Externally sponsored research and service expenditures provide a useful counterbalancing perspective for viewing teaching-load and instructional cost data. Although research universities teach fewer student credit hours and organized class sections than doctoral and comprehensive institutions, and do so at a greater cost, the magnitude of their research and service activity suggests that they are productive in those areas—an observation consistent with their institutional missions. Tenured and tenure-track faculty, on average, generate twice the volume of separately budgeted research and service activity per FTE than doctoral university faculty and ten times that for comprehensive institutions.

Although these global observations of the national benchmarks from the Delaware Study are interesting and useful, the real value and utility of the data become apparent when they are applied as an academic planning tool at the institutional level. The remainder of this chapter will focus on institutional uses of Delaware Study benchmarks.

Institutional Uses of Delaware Study Benchmark Data

A case study will illustrate the institutional uses of Delaware Study benchmarks. The first study involves two very different academic departments at the University of Delaware. The discussion will then move to the uses of benchmarks from Delaware Study data at other institutions.

The University of Delaware

It is fitting that the first analysis of how Delaware Study data might be used was done in the study's namesake institution. Delaware Study benchmarks were never intended as tools for rewarding or penalizing a given institution's academic departments or programs. Instead they are intended as tools for helping colleges and universities find out why their institutional data are similar to or different from national benchmarks.

Although this case study focuses on the uses of benchmark data at the University of Delaware, the strategies that will be presented are by no means unique to that institution. In fact, discussions with the vast majority of participating institutions suggest that, with very minor variations, most colleges and universities make similar uses of the data. Consequently, the uses of the data shown in Table 6.2 should be viewed through a generic template that is easily applied to any college or university accessing the study's national benchmark data.

The logical starting point for using Delaware Study benchmarks is to array an institution's data in the same format as the study's data collection instrument. Table 6.2 displays University of Delaware institutional data for two different academic departments, in each instance reflecting Fall 1996 teaching-load data and academic and fiscal year 1996–97 cost and productivity data. These are actual data taken from two very different academic departments at the University of Delaware, and they will be used to illustrate how institutional data are compared with Delaware Study national benchmarks.

The utility of the Delaware Study as an introspective tool is obvious in Table 6.2. The table provides detailed information on how much teaching is being done in each department by each of the four core categories of faculty. Academic year and fiscal year productivity and expenditure data are provided as well. The most frequent comment received from institutions participating in the Delaware Study concerning its general utility is a variation on the following: "Even if we did not receive benchmark data, the Delaware Study forced us to systematically look at how we are expending both personnel and fiscal resources at the academic program level. That, in and of itself, is invaluable."

Table 6.2 clearly demonstrates how entirely different two academic departments can be. Excluding teaching assistants (who do no credit-bearing teaching in either department), the faculty sizes are not all that different. Psychology is 27.15 FTE, of whom twenty-four are tenured or tenure-track, whereas chemical engineering is 22.56 FTE, of whom nineteen are tenured or tenure-track. Yet psychology generates nearly six times the volume of student credit hours as chemical engineering. Only 441 (4.5 percent) of all the student credit hours taught in psychology are at the graduate level; the proportion is 48.3 percent in chemical engineering—nearly half of the teaching workload. Not surprisingly, the fiscal year direct expense per student credit hour taught ratio is much lower in psychology at $173, compared with $1,139 in chemical engineering. However, separately budgeted research expenditures per FTE tenured tenure-track faculty are $43,800—quite respectable for a teaching department. Yet that ratio pales next to the $211,607 in chemical engineering.

It makes little sense to do head-to-head comparisons between two so dissimilar departments—dissimilar in disciplinary orientation, in emphasis on undergraduate teaching, and in volume of separately budgeted research. Yet without benchmarking data, these are precisely the sorts of inappropriate comparisons to which institutions, including the University of Delaware, were forced to resort. The Delaware Study benchmarks enable far more appropriate comparisons. They can be illustrated using the same two departments.

Other Institutions

In discussing the use of benchmarking data with Delaware Study participants across the nation, the first line of analysis is invariably tenured and tenure-track faculty. Within the psychology and chemical engineering faculties at the University of Delaware (excluding graduate teaching assistants), tenured and tenure-track faculty make up 88.4 percent and 83.1 percent of those faculties, respectively.

Tenured and tenure-track faculty are an appropriate starting point for analysis for the following reasons:

• They represent fixed costs. Personnel costs as a percentage of total instructional expenditures are 82 percent in psychology and 78 percent in chemical engineering. These percentages are typical of most academic departments and programs and are largely driven by the salaries and benefits of tenured and tenure-track faculty. Once tenure is conferred, these individuals are recurring costs until retirement, resignation, or death.

• Tenured and tenured-track faculty are the most visible of the faculty categories. Criticisms from the government, media, and parents are not directed at the activities of nontenurable full-time faculty or part-time adjunct faculty. It is faculty in the tenured and tenure-track category that are accused of shirking teaching responsibilities and engaging in nonproductive research.

• Tenured and tenure-track faculty are those in whom a college or university has the greatest investment. It is fair to ask what the return on that investment is.

Most institutions participating in the Delaware Study find it most useful to display comparisons between institutional and benchmark data within the context of a time series. As noted earlier, institutions are strongly cautioned against using a single set of benchmarks as the basis for rewarding or penalizing an academic department. Institutional data can be idiosyncratic at any point in time. A department or program with two or three faculty sabbatical leaves in a given year will incur the salary costs associated with those faculty but will lose the teaching and research productivity during the leave period. It is best to view Delaware Study benchmark data over time and use the information to frame questions about why institutional data are similar to or different from the national benchmarks.

TABLE 6.2 WORKLOAD DISTRIBUTION PATTERNS FOR TWO ACADEMIC DEPARTMENTS AT THE UNIVERSITY OF DELAWARE

Psychology

	Faculty					Student Credit Hou	
	FTE Faculty			(D)	(E)	(F)	(G) Tota
		(B)		Lower	Upper	Undergrad	Unde
	(A)	Buy-	(C)	Division	Division	Individual	grad
CLASSIFICATION	Total	Out	Instructional	OC	OC	Instruction	SCH
Regular Faculty							
Tenured/Tenure-							
Eligible	24.00	0.00	24.00	2,934	4,153	146	7,23
Non-Tenure-Track	2.07	0.00	2.07	189	30	1	22
Supplemental Faculty	1.08	na	1.08	1,107	602	0	1,70
Teaching Assistants							
Credit-Bearing-							
Courses	0.00	na	0.00	0	0	0	
Non-Credit-Bearing							
Courses	14.50	na	14.50	na	na	na	r
TOTAL	41.65	0.00	41.65	4,230	4,785	147	9,16

Academic Year Student Credit Hours Taught: FY 97 Direct Instructional Expenditures
Undergraduate: 17,249   Personnel: $25,534,592
Graduate: 852   Other than Personnel: $569,646
Total: 18,101   Total: $31,231,052

Chemical Engineering

	Faculty					Student Credit Hou	
	FTE Faculty			(D)	(E)	(F)	(G) Tota
		(B)		Lower	Upper	Undergrad	Unde
	(A)	Buy-	(C)	Division	Division	Individual	grad
CLASSIFICATION	Total	Out	Instructional	OC	OC	Instruction	SCH
Regular Faculty							
Tenured/Tenure-							
Eligible	19.00	0.00	19.00	165	445	30	64
Non-Tenure-Track	1.44	0.00	1.44	0	195	0	19
Supplemental Faculty	2.42	na	2.42	0	0	0	
Teaching Assistants							
Credit-Bearing-							
Courses	0.00	na	0.00	0	0	0	
Non-Credit-Bearing							
Courses	3.00	na	3.00	na	na	na	
TOTAL	25.86	0.00	25.86	165	640	30	83

Academic Year Student Credit Hours Taught: FY 97 Direct Instructional Expenditures
Undergraduate: 1,912   Personnel: $29,661,132
Graduate: 1,361   Other than Personnel: $762,171
Total: 3,273   Total: $37,282,842

(H) Graduate OC	(I) Graduate Individual Instruction	(J) Total Graduate SCH	(K) TOTAL STUDENT CREDIT HRS	(L) Lab/ Discuss/ Recitation Sections	Organized Class Sections — Other Section Types (Lecture, Seminar, Etc.)			(P) TOTAL SECTIONS
					(M) Lower Div.	(N) Upper Div.	(O) Graduate	
209	229	438	7,671	32	3	38	12	85
0	3	3	223	0	3	1	0	4
0	0	0	1,709	0	1	3	0	4
0	0	0	0	0	0	0	0	0
na	na	na	na	29	0	0	0	29
209	232	441	9,603	61	7	42	12	122

Y 97 Direct Research Expenditures: $1,051,166
Y 97 Direct Service Expenditures: $39
otal: $1,051,205

(H) Graduate OC	(I) Graduate Individual Instruction	(J) Total Graduate SCH	(K) TOTAL STUDENT CREDIT HRS	(L) Lab/ Discuss/ Recitation Sections	Organized Class Sections — Other Section Types (Lecture, Seminar, Etc.)			(P) TOTAL SECTIONS
					(M) Lower Div.	(N) Upper Div.	(O) Graduate	
416	194	610	1,250	10	3	7	9	29
0	0	0	195	0	0	3	0	3
145	24	169	169	0	0	0	6	6
0	0	0	0	0	0	0	0	0
na	na	na	na	0	0	0	0	0
561	218	779	1,614	10	3	10	15	38

Y 97 Direct Research Expenditures: $4,020,533
Y 97 Direct Service Expenditures: $0
otal: $4,020,533

Data Comparisons from a Provost's Perspective

The first question is, Whom do we compare ourselves with? The provost at the University of Delaware prefers to start comparisons by looking at university departments and programs compared with those at research universities across the nation. Because the University of Delaware is a Carnegie research university, the provost begins with the assumption that university departments should be roughly comparable to those at other research institutions. Because the Delaware Study offers several options in arraying benchmarks, one of which is by Carnegie institution type, it is easy to accommodate the provost. University data can also be compared with Delaware Study benchmarks based on highest degree offered in the discipline or by the relative emphasis on undergraduate teaching in the department. The comparison with research university benchmarks is simply a first cut at a comprehensive analysis.

Figure 6.1 shows a comparison of the Psychology Department's data with the national benchmarks *for research universities* in 1994–95, 1996–97, and 1997–98. It shows six key indicators:

- Undergraduate student credit hours taught per FTE tenured and tenure-track faculty
- Total student credit hours taught per FTE tenured and tenure-track faculty
- Class sections taught per FTE tenured and tenure-track faculty
- Total student credit hours taught per FTE faculty (all faculty categories)
- Direct instructional expense per student credit hour taught
- Separately budgeted research and service expenditures per FTE tenured and tenure-track faculty

The most effective way to present comparative data to provosts, deans, and other academic planners and managers is to do so graphically. It is sometimes difficult to capture the full attention of busy academicians if they expect to have to wade through tabular data and gauge the significance of the comparisons displayed. It is far more effective to "paint a picture" with the data. Figure 6.1 does precisely that. It is immediately clear that, for each of the Fall semesters under examination, tenured and tenure-track faculty in psychology at the University of Delaware had heavier undergraduate teaching loads, as measured in student credit hours taught, than the national benchmark for research universities. The total teaching load for tenured and tenure-track faculty, as measured in terms of student credit hours and class sections taught, is heavier each year in the Psychology Department than the respective benchmark for research universities. When the teaching load of all faculty categories combined is examined, the Psychology Department is lower than the national benchmark for research universities. Taken in conjunction with the previous benchmarks, the data strongly suggest that other research university psychology departments make more extensive use of non-tenure-track faculty than does the Psychology Department under analysis, thereby generating a heavier overall teaching load.

Although the direct expense per student credit hour taught is greater than the national benchmark, this is mitigated by the fact that tenured and tenure-track faculty in the Psychology Department at the University of Delaware teach most of the load. It is their salaries—as opposed to less expensive, nontenurable and adjunct faculty at other research universities—that drive the costs. However this becomes acceptable in light of the fact that, in addition to teaching heavier loads than their peers at research universities, psychology faculty at the University of Delaware consistently generate more research output, as measured in terms of direct expenditures, than their counterparts at other research institutions.

Care must be taken in interpreting comparative expenditure data. Although all of the foregoing comments concerning cost drivers for instructional expenditures at the University of Delaware are accurate, comparisons with national benchmarks are further mitigated by the fact that neither the institutional nor the national benchmark has been adjusted to reflect differences in cost of living. The national benchmarks for research universities include institutions from across the country in regions where the cost of living is substantially lower than in Newark, Delaware. Newark is located in the Washington to New York City corridor, which is noted for its high cost of living. Consequently, the competitive salaries paid to attract and retain faculty in high-cost areas may artificially inflate direct instructional costs when compared to national benchmarks that have not been adjusted for cost-of-living differentials.

Figure 6.2 does a similar comparison between the University of Delaware's Chemical Engineering Department and similar departments at research universities across the nation. The comparative data initially pose a sharp contrast to the Psychology Department. However, the comparisons underscore the critical importance of understanding the institutional context of academic departments and programs. The University of Delaware's Chemical Engineering Department, as noted earlier, has its student credit hour generation split roughly in half between undergraduate and graduate education. It is a research department, consistently ranked among the best in the nation by the National Research Council and other reputable assessment groups. It is therefore not surprising that the undergraduate teaching load in the Chemical Engineering Department at the University of Delaware is lower than the benchmark for research universities.

It is clear when comparing the national benchmarks for undergraduate student credit hours and total student credit hours that undergraduate teaching makes up the majority of the teaching load nationally in chemical engineering

FIGURE 6.1. PSYCHOLOGY: UNIVERSITY OF DELAWARE, COMPARED WITH NATIONAL BENCHMARKS.

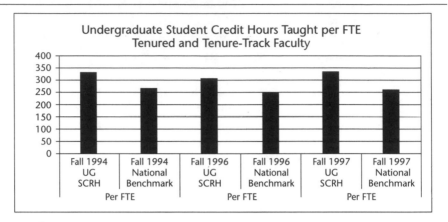

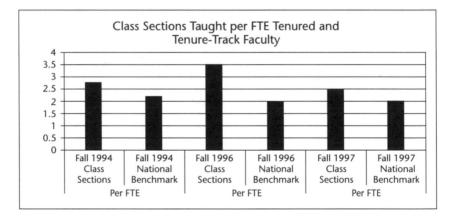

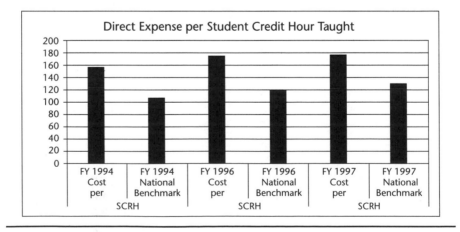

FIGURE 6.1. (*continued*)

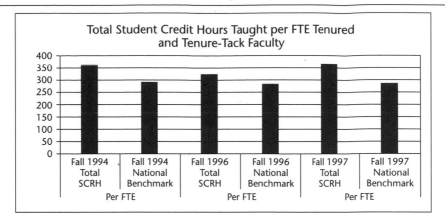

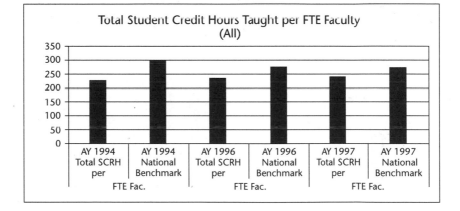

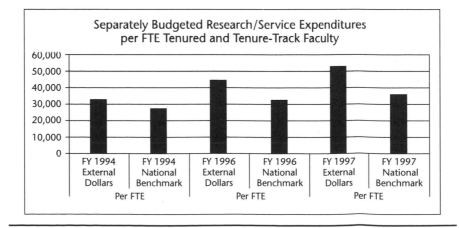

FIGURE 6.2. CHEMICAL ENGINEERING: UNIVERSITY OF DELAWARE, COMPARED WITH NATIONAL BENCHMARKS.

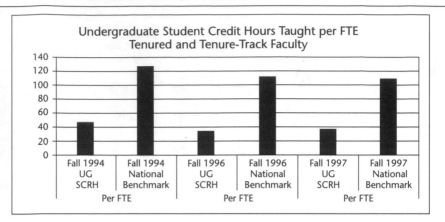

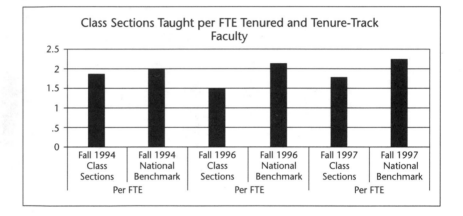

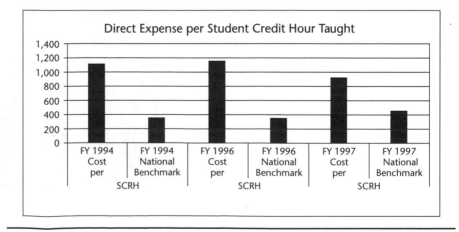

FIGURE 6.2 (*continued*)

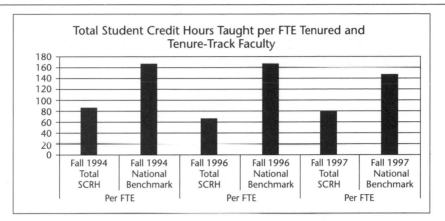

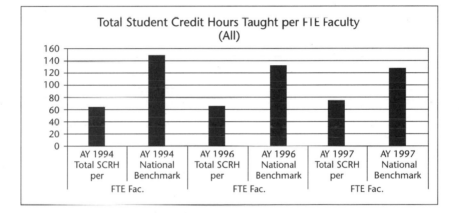

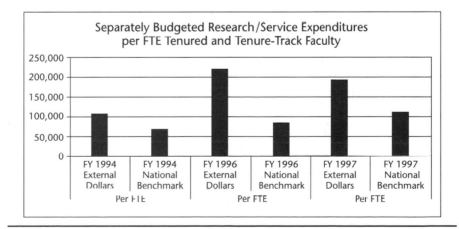

departments at research universities. This is a pattern distinctly different from the University of Delaware, where half the teaching is at the graduate level.

Because graduate education is more expensive than undergraduate teaching, it is not surprising to see that the direct expense per student credit hour taught in chemical engineering is substantially higher than the national benchmark. But in this instance "instruction" is not to be measured solely in terms of student credit hour generation. Graduate teaching in the sciences and engineering is far more likely to occur in the laboratory within the context of the interaction between the faculty member and his or her research assistant. That this is occurring at the University of Delaware is evident in the volume of research generated, as measured in terms of dollars expended. The Chemical Engineering Department at the University of Delaware generates research expenditures at a rate double that for the national benchmark. And these research expenditures support the graduate students who are in the laboratory with the faculty researcher. As I noted earlier, this sort of teaching and learning activity cannot be assessed strictly in terms of student credit hours taught.

The strength of the Delaware Study rests in its versatility. Although the University of Delaware's provost prefers to concentrate on the productivity of tenured and tenure-track faculty, the same sorts of analyses that were described for that faculty category in psychology and chemical engineering could as easily have been performed for permanent nontenurable faculty, supplemental or adjunct faculty, graduate teaching assistants, or any combination thereof. The Delaware Study provides benchmarks for virtually any discipline that is taught at an American four-year college or university. The sole exception is medical education, for which data are not collected at all, and those even more obscure disciplines for which, in any given data collection cycle, fewer than five institutions submit data. Moreover, any variable for which data are collected (refer to the data collection form in Chapter Five) has been benchmarked and can be analyzed within the context of a given department's activity.

Other Perspectives

As I noted earlier, the strategies discussed in the preceding section for analyzing and using Delaware Study national benchmark data are hardly unique to the University of Delaware. They are user-tested and reliable approaches to ensuring that benchmark data are not only seen by senior administrators but are used. It is nonetheless worthwhile to extend this discussion to examine other institutional approaches to national benchmark data.

The Delaware Study is first and foremost a comparative database that encourages inter-institutional benchmarking of productivity and expenditure measures. In addition to the national benchmarks based on Carnegie institutional classification, highest degree offered, and so on, that are produced by the Delaware Study, participating institutions are strongly encouraged to define their own custom peer groups from among the institutions that participate in the study. In defining peer groups with the Delaware Study, participating institutions are assured of the confidentiality of their data. For example, if a group of twelve universities is selected by a given institution, the requesting institution will know which twelve institutions are in the data pool but have no way of identifying or associating discrete data elements with a specific institution.

There are exceptions to this rule, however. The Delaware Study has become the clearinghouse for productivity and expenditure data for a number of national data-sharing consortia, including the Association of American Universities Data Exchange (AAUDE), the Southern Universities Group (SUG), and the Higher Education Data Sharing (HEDS) Consortium. In providing data to these consortia, by their own request, institutional identities are unmasked and members of the respective consortium can see the institutional data for all of the other members of that consortium. But unless specific institutional permission is granted to unmask data, the Delaware Study treats all institutional submissions as confidential.

The University of South Carolina

Harry Matthews, director of institutional research and planning at the University of South Carolina (USC), reports that they initially used Delaware Study data to prepare departmental profiles for their provost and academic deans in much the same fashion as the University of Delaware did in the preceding discussion. They have extended their analysis, however, by incorporating study data into a Web-based data warehouse. Within that Web-based framework, USC creates departmental profiles wherein departmental productivity and expenditure measures are compared with benchmarks for discrete groupings of a dozen or so peer institutions identified by USC, as opposed to larger aggregate groupings such as "research universities." Deans and department chairs at USC are expected to use these Web-based comparisons as a component of their annual strategic planning process and to use them when justifying requests for modified funding levels.

USC also uses departmental comparisons in their discussions with their state legislature on issues related to performance funding. The Delaware Study productivity and expenditure measures are clearly more comprehensive and precise than those established by the State of South Carolina (discussed in Chapter Two). Having this more comprehensive portrait of productivity and costs is an advantage for USC as they deal with the legislature.

The USC concept of using a customized peer group underscores one of the distinct advantages of the Delaware Study. In addition to the broad national benchmarks arrayed by Carnegie institution type, highest degree offered, and so on, it has been possible over the years for USC to identify a customized peer group from among all the colleges and universities participating in the project. As a member of the Southern Universities Group, USC receives the data from that consortium but is free to select additional peers. The peer group must be no smaller than five institutions, but the upper limit of the peer group is defined by the requesting institution.

The University of Utah

The University of Utah takes a somewhat different approach to benchmarking in that it focuses largely on a single measure—student credit hours taught per FTE faculty—and concentrates the analysis on two faculty groups: tenured and tenure-eligible faculty and other full-time faculty who are nontenurable. The volume of teaching activity, as measured in terms of student credit hour generation within these two faculty categories and compared with national and customized Delaware Study benchmarks, places departments in one of three groups: (1) highly productive, (2) normal, and (3) underproductive. Departments that are "highly productive" are advantaged in budget decisions, whereas "underproductive" departments are disadvantaged and are targets for budget reductions. The University of Utah does not, however, make resource allocation and reallocation decisions solely on a single quantitative measure. A number of other quantitative and qualitative factors enter the budget decisions at that institution.

In setting the productivity parameters for designating a program as highly productive, normal, or underproductive, the University of Utah uses considerable latitude. Data are viewed over time to establish trend information, as measures for any single year may be idiosyncratic. Understanding that Delaware Study measures are not empirical absolutes but simply reasonable comparative indicators that can be used for academic policy and planning, the university suggests that a department's measures have to be considerably out of line with its peers before budgetary implications come into play.

Paul Brinkman, associate vice president for budget and planning at the University of Utah and a major contributor to the development of the methodology of the Delaware Study, reports:

> In the current budget model, wherein a department's share of an enrollment-related, soft money pool is a function of year-to-year changes in the department's student credit hour production, only a handful of departments fall outside of the normal group. We forgive the highly productive departments if they owe the central pool because of a short-term decline in student credit

hours, and we sequester the funds that under-productive departments would otherwise be entitled to because of a short-term increase in student credit hours. In the latter case, the relative lack of productivity leads to planning meetings which entail further review of comparative data, an assessment of the reasons behind the low level of production, and a discussion of what the future likely holds, all of which may or may not result in releasing the funds in question to the department. [personal correspondence, April 2, 2000]

The Delaware Study measures are used precisely as they were intended at the University of Utah, that is, to identify trends in productivity, to frame questions as to the causes of apparent underproductivity, and in the long term to serve as a tool for making rational resource allocation and reallocation decisions.

The University of North Carolina System

A number of state higher education systems have elected to participate in the Delaware Study over the years. These include the University of North Carolina general administration, the University of Missouri System, the California State University System, the State University of New York, the South Dakota State Board of Regents, and the Louisiana Board of Regents. Gary Barnes, vice president for program assessment and public service in the University of North Carolina (UNC) general administration, and Troy Barksdale, associate vice president for planning in the same office, were the two key individuals in determining that all of the constituent institutions of the University of North Carolina would become participants in the Delaware Study. As with many large state university systems (I spent a number of years working on State University of New York campuses), the University of North Carolina system collected detailed information on teaching loads from its campuses every year but found itself in need of consistent and credible information on instructional costs. State university systems tend to be insular with data; variables are defined for system needs only and are collected in a manner that allows for little or no external benchmarking.

This was the primary concern that Barnes and Barksdale voiced when considering the Delaware Study. They were seeking national benchmarks from a data-sharing consortium that embraced a large enough and diverse enough universe of institutions that comparisons with UNC would make sense. The UNC system embraces two major research universities (one of which is land grant), three doctoral universities, seven comprehensive institutions, and four baccalaureate colleges. The Delaware Study provided precisely the critical mass of institutions that would enable appropriate benchmarking for each of the institution types within the UNC system.

At this writing, UNC is in its initial year of full, systemwide participation in the study. This is not, however, the UNC general administration's first contact with Delaware Study data. The administration, using historical national benchmark data provided to them in 1998, developed a twelve-cell cost-data matrix that embraced three student levels (undergraduate, graduate, and doctoral) within four broad curricular groupings that embraced the spectrum of academic programs offered within the system. The result was an algorithm by which student credit hours were converted to fundable faculty positions.

The intention of the UNC general administration in embracing and using the Delaware Study data is two-fold: (1) to better understand how their institutions perform when compared with similar institutions throughout the country, particularly those in other state systems and (2) to use that information to build a rational and cohesive case for state funding of instructional costs in a fashion that ensures that the UNC system has sufficient resources to perform at levels that compare favorably with national benchmarks.

The UNC system is not alone in these objectives. Increasingly, state higher education system offices and state boards of higher education are recognizing the necessity for national benchmarks data at the level of the academic program. Clearly, when one analyzes the cost of instruction on a campus, that cost is shaped in no small way by the academic disciplines that make up the curriculum. The need for comparative data that show how academic departments on a campus compare with national as well as systemwide benchmarks is causing increasing numbers of state systems to seek out the Delaware Study, as it is the only data consortium that deals with teaching productivity and expenditure data at the discipline level of analysis. The UNC system is charting the course in defining creative ways in which state university systems can use national benchmark data to enhance not only the productivity levels within its component institutions but the overall stewardship of fiscal and human resources on campus.

Other Institutional Uses of Delaware Study Data

One of the more difficult tasks confronting land grant universities is explaining to those outside the institution precisely who the faculty are and what they do. The problem stems from the fact that some land grant institutions include their agricultural extension personnel as faculty, even though they do not teach and were never supposed to teach. The University of Delaware, itself a land grant university and the custodian of the Delaware Study database, has for the past several years been working with a consortium of land grant universities to address the agricultural extension issue. Led by North Carolina State University, representatives from the University of Maryland, Virginia Polytechnic Institute and State University, Clemson University, Texas A&M University, and Louisiana State University met with me in my role as director of the Delaware Study and developed a common protocol for addressing faculty in agricultural extension units. If an institution defines extension personnel as faculty, it is not the place of the study to tell them what is or is not appropriate. However, it is imperative to get the correct count for instructional faculty for any national or local teaching activity benchmarks. Consequently, the group started with the Delaware Study data collection form (see Chapter Five) and encouraged each respective institution to count all individuals designated as faculty within their agricultural units and include them in the FTE Faculty total under Column A in the faculty grid on the data collection form. However, because extension personnel are almost always supported by a budget separate from an academic department's instructional budget, the FTE for those separately budgeted personnel are backed out in Column B on the data collection form, leaving a correct Instructional Faculty FTE in Column C.

This may sound like a trivial book-keeping exercise, but to those who work on land grant campuses, accounting for faculty who do not teach but who engage in research and public service activity as primary components of their jobs is essential. In addition to establishing the appropriate means for identifying total faculty versus instructional faculty, this consortium of land grant universities also identified appropriate methods for capturing all of the research and public service expenditures that help explain what nonteaching faculty do with their time. This underscores the flexibility and utility of the Delaware Study. Even for specialized disciplines in agriculture, the methodology is sufficiently flexible and cognizant of the inner workings of higher education to accommodate accurate instruction, research, and service activity in these units.

As noted earlier, the Delaware Study has become the official teaching-workload database for major data-sharing consortia such as the Association of American Universities Data Exchange, the Southern Universities Group, and the Higher Education Data Sharing Consortium. Each of these groups has a tradition of sharing information among themselves. However, economic conditions in the 1990s made it abundantly clear to each of the groups that, while their own historical data were important, the information becomes far more useful when cast against appropriate national benchmarks. With that as an approach, the Delaware Study has evolved as the official data collection agent for each of these groups with respect to information about teaching loads, instructional productivity, and costs. As the push for discipline-specific data becomes more pronounced, additional data-sharing consortia will follow suit.

Perhaps the most significant enhancement to the Delaware Study with respect to institutional use will be evident in the 2000–01 data collection cycle. There for the first time participating institutions will be given access to the complete data set from which the national benchmarks were calculated. This was not possible in past data cycles, owing to technical issues related to the security and confidentiality of the data. However, with a secure Web server in place, the vast majority of the data collection and editing will take place within a Web-based environment. And by granting institutions access to the full data set, it then becomes possible for a college or university to select different peer groups for different academic departments. This need has long been articulated by institutional participants but heretofore impossible to achieve. Now a dean can look at the list of Delaware Study participating institutions and choose the twelve that seem most appropriate for the music department while selecting a different set of twelve or so institutions for physics, and so on. Institutional identities will be protected with respect to individual data elements, but the user will know which peers constitute the data pool in each instance.

The intent of the Delaware Study since its inception has been to develop a data-sharing consortium and tools that are of maximum use to institutional participants. The introduction of secure, Web-based data that institutions can massage to meet their specific analytical needs is one more significant step in fully realizing that intention.

Conclusion

This chapter has provided a number of strategies for using national benchmark data from the Delaware Study as a quantitative basis for academic planning and policymaking. In Chapter Three, when the quantitative framework was developed for reporting teaching activity, instructional productivity, and expenditure data for teaching, research, and service, the point was made that quantitative data alone would not suffice. Chapter Four focused on thinking qualitatively at the institutional level. Consequently, if this chapter has established reasonable criteria for quantitatively benchmarking instructional productivity and cost data, it still remains to establish a comparable framework for qualitative benchmarking. Some critics argue that quality cannot be measured in the academic enterprise. It is clear from the current climate in state legislatures and among consumer groups that such claims will not be accepted. Chapter Seven will look at qualitative benchmarks. Although far more embryonic than the quantitative measures in the Delaware Study with respect to broad, national, comparative uses, qualitative benchmarks do exist and must be developed with the same rigor as their quantitative counterparts.

CHAPTER SEVEN

ESTABLISHING QUALITATIVE BENCHMARKS IN INDIVIDUAL DEPARTMENTS

Knowing how much instructional or research activity is occurring in an academic unit is different from knowing how good that activity is. Consider for a moment the following benchmarking of the Art Conservation Program at the University of Delaware with national data from the Delaware Study (Table 7.1).

Context is a crucial component in the examination of any quantitative information. In this example an academic department is teaching 25 percent less than the national benchmark for fine arts programs at research universities, generates a cost per credit hour nearly eight times larger than the benchmark, and a per FTE student taught expenditure rate that is double the benchmark. Should this program be allowed to continue operating at such levels? The answer lies in qualitative, contextual information.

The program is largely graduate in orientation. It is the only Ph.D.-granting art conservation program in the country. The program is personnel- and equipment-intensive, drawing heavily on the chemistry and chemical engineering departments at the university for advanced techniques in paint pigment analysis and other highly technical issues. Faculty work closely with their students, much as masters and apprentices did during the Renaissance. Graduates of the program have been highly successful and visible, enjoying curator positions in major art museums and galleries across the nation. The Art Conservation Department has an international reputation for excellence, and the philanthropic support it generates for the university is substantial. None of these characteristics is manifestly evident

TABLE 7.1. BENCHMARKING OF THE ART CONSERVATION PROGRAM AT THE UNIVERSITY OF DELAWARE.

	University of Delaware	National Benchmark
FTE Students Taught per FTE Faculty	8	12
Direct Instructional Cost per Student Credit Hour Taught	$894	$157
Direct Instructional Cost per FTE Student Taught	$8,943	$4,667

in a student-faculty ratio or assorted expenditure ratios. Understanding the qualitative dimension of teaching, research, and service is crucial to a full picture of what faculty do and how productive they are.

The importance of measuring faculty activity qualitatively is underscored by the current emphasis on outcomes assessment in regional and professional accreditation organizations. The Commission on Higher Education of the Middle States Association of Colleges and Schools, one of the six regional accrediting bodies in the United States, frames their accreditation criteria as "characteristics of excellence." The current edition of *Characteristics of Excellence,* published in 1994, offers the following observation:

> Outcomes assessment involves gathering and evaluating both quantitative and qualitative data which demonstrate congruence between the institution's mission, goals, and objectives and the actual outcomes of its educational programs and activities. The ultimate goal of outcomes assessment is the improvement of teaching and learning. The approaches may vary and need not be elaborate or dependent on quantitative criteria, but they should be systematic and thorough. . . . The plan for assessment of outcomes should attempt to determine the extent and quality of student learning. . . . The assessments should include frequent appraisals of the academic progress and goal achievement of students, of the progress of graduates, and of alumni opinions. In addition to assessing academic achievements, institutions should seek ways to assess the degree to which students' attitudes, social and ethical values, interests, and commitment to scholarship and lifelong learning develop as the result of their education. [p. 17]

Comparable outcomes statements are found in the accreditation standards of most regional and professional accrediting bodies. The emphasis on understanding the outcomes of teaching and learning activities, as well as other faculty activity related to a university's or college's mission, goals, and objectives, is not a passing fad in higher education. It is a direct response to the pressures and criticisms directed at higher education over the past decade. Indeed, the statements on assessment cited here are currently undergoing revision by the Middle States Association of Colleges and Schools to strengthen them and to provide even more direction on what should be assessed. It is clear that activities related to the assessment of academic programs and outcomes will become a critical component of faculty productivity over the next several years. The remainder of this chapter will focus on ways to address qualitative issues in addition to those already discussed.

National Sources of Qualitative Data

A number of data sources in the public domain contain benchmark data that can assist academic departments and programs in looking at the outputs of their faculty relative to those at other institutions. In considering where a departmental faculty is with regard to the overall quality of the academic program, as well as scholarly output of the faculty, *Research-Doctorate Programs in the United States* (Goldberg, Maher, and Flattau, 1995) is an excellent starting point. It ranks the leading academic programs, by institution and by discipline, in the arts and humanities, engineering, physical sciences and mathematics, social and behavioral sciences, and the biological sciences. The quality of faculty in a given institution's departments is assessed from responses to the National Survey of Graduate Faculty. The sample of program raters was drawn from a list of 65,470 faculty identified nationally as active in research-doctorate training programs at institutions. No fewer than two hundred raters were selected for any academic discipline. The result is a comprehensive ranking of departmental faculties, by discipline, within each of the fields listed.

To examine faculty scholarly output, the National Research Council looked specifically at papers published in refereed journals and monographs produced by recognized publishing houses; they also noted the impact of publications on the field, as evidenced by the number of times they were cited. These data are accessible in computerized form in the Institute for Scientific Information's (ISI) *U.S. University Science Indicators* database. This database contains summary publication and citation statistics that reflect scholarly production at over one hundred major universities throughout the United States. The data are drawn from publications indexed in ISI's *Science Citation Index, Social Science Citation Index,* and the *Arts and Humanities Citation Index.* It is accessible at most major research university libraries and enables institutions to identify the productivity of their own academic departments within the context of the hierarchical rankings of the major national programs in the field—often those that faculty aspire to join as peers.

Another extraordinary public resource for benchmarking the types of data identified earlier in this chapter is the NSF's Web-based WEB CASPAR (Computer Aided Science Policy Analysis and Research) database (http://caspar.nsf.gov). WEB CASPAR provides a longitudinal database that allows the retrieval and rank ordering of data, by institution and by discipline, from each of the following sources:

- *The NSF-NIH Survey of Graduate Students and Postdoctorates in Science and Engineering:* Provides detailed information on the numbers of graduate students and post-doctoral appointments, as well as information on sources of funding support, primary mechanism for support (fellowship, assistantship), as well as basic demographic information.
- *IPEDS Completions Survey:* Provides information on the volume of degrees awarded annually by institutions, by degree type, by discipline.
- *NSF Survey of Research and Development Expenditures at Universities and Colleges:* Collects data annually from roughly five hundred colleges and universities that account for virtually all of the funded R&D activity in the United States. The data reflect volume of funding, by institution, by discipline, by funding source.

The CASPAR data are not limited to these sources, but they most readily lend themselves to the benchmarking needed for a department to determine its relative position in the universe of higher education institutions.

The foregoing "benchmarkable" databases tend to focus on variables that are more characteristic of large research and doctoral institutions. What about comprehensive, baccalaureate, and two-year institutions? The fact that no standard, public domain database exists does not mean that data cannot be collected. Commencing with the 2000–01 data collection cycle, the Delaware Study will provide to participating institutions electronic versions of the Qualitative Measures of Faculty Activity discussed in Chapter Four. The checklist is still prototypic but will represent the first major attempt to collect qualitative information that can be married to quantitative data to give a richer and fuller picture of faculty productivity at the level of the academic discipline. As mentioned earlier, research universities have access to large national databases that speak to issues of academic quality. The Delaware Study initiative will bring comparable information to academic departments and programs in doctoral, comprehensive, and baccalaureate institutions. National benchmarks for these qualitative measures, by Carnegie institution type, will be available and incorporated into the next revision of this volume.

Problem-Based Learning (PBL)

Perhaps the most exciting area of faculty productivity over the next decade will be in curriculum development, especially in view of the impact of technology on campuses. New teaching paradigms such as PBL are transforming the ways faculty teach and students learn on campuses across the nation. Thus the volume of credit hour production will be supplemented with information on how and how well those credit hours are delivered. PBL is a means of instruction based on complex problems that have real-world implications.

To illustrate, the Physics Department at the University of Delaware, one of several units across the country being funded by the Pew Charitable Trusts to engage in PBL, uses the approach in several of their courses. By investigating, for example, how quickly electrical current moves through different materials, students are motivated to discover important concepts for themselves. Working together in groups, students learn to analyze such problems, identify central questions, and locate information through independent research. Findings are shared with group members, who then suggest and evaluate solutions to the problem. Throughout the process, the faculty member serves as a guide and facilitator. Carefully constructed, open-ended problems help students develop critical thinking skills such as analyzing, synthesizing, and evaluating. And by encouraging students to assess their knowledge base and to recognize and remedy areas of deficiency, PBL sets the stage for lifelong learning. Working in groups fosters communication and interpersonal skills, as well as a recognition that group diversity is a strength.

Paradigms such as PBL require that faculty retool. The new curricula force faculty to change the way they teach, focusing more on hands-on activities for the students than on the old techniques of lecture and rote memorization. Faculty must be trained in these new teaching techniques, which requires a significant investment in faculty development programs at colleges and universities. It appears to be well worth doing. Among University of Delaware students completing PBL-based courses, over 70 percent indicated that they had become more active participants in learning and had improved their research skills, as well as their ability to solve real-world problems, while working in teams. These findings are being compared with results from other Pew-funded institutions, such as Samford University in Alabama, to better understand PBL's effectiveness. The challenge to faculty is to provide instructional techniques that meet the real cognitive and skill needs of twenty-first century college students. The old lecture paradigm simply is not viable in the current age of instant information. Faculty products such as PBL are essential to the continuing relevance of a college education.

Measuring what and how students learn is another faculty product that is undergoing significant transformation. A letter grade used to be the sole indicator for assessing what students learned in courses. Although mastery of course content continues to be essential, there is a national emphasis on what students learn as the result of their total undergraduate experience. There are well-established psychometric instruments for measuring skills in critical thinking, problem solving, and communicating, among other skills. Web-based electronic portfolios that integrate and synthesize the knowledge gained through a broad cross-section of courses is yet another tool for measuring student learning. In the final analysis, however, the individual faculty member bears ultimate responsibility for assessing cognitive gains in students. And the development of appropriate tools for making those assessments is quickly becoming part of the overall productivity of faculty in the twenty-first century. That these sorts of curriculum development activities are occurring and ongoing within academic departments will be captured—at least as a baseline measure—in the Delaware Study Measures of Qualitative Activities Checklist (see Chapter Four).

Research and Public Service Activity

In Chapter Four I made the argument that the quality and worth of pure and applied research at U.S. colleges and universities is all too often a subjective judgment call. I also argued that the economic impact of university research on local, state, and national economies is, more often than not, a compelling reason for encouraging research and service activity. Major research universities have become expert at developing public relations packets that not only highlight the economic impact of their research activities but do so in ways that describe the benefits of such activity to both the surrounding population and society at large.

Institutions wishing to benchmark the nature and scope of their research and service activity, as measured in terms of dollars expended for those respective functions, are encouraged to begin with the Web-based databases referenced earlier in this chapter. WEB CASPAR is the Web site of the NSF's Division of Science Resources Studies (SRS). It provides three-year trend data for all colleges and universities who reported information on one or more of the following surveys, conducted annually by the NSF:

- The *NSF Survey of Research and Development Surveys at Universities and Colleges.* This data source provides detailed information on funds expended for research and development, by discipline, and by funding source.

- The *NSF/National Institutes for Health Survey of Graduate Students and Postdoctorates in Science and Engineering.* Provides detailed data on number of students, by category, and primary funding source (fellowship, assistantship, and so on).
- The *NSF Survey of Federal Funds for Research and Development.* Provides data on federal obligations for research performance at colleges and universities, including obligations for plant funds.

Each of these surveys represents a rich data source for benchmarking externally funded research activity. The data will benefit institutions with a substantial research component in their mission most. But for institutions aspiring to the top one hundred institutions in externally sponsored research and development funds, or for those institutions simply wishing to know their relative position in the higher education community with respect to externally funded research, these are excellent benchmarking sources.

The University of Florida, in particular, has made exceptionally creative use of benchmarking data for research and public service activity. Elizabeth Capaldi and John Lombardi, now senior faculty members at the University of Florida, were architects of a construct referred to as the Florida Bank—a measure of the relative productivity and quality of academic units at the university. It does so by comparing productivity and quality measures with those of comparator colleges at appropriate peer institutions. The term *the Florida Bank* implies what is true in practice—that performance is financially rewarded as productivity and quality increase. Productivity is measured in terms of weighted student credit hours, sponsored research expenditures, fundraising, and other income. The University of Florida is a member of both the American Association of Universities Data Exchange and the Southern Universities Group. As members they have access to detailed student credit hour data from the Delaware Study for both consortia and can benchmark sponsored research productivity using either Delaware Study expenditure data or expenditure data from WEB CASPAR data sources. Readers interested in a more detailed discussion of the Florida Bank are encouraged to read the Capaldi and Lombardi (2000) paper or *A Decade of Performance,* published by the University of Florida development office.

The quality dimension is more difficult to assess than research and service. Typical measures would be those specified in the Qualitative Measures Checklist in Chapter Four; there is little debate as to their appropriateness. The difficulty for the University of Florida, as for most colleges and universities, is in collecting data on these measures, over time, from a pool of institutions sufficiently large and comparable in mission to constitute an appropriate benchmarking pool.

Conclusion

The fact that the Delaware Study will begin such a systematic data collection commencing with the 2000–01 data collection cycle holds considerable promise. The study is a well-established data-sharing consortium with a proven track record in data collection and analysis at the academic discipline level. Granted, it will require close collaboration between the Delaware Study data collection office on a given campus, as well as that campus's academic department chairs, to ensure the accuracy and completeness of qualitative productivity measures collected. However, given the current climate in higher education that demands accountability with respect to both productivity and program quality, we may be witnessing the same confluence of events that will promote qualitative data sharing that led to quantitative data sharing through the Delaware Study.

CHAPTER EIGHT

LOOKING TO THE FUTURE

The need for reliable and consistent benchmark data for higher education institutions has never been more pronounced than in the past few years. In
1997, Public Law 105–18 (Title IV, Cost of Higher Education Review, 1997) established the National Commission on the Cost of Higher Education. This body
was to report directly to Congress and to provide a comprehensive analysis of what
drives college costs and prices.

The commission was directed to look at the following issues:

- The increase in college tuition, over time, as compared with other commodities
  and services
- Innovative methods of reducing or stabilizing tuition
- Trends in college and university administrative costs, including administrative
  staff levels, the ratio of administrative staff to instructors, the ratio of administrative staff to students, remuneration of administrative staff, and remuneration
  of college and university presidents and chancellors
- Trends in faculty workload and remuneration (including the use of adjunct faculty), faculty-to-student ratios, the number of hours faculty spent in the classroom, tenure practices, and the impact of such trends on tuition
- Trends in the construction and renovation of academic and other collegiate facilities, the modernization of facilities to access and use new technologies, and
  the impact of such trends on tuition

- The extent to which increases in student financial aid and tuition discounting have affected tuition increases, including the demographics of students receiving such aid, the extent to which such aid is provided to students with limited need in order to attract such students to particular institutions or major fields of study, and the extent to which federal financial aid, including loan aid, has been used to offset such increases
- The extent to which federal, state, and local laws, regulations, and other mandates contribute to increasing tuition, and recommendations on reducing those mandates
- The establishment of a mechanism for a more timely and widespread distribution of data on tuition trends and other costs of operating colleges and universities
- The extent to which student financial aid programs have contributed to changes in tuition
- Trends in state fiscal policies that have affected college costs
- The adequacy of existing federal and state financial aid programs in meeting the cost of attending colleges and universities [pp. xiii and xiv]

This charge of responsibilities is as remarkable in what it does *not* say as in what it does. Implicit in the charge is the assumption that college tuition costs are escalating, with no fair return on value. Also implicit in the charge is the assumption that rising college costs are related to declining workloads among tenured and tenure-track faculty, accompanied by increasing use of adjunct faculty as a cost add-on over and above compensation paid to tenured and tenure-track faculty. And finally, there is an assumption that tuition costs are being driven by unrestrained attempts to incorporate new technologies into institutions while using federal and other sources of financial aid to drive up tuition costs.

Efforts to Create a Cost Model

The National Commission on the Cost of Higher Education reported to Congress in 1998. That report, titled *Straight Talk About College Costs and Prices,* is worthwhile reading (see the References for publication information).

In response to the commission and to Congress, as a component of the provisions of the 1999 Higher Education Reauthorization Act, the National Center for Education Statistics (NCES) was to conduct a major study of the cost of higher education, focusing on the following expenditures: faculty salaries and benefits, administrative salaries and benefits, academic support services, student support services, and student aid. Moreover, the study was to focus specifically on expenditures associated with technology on campuses and those associated with the construction or renovation of instructional facilities.

At the time of this writing, Congress had repeatedly failed to fund the NCES National Cost Study, and the project has not gone forward. However, the National Association of Collegiate and University Business Officers (NACUBO) has begun a study of higher education costs that is conceptually similar to the congressionally mandated NCES study. It examines instructional and student services expenditures, institutional support expenditures (that is, administrative and plant operations costs), and student financial aid expenditures; it also develops a ratio for each expenditure category against a student FTE calculated from headcount enrollment. It too attempts to capture the extent to which capital costs contribute to the overall cost of higher education.

Although there is something to be said for both the NCES and NACUBO efforts to develop a comprehensive model for explaining the cost of higher education, both studies suffer from significant flaws. Both studies will provide a number that defines the cost of educating a student at a college or university, but neither ties that cost to any measure of productivity or return on investment. If it costs $20,000 to educate an undergraduate at University X but only $15,000 at University Y, does that mean that University X is overpaying? Or conversely, if there is a real relationship between tuition (the sticker price) for a college education and what the institution pays to educate a student, does the student who pays a $20,000 tuition get more for his or her money than the student who pays $15,000 in tuition? Neither the NCES nor the NACUBO cost study can answer these questions because, as is the case with cost studies that preceded them, they focus on inputs—how much money is spent on how many students—without any consideration of the outcomes or products of a college or university education.

The Joint Commission on Accountability Reporting (JCAR) project that was described in Chapter Two made an initial attempt to link costs with outcomes. The JCAR reporting methodology provides clear and consistent conventions for reporting the tuition and mandatory fees that an institution charges a student with outcomes such as student graduation rates, licensure examination pass rates, and placement in the workforce after graduation. This is extremely valuable information, framed within a clear construct that allows comparability across institutions. But it does not address the relationship between cost (dollars an institution spends to provide an education, as opposed to the price a student pays for that education) and productivity. In fairness to JCAR, it was never their purpose to explain such a relationship. But it is a relationship that must be explained if colleges and universities are serious about accountability.

The Delaware Study is the only data collection and data-sharing project that makes a serious attempt to link direct expenditures for instruction, research, and public service with instructional outcomes. Moreover, the data are collected at the academic discipline level of analysis. Both the NCES and NACUBO studies look at data aggregated at the institutionwide level. Because of this aggregation, both studies are insensitive to the disciplinary mix within the institution's curriculum. Disciplines such as the natural and physical sciences and engineering are highly equipment-intensive and require laboratory instruction in addition to traditional lecture; also, class sizes must be small enough to allow frequent faculty-student interaction, especially in the laboratory. Social sciences and humanities, however, lend themselves to a lecture pedagogy and are not hampered by restrictions on class size that are imposed by equipment and hazardous materials issues. Consequently, the discipline mix at an institution becomes important in any analysis of the cost of educating a student.

Tables 17 and 18 in Appendix B at the end of this volume contain the national benchmarks for four years of Delaware Study data in twenty-four disciplines that are typically found at most colleges and universities. Among research universities, the fiscal year 1998 national benchmark (that is, the refined mean value from reporting institutions) for direct instructional expense per student credit hour taught in engineering was $395; for nursing, $300; for biological sciences, $261; for physics, $249. Contrast those values with the 1998 research university benchmark for history, $129; for English, $122; for philosophy; $123, and for sociology, $108. Examination of Tables 17 and 18 will quickly demonstrate that these patterns are consistent over time and across Carnegie institution type.

Obstacles to Creating a Cost Model

Clearly, the disciplines contained in a college or university's curriculum make a difference in the cost of educating a student, as does the volume of teaching done in the respective disciplines. The NCES and NACUBO cost studies are silent on the issue of disciplinary mix. One can only assume that the comparatively inexpensive disciplines are expected to cancel out the more expensive programs. But colleges and universities do not structure curricula to achieve a financial balance between and among departments; structure is in place because it is consistent with the institutional mission and the academic needs of students. Consequently, using either the NCES or NACUBO methodology, institutions that are heavily weighted with disciplines in the sciences and engineering will clearly be disadvantaged in cost comparisons with institutions weighted in the arts, humanities, and social sciences. Both NCES and NACUBO argue that technological costs and capital costs affect the overall expenditures in educating a student. One need only examine the NSF publication, *The National Science Foundation Survey of Federal Funds for Research and Development,* for any given fiscal year, and it becomes readily apparent that the more scientifically oriented the curriculum, the more expensive the technology and capital costs incurred.

Contributions of the Delaware Study to a Model

The Delaware Study, however, captures these disciplinary differences as they are measured in terms of direct expenditures for instruction. By capturing direct instructional costs with reasonable accuracy, it is possible to use the discipline-specific data in the Delaware Study to model a university that mirrors the curriculum mix at a given institution or to predict the direct costs at a new institution, given the projected curricular mix. With national benchmarks for basic measures such as direct expense per student credit hour taught and direct expense per FTE student taught, one need only estimate the amount of teaching done in a given discipline to create the model. Frances Dyke, director of institutional research and member of the Delaware Study Advising Committee, has created just such a virtual university against which she benchmarks her institution's departments.

For example, if an academic department teaches 9,000 student credit hours per year, multiplying the appropriate Delaware Study benchmark by 9,000 results in the national comparator value. By repeating this process for all of the disciplines at a college or university, it is possible to arrive at a hypothetical national comparator institution modeled from Delaware Study data. This model would be a far more appropriate comparator for any institution than the generic, non-discipline-sensitive NCES or NACUBO construct.

Similarly, Delaware Study data can be used to capture the direct cost of educating a student in virtually any academic major at a four-year college or university. Suppose one wished to know the cost of educating an English major. Most colleges and universities maintain a database commonly referred to as an induced course load matrix (ICLM). The ICLM simply looks at the course consumption patterns throughout the institution by a given group of academic majors. In the example at hand, it would examine not only the number of English student credit hours consumed by English majors but also the number of student credit hours that English majors consume in foreign languages, mathematics, biology, sociology, and so on. By multiplying the Delaware Study benchmark for direct cost per credit hour in each of these disciplines by the average number of hours consumed by English majors in those disciplines at a given institution, it is possible to arrive at a realistic national estimate for the *direct* cost of educating a student in that major.

One might argue that any cost model derived from Delaware Study data suffers in that it accounts for direct expenditures only. Research Associates of Washington, D.C., have, for years, produced a volume titled *Higher Education Revenues and Expenditures,* in which they calculate the full cost of educating a student, using data from the Integrated Postsecondary Educational Data System's (IPEDS) *Finance Survey*. They apply the following algorithm to expenditure data: "Full instructional cost per FTE student equals the sum of direct costs for instruction and student services plus indirect costs equal to total academic and institutional support and plant, less overhead for funded research and public service estimated at 33.3 percent of the expenditures for these two activities" (p. 1). Although this algorithm initially seems unwieldy, several of its components—direct expense for instruction, research, and public service—are accurately captured at the academic department or program level in the Delaware Study. As the study itself moves toward a full-cost model, its advisory panel may be able to use this algorithm as a starting point and modify it in ways that are appropriate to bring expenditures such as student services, academic and institutional support, and plant costs to the departmental level.

The movement toward a full-cost model using Delaware Study data should proceed with the same deliberation and caution that has gone into its maturation to this point. It enjoys widespread credibility because it does not do more than it claims to do, which at this point, is to explain instructional productivity and costs in terms of direct expenditures. These expenditures, as noted in Chapter Three, are verifiable and auditable. Indirect costs are more amorphous, and any algorithm that hopes to explain them must stand up to basic tests of credibility and have some grounding in institutional accounting practices. This will become increasingly important as those costs become more pronounced in emerging pedagogies such as the Web-based delivery of courses and enhanced distance learning. That said, the best hope for explaining the full cost of educating a student rests in a model that is sensitive to academic discipline and institutional mission. That is a description of the Delaware Study.

Perhaps the most important modifications to the study are those described in the preceding chapter that incorporate qualitative measures of faculty activity into current departmental profiles that describe teaching activity, instructional productivity, and cost data strictly in quantitative terms. Constructs that measure the outcomes of teaching activity, that is, graduation rates, postgraduation placement, licensure and accreditation rates, and so on, are critical to providing a full picture of the quantity and quality of faculty work. Equally important is a mechanism for describing faculty involvement in such curriculum-developing and curriculum-enriching activity as PBL and formal opportunities for undergraduate research. And finally, describing faculty research and service activity not simply in terms of dollars expended at the department level but in terms of the economic and social impact on the region and nation is a far more effective way of communicating the importance of those functions.

Conclusion

American higher education is a complex enterprise in which various types of institutions deliver teaching, research, and service; the relative emphasis on each of those components relates to institutional mission and to the diversity of the populations they serve.

Historically, colleges and universities have taken a generic approach to explaining what faculty and the institutions themselves do. In years past this sufficed. But since 1990, higher education has clearly been a prime target for accountability in terms of how faculty spend their time, what the products of higher education are, and what costs are associated with those products. This volume has provided some strategic approaches to new ways of describing and explaining each of those issues. A meaningful dialogue between and among higher education institutions, legislators, parents, and benefactors has just begun. As with most complex conversations, it will take on a new language with new constructs and definitions. This volume might well help shape those conversations with useful and usable tools for describing what colleges and universities, faculty, and administrators do and how well they do it.

As this conversation continues, if it is carried out in an honest and frank manner that allows all parties to speak and be heard, the logical outcome should be a restoration of public trust in higher education that was evident throughout most of the twentieth century. If this book helps in that conversation, it will have been well worth writing.

DELAWARE STUDY DEFINITIONS AND CONVENTIONS

As you read the definitions and calculations that follow, please examine the copy of the data collection form also found in this packet. *(See Chapter Five.)*

Definitions of Terms

Academic Department or Discipline

The disciplines selected for benchmarking in this study are found in the Classification of Instructional Programs taxonomy, which is derived directly from the National Center for Education Statistics (NCES) CIP code system. Wherever possible, we are benchmarking data at the four-digit CIP code level. That is, we will be looking at discrete disciplines within a broad curricular field.

For example, in engineering (CIP Code 14.XX) you will be asked to provide data for the engineering disciplines at your institution. Suppose you have five engineering departments—agricultural, chemical, civil, electrical, and mechanical. You would provide data for five discrete CIP codes: 14.03 (Agricultural Engineering), 14.07 (Chemical Engineering), 14.08 (Civil Engineering), 14.10 (Electrical Engineering), and 14.19 (Mechanical Engineering). Institutions with different engineering departments would report data for the appropriate four-digit engineering CIP codes. The pattern would be repeated across other curricular areas

If you have difficulty disaggregating categories within a specific disciplinary area, a general CIP code, typically XX.01, should be used. For example, if your Department of Foreign Languages offers French, Spanish, Russian, Chinese, Greek, and Latin, and you cannot cleanly disaggregate teaching-workload and cost data into each of these disciplines, simply report the data as Foreign Languages and Literature, CIP Code 16.01. If a disciplinary area provides no "general" option, and you cannot cleanly disaggregate to specific curricular area, report a two-digit CIP code. For example, Engineering-Related Technologies would be 15.00.

Note: Members of the Southern Universities Group and a number of other institutions have asked to benchmark at the six-digit CIP level. *All* participating institutions are encouraged to provide six-digit CIP codes in as many instances as feasible, and we will benchmark at that level wherever possible. Those data will then be rolled up to the four-digit level, at which all institutions will be benchmarked, consistent with the preceding discussion.

Degree Offerings

The term *degree offerings* refers to all degrees offered in this discipline at your institution. In the space next to each degree, provide the average number of degrees awarded in the discipline for each of the past three academic years (1996–97, 1997–98, and 1998–99), as reported to IPEDS. We will again benchmark (in a separate section of the report) the data, based on *highest degree offered.*

Part A: Instructional Workload—Fall 1999 Semester

Note: The following discussion of faculty should be read within the context of your institution's Fall 1999 census data. *Reminder:* the due date for submission of data is January 28, 2001.

Regular Faculty

Regular faculty are hired to teach but may also do research or perform service, or both. They are characterized by a *recurring* contractual relationship in which the individual and the institution both assume a continuing appointment. These faculty typically fall into two categories: (1) tenured and tenure-track individuals or those for whom tenure is an expected outcome (usually full, associate, and assistant professors), and (2) non-tenure-track individuals. These individuals teach on a recurring contractual basis, but their academic title renders them ineligible for academic tenure. At most institutions these titles include instructor, lecturer, and visiting faculty.

Supplemental Faculty

Supplemental faculty are hired to teach and are usually paid out of a pool of temporary funds. Their appointment is nonrecurring, although the same individual might receive a temporary appointment in successive terms. The key point is that the funding is, by nature, temporary, and there is no expectation of continuing appointment.

This category includes adjuncts, administrators, or professional personnel at the institution who teach but whose primary job responsibility is nonfaculty, contributed service personnel, and so on.

Teaching Assistants

Teaching assistants are students at the institution who receive a stipend strictly for teaching. The category includes teaching assistants who are instructors of record, as well as teaching assistants who function as discussion section leaders, laboratory section leaders, and other types of organized class sections in which instruction takes place but credit is not awarded and there is no formal instructor of record. For purposes of this study, graduate research assistants are not included.

Note: In calculating FTE for each of the faculty categories described, the following conventions are recommended:

FTE for Regular Faculty

Take the total FTE for *filled* faculty positions as they appear in the Fall 1999 personnel file at your institution, and report this in the "Total FTE Faculty" data field (Column A). Be sure to report filled positions only. Filled positions have salaries associated with them. Include paid leaves such as sabbaticals wherein the individual is receiving a salary, but exclude unpaid leaves of absence. In Column B, report the FTE portion of faculty lines that are supported by external or separately budgeted funds for purposes other than teaching (research or service). The remainder is the departmental or program instructional faculty FTE and should be reported in the "Instructional" FTE faculty data field. That is, the FTE for Column C is computed by subtracting Column B from Column A.

For example, suppose Professor Jones is a full-time member of the chemistry faculty. He would be reflected as 1.0 FTE in Column A. Professor Jones has a research grant that contractually obligates him to spend one-third of his time in research. The externally supported portion of his position is 0.33 FTE, which would be reflected in Column B. As a result, 0.66 FTE is the instructional faculty, which would appear in Column C, that is, 1.0 FTE (Column A) minus 0.33 FTE (Column B).

FTE for Supplemental Faculty

FTE for supplemental faculty can be arrived at by taking the total teaching credit hours (which are generally equivalent to the credit value of the course or courses taught) for each supplemental faculty and dividing by 12. Twelve hours is a broadly accepted standard for a full-time teaching load. (If your institution assigns one course unit instead of three or four credit hours to a course being taught, use a divisor of 4.) Because supplemental faculty are not usually supported by external funds, Column C will typically equal Column A.

FTE for Teaching Assistants

You are asked to assign an FTE value to teaching assistants, apportioned between credit-bearing course activity where the teaching assistant is the instructor of record and non-credit-bearing course activity such as being section leader for zero-credit laboratories, discussion sections, or recitation sections. To do this, take the FTE value for teaching assistants in a given academic department or program, as it appears in your personnel file. Then apportion the FTE as follows.

Credit-Bearing Courses. Use the same convention as with supplemental faculty. Take all courses that are credit bearing and for which teaching assistants are the instructors of record, and divide the total teaching credit hours by 12. The resulting quotient is the teaching assistant FTE for credit-bearing course activity.

Non-Credit-Bearing Activity. From the total teaching assistant FTE, taken from your personnel file, subtract the calculated FTE for credit-bearing activity as described. The difference is the FTE for non-credit-bearing activity. It is understood that on many campuses, the non-credit-bearing activity is not exclusively instructional and may include activities such as grading papers. However, the decision to allow teaching assistants to do things other than teach is analogous to allowing other departmentally paid faculty to take reduced loads to engage in activity other than teaching. In both instances, salaries are associated with personnel, and in the interest of consistency, personnel should be counted as a component of common practice in higher education.

Note: When looking at student credit hours generated, by level of instruction and number of organized class sections taught, refer only to your institution's Fall 1999 semester workload file. Do *not* report data here for the full academic year.

Course

A course is an instructional activity, identified by academic discipline and number, in which students enroll, typically to earn academic credit applicable to a degree objective; excludes noncredit courses but includes zero-credit course sections that are requirements of or prerequisites to degree programs and are scheduled and consume institutional or departmental resources in the same manner as credit courses. Zero-credit course sections are typically supplements to the credit-bearing lecture portion of a course. Zero-credit sections are frequently listed as laboratory, discussion, or recitation sections in conjunction with the credit-bearing lecture portion of a course.

Organized Class Course

An organized class course is provided by means of regularly scheduled classes meeting in classrooms or similar facilities at stated times.

Individual Instruction

An individual instruction course is when instruction is not conducted in regularly scheduled class meetings. Such a course includes "readings" or "special topics" courses, "problems" or "research" courses, including dissertation and thesis research, and "individual lesson" courses (typically in music and fine arts).

Course Section

A course section is a unique group of students that meets with one or more instructors.

Note: In reporting the number of sections taught at the respective levels of instruction, to the extent that your database allows, please make certain not to double count dual-listed (undergraduate and graduate sections of a single course meeting concurrently) and cross-listed courses, that is, single courses in which students from two or more disciplines may register under their respective department call letters.

Course Credit

Course credit refers to the academic credit value of a course. It is the value recorded for a student who successfully completes the course.

Lower-Division Instruction

Lower-division instruction refers to courses typically associated with the first and second year of college study.

Upper-Division Instruction

Upper-division instruction refers to courses typically associated with the third and fourth year of college study.

Graduate-Level Instruction

Graduate-level instruction refers to courses typically associated with postbaccalaureate study.

Student Credit Hours

Student credit hours refers to the credit value of a course (typically three or four credits) multiplied by the enrollment in the course.

Student credit hours should be aggregated and reported on the data form on the basis of course level of instruction and classification of the faculty member. It is important to underscore that the criterion is the level of the course, as opposed to level of the student registered in the course. For example, the student credit hours generated by a second-semester senior taking an introductory graduate course would be reported in the "graduate" column. Similarly, those generated by a first-semester graduate student taking an upper-division prerequisite undergraduate course would be reported in the "upper division" column. (If your institution assigns one credit unit instead of three or four credit hours to a course, convert the units to credit hours by multiplying by 3 or 4, as appropriate.)

For institutions with doctoral-level instruction, in the box below the total for "Individual Instruction Graduate Student Credit Hours," please indicate the number of student credit hours from that total that are devoted to dissertation supervision.

If you cannot differentiate between Organized Class and Individualized Instruction student credit hours, assign all credit hours to the appropriate OC column. Similarly, if you cannot differentiate between lower-division and upper-division undergraduate student credit hours, report all those credit hours under Total Undergraduate Credit Hours.

In addition to aggregation by course level, student credit hours should also be aggregated and reported, based on the classification of the instructors teaching the respective courses. Student credit hours should be reported for all courses taught by a faculty member who is budgeted to a given department, regardless of whether the course is taught in that department or elsewhere. For example, a faculty member who is budgeted to the History Department and whose teaching load includes two history courses and one political science course should have all of the student credit hours generated from these courses credited to the History Department.

To the extent possible, deal with team teaching situations by prorating student credit hours to individual faculty in an appropriate fashion. If two faculty members are sharing instructional responsibilities equally for a three-credit course with thirty students enrolled (ninety student credit hours), forty-five credit hours would be apportioned to Faculty A and forty-five credit hours to Faculty B. The same allocation would hold in appropriating the organized class section to the two faculty, that is, 0.5 section to each. This is especially important when the faculty members in a team teaching situation are budgeted to different departments. The student credit hours should follow the faculty member. Use your institutional convention in making these prorating decisions.

The same conventions apply to reporting counts of organized class sections. The first column asks for the number of lab or discussion or recitation sections taught by each type of faculty. The remainder of the grid looks at all other organized class sections, disaggregated by level of instruction and by faculty type.

Note: The foregoing data collection discussion refers to the Fall 1999 term. All institutions are expected to submit data for Fall 1999. *Reminder:* the due date for submission of data is January 28, 2001.

Part B: Cost And Productivity Information

The data collected on this portion of the data form require financial information for all of FY 2000 and student credit hour data for the major terms in academic year 1999–2000 that are supported by an academic department's basic operating budget. These major terms are generally Fall and Spring at institutions on a semester calendar and Fall, Winter, and Spring at institutions on a quarter calendar. *Reminder:* the due date for submission of data is January 28, 2001.

Student Credit Hour Data

You are asked to provide the total number of student credit hours taught at the undergraduate and graduate levels, respectively, during the 1999–2000 academic year. "1999–2000 Academic Year" refers only to terms that are funded by the department's instructional budget. At most institutions on the semester system, this refers to the Fall and Spring terms; at institutions on the quarter system, Fall, Winter, and Spring terms are generally included. If instructional activity in a given term is funded by a source other than the departmental instructional budget (for example, if the Summer term teaching is funded by the Special Sessions Office or Continuing Education), student credit hours associated with that term are to be excluded.

Direct Expenditure Data

This study asks for total direct expenditure data in the areas of instruction, research, and public service. Direct expenditure data reflect costs incurred for personnel compensation, supplies, and services used in the conduct of each of these functional areas. They include acquisition costs of capital assets such as equipment and library books, to the extent that funds are budgeted for and used by operating departments for instruction, research, and public service. For purposes of this report, exclude centrally allocated computing costs and centrally supported computer labs, as well as graduate student tuition remission and fee waivers.

Instruction

The instruction function, for purposes of this study, includes general academic instruction, occupational and vocational instruction, community education, preparatory and adult basic education, and remedial and tutorial instruction conducted by the teaching faculty for the institution's students. Departmental research and service *that are not separately budgeted* should be included under instruction. In other words, department research that is externally funded should be excluded from instructional expenditures, as should any departmental funds that were expended for the purpose of matching external research funds as part of a contractual or grant obligation. Expenditures for academic administration where the primary function is administration should be excluded. For example, deans would be excluded but department chairs would be included.

You are asked to disaggregate total instructional expenditures for each discipline into three pieces of data: salaries, benefits, and nonpersonnel costs.

Salaries. Report all wages paid to support the instructional function in a given department or program during FY 2000. Although these will mostly be faculty salaries, be sure to include clerical (for example, the departmental secretary), professional (for example, lab technicians), and graduate student (stipends but not tuition waivers) salaries, and any other personnel who support the teaching function and whose salaries and wages are paid from the department or program's instructional budget.

Benefits. Report expenditures for benefits associated with the personnel for whom salaries and wages were reported on the previous entry. If you cannot separate benefits from salaries, but benefits are included in the salary figure you have entered, indicate "Included in Salaries" in the data field. Some institutions book benefits centrally and do not disaggregate to the department level. If you can compute the appropriate benefit amount for the department or program, please do so and enter the data. If you cannot, enter "NA" in the field, and we will impute a cost factor based on the 1999–2000 benefit rate for your institution, as published in *Academe*. If no rate is available, we will use a default value of 28 percent.

Nonpersonnel Costs. This category includes nonpersonnel items such as travel, supplies and expense, noncapital equipment purchases, and so on, that are typically part of a department or program's cost of doing business. *Excluded* from this category are items such as central computing costs, centrally allocated computing labs, and graduate student tuition remission and fee waivers.

Research. This category includes all funds expended for activities specifically organized to produce research outcomes and commissioned by an agency either external to the institution or separately budgeted by an organizational unit within the institution. Report total research expenditures only. It is not necessary to disaggregate costs for this category.

Public Service. Report all funds that are budgeted separately for public service and expended for activities established primarily to provide noninstructional services beneficial to groups external to the institution. Examples include cooperative extension and community outreach projects. Report total service expenditures only. It is not necessary to disaggregate costs for this category.

Note: Respondents at institutions with "centers" for interdisciplinary research and service should make every attempt to disaggregate expenditures in those centers on a pro rata basis to component disciplines or departments. For institutions with separate foundations for handling external research and service contracts and grants, funds processed by those foundations to departments or disciplines should be included. *Reminder:* the due date for submission of data is January 28, 2001.

DELAWARE STUDY BENCHMARKS FOR TYPICAL ACADEMIC DEPARTMENTS

TABLE B.1. PROPORTION OF LOWER-DIVISION STUDENT CREDIT HOURS TAUGHT BY TENURED AND TENURE-TRACK FACULTY IN TWENTY-FOUR SELECTED DISCIPLINES: RESEARCH AND DOCTORAL UNIVERSITIES: FALL 1993, 1994, 1996, AND 1997.

DEPARTMENT/PROGRAM		% LD SCRH Taught T-TT Faculty RESEARCH Fall 1993	% LD SCRH Taught T-TT Faculty RESEARCH Fall 1994	% LD SCRH Taught T-TT Faculty RESEARCH Fall 1996	% LD SCRH Taught T-TT Faculty RESEARCH Fall 1997	% LD SCRH Taught T-TT Faculty DOCTORAL Fall 1993	% LD SCRH Taught T-TT Faculty DOCTORAL Fall 1994	% LD SCRH Taught T-TT Faculty DOCTORAL Fall 1996	% LD SCRH Taught T-TT Faculty DOCTORAL Fall 1997
Communications	9.00	53	56	54	55	52	46	48	53
Computer and Information Sciences	11.00	36	33	37	33	30	24	30	30
Education	13.00	34	32	19	32	43	27	22	22
Engineering	14.00	75	64	67	66	68	56	62	58
Foreign Languages and Literature	16.00	28	34	30	34	36	37	29	27
English	23.00	21	20	23	21	29	27	23	25

		53.4	52.9	51.8	52.5	55.0	55.5	53.9	52.0
Biological Sciences	26.00	70	62	60	59	73	72	72	56
Mathematics	27.00	37	38	32	34	41	41	41	42
Philosophy	38.01	65	63	64	61	66	76	70	67
Chemistry	40.05	65	67	61	63	76	73	74	69
Geology	40.06	81	82	79	81	77	80	74	79
Physics	40.08	76	80	77	76	81	75	69	66
Psychology	42.00	62	57	55	61	53	53	45	41
Anthropology	45.02	70	72	70	65	70	78	72	66
Economics	45.06	53	60	65	61	67	74	69	65
Geography	45.07	84	75	72	70	76	69	75	65
History	45.08	67	68	65	66	68	70	74	77
Political Science	45.10	65	63	69	65	67	72	73	68
Sociology	45.11	68	63	63	64	69	72	65	51
Visual and Performing Arts	50.00	55	60	60	55	63	59	59	58
Nursing	51.16	55	52	38	48	48	42	30	50
Business Administration	52.02	36	33	30	32	19	37	42	30
Accounting	52.03	20	25	28	31	38	45	36	33
Financial Management	52.08	5	11	24	26	10	27	40	49
Mean Benchmark		53.4	52.9	51.8	52.5	55.0	55.5	53.9	52.0

TABLE B.2. PROPORTION OF LOWER-DIVISION STUDENT CREDIT HOURS TAUGHT BY TENURED AND TENURE-TRACK FACULTY IN TWENTY-FOUR SELECTED DISCIPLINES: COMPREHENSIVE AND BACCALAUREATE INSTITUTIONS: FALL 1993, 1994, 1996, AND 1997.

DEPARTMENT/ PROGRAM		% LD SCRH Taught T-TT Faculty COMP. Fall 1993	% LD SCRH Taught T-TT Faculty COMP. Fall 1994	% LD SCRH Taught T-TT Faculty COMP. Fall 1996	% LD SCRH Taught T-TT Faculty COMP. Fall 1997	% LD SCRH Taught T-TT Faculty BACC. Fall 1993	% LD SCRH Taught T-TT Faculty BACC. Fall 1994	% LD SCRH Taught T-TT Faculty BACC. Fall 1996	% LD SCRH Taught T-TT Faculty BACC. Fall 1997
Communications	9.00	62	56	53	51	na	na	91	59
Computer and Information Sciences	11.00	69	59	50	53	na	63	85	65
Education	13.00	71	50	46	45	na	46	58	86
Engineering	14.00	90	62	69	81	na	na	na	na
Foreign Languages and Literature	16.00	67	60	56	60	na	67	55	70
English	23.00	59	52	50	48	na	68	61	60

		73.8	68.3	65.2	65.6	na	74.8	76.4	73.6
Biological Sciences	26.00	80	75	76	73	na	63	79	78
Mathematics	27.00	71	66	58	56	na	79	70	65
Philosophy	38.01	78	73	77	81	na	69	87	83
Chemistry	40.05	80	75	71	72	na	74	91	91
Geology	40.06	88	86	78	80	na	na	na	na
Physics	40.08	84	81	80	79	na	84	88	75
Psychology	42.00	74	69	72	67	na	84	76	86
Anthropology	45.02	84	82	72	69	na	54	na	na
Economics	45.06	83	85	79	88	na	65	80	69
Geography	45.07	85	88	65	79	na	na	na	na
History	45.08	80	74	74	73	na	84	83	72
Political Science	45.10	84	74	79	74	na	84	85	86
Sociology	45.11	76	74	74	73	na	84	79	85
Visual and Performing Arts	50.00	74	68	65	64	na	61	62	68
Nursing	51.16	54	57	53	40	na	na	na	na
Business Administration	52.02	51	51	46	50	na	68	68	54
Accounting	52.03	75	69	65	68	na	na	na	na
Financial Management	52.08	53	53	57	51	na	na	na	na
Mean Benchmark		73.8	68.3	65.2	65.6	na	74.8	76.4	73.6

TABLE B.3. PROPORTION OF UNDERGRADUATE STUDENT CREDIT HOURS TAUGHT BY TENURED AND TENURE-TRACK FACULTY IN TWENTY-FOUR SELECTED DISCIPLINES: RESEARCH AND DOCTORAL UNIVERSITIES: FALL 1993, 1994, 1996, AND 1997.

DEPARTMENT/PROGRAM		% UG SCRH Taught T-TT Faculty RESEARCH Fall 1993	% UG SCRH Taught T-TT Faculty RESEARCH Fall 1994	% UG SCRH Taught T-TT Faculty RESEARCH Fall 1996	% UG SCRH Taught T-TT Faculty RESEARCH Fall 1997	% UG SCRH Taught T-TT Faculty DOCTORAL Fall 1993	% UG SCRH Taught T-TT Faculty DOCTORAL Fall 1994	% UG SCRH Taught T-TT Faculty DOCTORAL Fall 1996	% UG SCRH Taught T-TT Faculty DOCTORAL Fall 1997
Communications	9.00	63	62	60	59	58	54	53	58
Computer and Information Sciences	11.00	48	46	48	44	41	37	43	40
Education	13.00	50	53	47	50	52	51	51	41
Engineering	14.00	79	81	80	82	76	77	80	77
Foreign Languages and Literature	16.00	37	43	40	43	47	45	39	37
English	23.00	34	33	37	35	42	38	35	36

Biological Sciences	26.00	74	81	80	77	76	78	75	67
Mathematics	27.00	43	43	41	42	47	48	47	47
Philosophy	38.01	69	67	69	65	72	73	69	67
Chemistry	40.05	67	70	65	66	77	75	79	72
Geology	40.06	84	81	80	82	81	82	75	80
Physics	40.08	77	80	77	77	82	79	73	69
Psychology	42.00	63	66	66	67	62	60	59	54
Anthropology	45.02	70	75	74	72	70	74	72	62
Economics	45.06	64	63	66	63	72	77	73	65
Geography	45.07	80	79	76	72	74	75	75	68
History	45.08	72	72	71	72	73	75	77	78
Political Science	45.10	70	68	71	68	72	70	74	70
Sociology	45.11	68	68	64	68	69	70	70	60
Visual and Performing Arts	50.00	63	64	65	60	65	64	63	61
Nursing	51.16	67	59	49	53	62	59	54	51
Business Administration	52.02	58	53	54	58	61	63	61	60
Accounting	52.03	49	44	47	48	58	61	57	50
Financial Management	52.08	62	58	58	63	65	75	76	66
Mean Benchmark		63.0	62.9	61.9	61.9	64.8	65.0	63.8	59.8

TABLE B.4. PROPORTION OF UNDERGRADUATE STUDENT CREDIT HOURS TAUGHT BY TENURED AND TENURE-TRACK FACULTY IN TWENTY-FOUR SELECTED DISCIPLINES: COMPREHENSIVE AND BACCALAUREATE INSTITUTIONS: FALL 1993, 1994, 1996, AND 1997.

DEPARTMENT/ PROGRAM		% UG SCRH Taught T-TT Faculty COMP. Fall 1993	% UG SCRH Taught T-TT Faculty COMP. Fall 1994	% UG SCRH Taught T-TT Faculty COMP. Fall 1996	% UG SCRH Taught T-TT Faculty COMP. Fall 1997	% UG SCRH Taught T-TT Faculty BACC. Fall 1993	% UG SCRH Taught T-TT Faculty BACC. Fall 1994	% UG SCRH Taught T-TT Faculty BACC. Fall 1996	% UG SCRH Taught T-TT Faculty BACC. Fall 1997
Communications	9.00	67	64	54	57	na	na	89	64
Computer and Information Sciences	11.00	71	65	57	59	na	84	85	64
Education	13.00	74	67	60	65	na	67	67	76
Engineering	14.00	88	80	81	81	na	na	na	na
Foreign Languages and Literature	16.00	70	66	62	63	na	73	59	72
English	23.00	66	62	58	55	na	75	68	63

Biological Sciences	26.00	83	79	80	77	na	82	84	82
Mathematics	27.00	74	70	61	60	na	81	72	66
Philosophy	38.01	80	76	76	81	na	85	89	81
Chemistry	40.05	84	79	77	75	na	90	91	90
Geology	40.06	88	85	78	83	na	na	na	na
Physics	40.08	87	81	79	79	na	87	90	74
Psychology	42.00	79	73	74	73	na	83	77	86
Anthropology	45.02	83	86	69	71	na	77	na	na
Economics	45.06	86	88	83	87	na	88	83	78
Geography	45.07	87	87	69	77	na	na	na	na
History	45.08	82	75	77	76	na	88	84	75
Political Science	45.10	85	80	82	76	na	84	83	84
Sociology	45.11	80	80	76	76	na	84	81	84
Visual and Performing Arts	50.00	74	70	69	67	na	69	62	69
Nursing	51.16	76	74	73	65	na	na	na	na
Business Administration	52.02	76	72	73	65	na	76	72	55
Accounting	52.03	78	74	72	76	na	na	na	na
Financial Management	52.08	86	81	85	81	na	na	na	na
Mean Benchmark		79.3	75.6	71.9	71.9	na	85.8	78.6	74.3

TABLE B.5. PROPORTION OF LOWER-DIVISION ORGANIZED CLASS SECTIONS TAUGHT BY TENURED AND TENURE-TRACK FACULTY IN TWENTY-FOUR SELECTED DISCIPLINES: RESEARCH AND DOCTORAL UNIVERSITIES: FALL 1993, 1994, 1996, AND 1997.

DEPARTMENT/ PROGRAM		% LD Sects. Taught T-TT Faculty RESEARCH Fall 1993	% LD Sects. Taught T-TT Faculty RESEARCH Fall 1994	% LD Sects. Taught T-TT Faculty RESEARCH Fall 1996	% LD Sects. Taught T-TT Faculty RESEARCH Fall 1997	% LD Sects. Taught T-TT Faculty DOCTORAL Fall 1993	% LD Sects. Taught T-TT Faculty DOCTORAL Fall 1994	% LD Sects. Taught T-TT Faculty DOCTORAL Fall 1996	% LD Sects. Taught T-TT Faculty DOCTORAL Fall 1997
Communications	9.00	41	40	44	43	40	43	47	45
Computer and Information Sciences	11.00	29	32	29	29	31	30	35	32
Education	13.00	30	24	18	32	31	23	21	20
Engineering	14.00	65	63	66	69	60	54	61	58
Foreign Languages and Literature	16.00	30	32	31	29	39	38	32	27
English	23.00	17	15	15	14	26	23	19	23

Biological Sciences	26.00	31	58	60	53	43	71	71	61
Mathematics	27.00	30	35	30	29	38	37	40	40
Philosophy	38.01	55	58	58	54	61	74	64	64
Chemistry	40.05	31	68	67	65	56	75	78	70
Geology	40.06	51	77	81	79	52	82	78	80
Physics	40.08	35	84	77	75	59	75	73	72
Psychology	42.00	48	52	49	53	48	49	45	42
Anthropology	45.02	44	73	67	61	67	77	73	67
Economics	45.06	34	54	55	54	62	71	69	57
Geography	45.07	52	73	75	67	57	70	74	64
History	45.08	58	65	65	60	62	68	70	70
Political Science	45.10	50	58	66	64	66	70	71	62
Sociology	45.11	51	58	60	59	65	70	67	50
Visual and Performing Arts	50.00	49	52	52	46	56	58	57	58
Nursing	51.16	56	53	41	52	45	37	33	51
Business Administration	52.02	31	33	22	23	23	34	41	28
Accounting	52.03	20	24	28	28	40	43	35	33
Financial Management	52.08	7	9	24	28	6	27	39	38
Mean Benchmark		39.4	49.6	49.2	48.6	47.2	54.1	53.9	50.5

TABLE B.6. PROPORTION OF LOWER-DIVISION ORGANIZED CLASS SECTIONS TAUGHT BY TENURED AND TENURE-TRACK FACULTY IN TWENTY-FOUR SELECTED DISCIPLINES: COMPREHENSIVE AND BACCALAUREATE INSTITUTIONS: FALL 1993, 1994, 1996, AND 1997.

DEPARTMENT/ PROGRAM		% LD Sects. Taught T-TT Faculty COMP. Fall 1993	% LD Sects. Taught T-TT Faculty COMP. Fall 1994	% LD Sects. Taught T-TT Faculty COMP. Fall 1996	% LD Sects. Taught T-TT Faculty COMP. Fall 1997	% LD Sects. Taught T-TT Faculty BACC. Fall 1993	% LD Sects. Taught T-TT Faculty BACC. Fall 1994	% LD Sects. Taught T-TT Faculty BACC. Fall 1996	% LD Sects. Taught T-TT Faculty BACC. Fall 1997
Communications	9.00	60	53	53	49	na	na	90	52
Computer and Information Sciences	11.00	68	60	50	53	na	65	84	63
Education	13.00	62	49	44	43	na	43	52	59
Engineering	14.00	88	65	76	77	na	na	na	na
Foreign Languages and Literature	16.00	64	59	57	61	na	66	64	66
English	23.00	57	50	48	46	na	64	59	59

Biological Sciences	26.00	76	72	75	74	na	67	77	81
Mathematics	27.00	72	65	59	55	na	77	70	62
Philosophy	38.01	78	73	74	82	na	66	82	83
Chemistry	40.05	72	75	71	74	na	72	84	91
Geology	40.06	80	84	78	85	na	na	na	na
Physics	40.08	84	79	78	80	na	81	82	83
Psychology	42.00	75	69	71	68	na	84	76	85
Anthropology	45.02	83	80	71	64	na	56	na	na
Economics	45.06	84	84	77	85	na	66	81	69
Geography	45.07	84	88	71	77	na	na	na	na
History	45.08	79	72	73	74	na	82	84	70
Political Science	45.10	82	73	80	74	na	83	76	85
Sociology	45.11	75	73	74	71	na	83	77	75
Visual and Performing Arts	50.00	71	67	65	64	na	58	57	61
Nursing	51.16	51	56	47	40	na	na	na	na
Business Administration	52.02	50	48	44	49	na	67	51	58
Accounting	52.03	76	68	66	67	na	na	na	na
Financial Management	52.08	51	50	59	50	na	na	na	na
Mean Benchmark		71.8	67.2	65.0	65.1	na	73.8	73.3	70.7

TABLE B.7. PROPORTION OF UNDERGRADUATE ORGANIZED CLASS SECTIONS TAUGHT BY TENURED AND TENURE-TRACK FACULTY IN TWENTY-FOUR SELECTED DISCIPLINES: RESEARCH AND DOCTORAL UNIVERSITIES: FALL 1993, 1994, 1996, AND 1997.

DEPARTMENT/ PROGRAM		% UG Sects. Taught T-TT Faculty RESEARCH Fall 1993	% UG Sects. Taught T-TT Faculty RESEARCH Fall 1994	% UG Sects. Taught T-TT Faculty RESEARCH Fall 1996	% UG Sects. Taught T-TT Faculty RESEARCH Fall 1997	% UG Sects. Taught T-TT Faculty DOCTORAL Fall 1993	% UG Sects. Taught T-TT Faculty DOCTORAL Fall 1994	% UG Sects. Taught T-TT Faculty DOCTORAL Fall 1996	% UG Sects. Taught T-TT Faculty DOCTORAL Fall 1997
Communications	9.00	54	54	54	53	51	54	51	51
Computer and Information Sciences	11.00	43	53	47	46	43	45	48	45
Education	13.00	48	49	41	45	48	46	45	41
Engineering	14.00	71	81	81	82	71	77	80	77
Foreign Languages and Literature	16.00	41	45	43	42	51	51	49	45
English	23.00	34	30	30	29	39	36	33	37

Subject	Code								
Biological Sciences	26.00	51	78	79	76	56	78	77	71
Mathematics	27.00	40	45	46	45	48	50	50	49
Philosophy	38.01	64	68	68	64	66	73	70	68
Chemistry	40.05	38	74	71	70	62	80	83	78
Geology	40.06	63	81	84	81	63	86	81	82
Physics	40.08	40	84	81	78	63	80	79	77
Psychology	42.00	60	62	65	66	61	63	62	56
Anthropology	45.02	59	78	74	72	68	73	74	68
Economics	45.06	59	65	64	65	72	79	76	67
Geography	45.07	62	77	76	73	66	78	77	67
History	45.08	70	73	74	71	68	74	75	75
Political Science	45.10	63	67	72	67	71	71	77	72
Sociology	45.11	63	67	64	65	67	71	73	62
Visual and Performing Arts	50.00	62	63	60	61	62	65	63	64
Nursing	51.16	61	59	48	50	59	49	51	50
Business Administration	52.02	54	55	54	57	64	64	66	61
Accounting	52.03	53	52	54	51	61	67	60	54
Financial Management	52.08	58	59	60	62	64	76	75	65
Mean Benchmark		54.6	63.3	62.1	61.3	60.2	66.1	65.6	61.8

TABLE B.8. PROPORTION OF UNDERGRADUATE ORGANIZED CLASS SECTIONS TAUGHT BY TENURED AND TENURE-TRACK FACULTY IN TWENTY-FOUR SELECTED DISCIPLINES: COMPREHENSIVE AND BACCALAUREATE INSTITUTIONS: FALL 1993, 1994, 1996, AND 1997.

DEPARTMENT/ PROGRAM		% UG Sects. Taught T-TT Faculty COMP. Fall 1993	% UG Sects. Taught T-TT Faculty COMP. Fall 1994	% UG Sects. Taught T-TT Faculty COMP. Fall 1996	% UG Sects. Taught T-TT Faculty COMP. Fall 1997	% UG Sects. Taught T-TT Faculty BACC. Fall 1993	% UG Sects. Taught T-TT Faculty BACC. Fall 1994	% UG Sects. Taught T-TT Faculty BACC. Fall 1996	% UG Sects. Taught T-TT Faculty BACC. Fall 1997
Communications	9.00	67	63	55	56	na	na	86	60
Computer and Information Sciences	11.00	73	68	63	62	na	63	83	64
Education	13.00	70	66	59	62	na	52	63	61
Engineering	14.00	87	81	78	81	na	na	na	na
Foreign Languages and Literature	16.00	68	66	64	65	na	71	68	67
English	23.00	65	62	57	55	na	71	69	63

	1	2	3	4	5	6	7	8	9
Biological Sciences	26.00	80	81	81	80	na	86	na	83	85
Mathematics	27.00	75	71	64	63	na	79	na	73	66
Philosophy	38.01	80	77	78	84	na	66	na	85	80
Chemistry	40.05	80	83	78	80	na	86	na	91	89
Geology	40.06	84	85	82	87	na	na	na	na	na
Physics	40.08	84	81	79	82	na	85	na	91	84
Psychology	42.00	81	75	75	74	na	84	na	77	82
Anthropology	45.02	81	87	70	70	na	59	na	na	na
Economics	45.06	86	88	82	87	na	68	na	82	80
Geography	45.07	83	87	75	80	na	na	na	na	na
History	45.08	82	76	78	77	na	85	na	83	77
Pol tical Science	45.10	83	79	82	77	na	84	na	80	82
Sociology	45.11	78	79	78	77	na	84	na	82	78
Visual and Performing Arts	50.00	73	71	69	68	na	69	na	61	65
Nursing	51.16	72	73	69	62	na	na	na	na	na
Business Administration	52.02	76	71	72	66	na	74	na	75	55
Accounting	52.03	80	76	75	75	na	na	na	na	na
Financial Management	52.08	88	82	84	81	na	na	na	na	na
Mean Benchmark		78.2	76.2	72.8	73.0	na	79.1	na	78.4	72.8

TABLE B.9. UNDERGRADUATE STUDENT CREDIT HOURS PER FTE TENURED AND TENURE-TRACK FACULTY IN TWENTY-FOUR SELECTED DISCIPLINES: RESEARCH AND DOCTORAL UNIVERSITIES: FALL 1993, 1994, 1996, AND 1997.

DEPARTMENT/PROGRAM		UG SCRH/ T-TT FTE Faculty RESEARCH Fall 1993	UG SCRH/ T-TT FTE Faculty RESEARCH Fall 1994	UG SCRH/ T-TT FTE Faculty RESEARCH Fall 1996	UG SCRH/ T-TT FTE Faculty RESEARCH Fall 1997	UG SCRH/ T-TT FTE Faculty DOCTORAL Fall 1993	UG SCRH/ T-TT FTE Faculty DOCTORAL Fall 1994	UG SCRH/ T-TT FTE Faculty DOCTORAL Fall 1996	UG SCRH/ T-TT FTE Faculty DOCTORAL Fall 1997
Communications	9.00	174	191	200	204	190	195	192	207
Computer and Information Sciences	11.00	136	143	152	159	106	138	156	143
Education	13.00	87	90	78	79	100	106	100	93
Engineering	14.00	113	112	104	104	172	120	119	106
Foreign Languages and Literature	16.00	141	127	123	115	160	158	163	134
English	23.00	139	143	149	145	172	157	155	136

Discipline	Code								
Biological Sciences	26.00	218	217	215	195	240	269	257	219
Mathematics	27.00	179	178	186	176	204	188	207	195
Philosophy	38.01	275	236	260	224	260	250	260	221
Chemistry	40.05	275	276	264	261	274	263	249	223
Geology	40.06	185	203	202	217	228	198	207	205
Physics	40.08	195	195	181	188	246	203	187	171
Psychology	42.00	241	263	251	258	222	261	216	202
Anthropology	45.02	223	256	246	220	252	254	226	221
Economics	45.06	214	213	245	239	224	226	224	212
Geography	45.07	296	274	276	247	310	303	284	284
History	45.08	263	249	236	234	291	274	257	223
Political Science	45.10	241	211	214	191	271	248	220	162
Sociology	45.11	291	269	266	282	328	314	284	245
Visual and Performing Arts	50.00	141	136	141	138	141	141	151	131
Nursing	51.16	98	108	79	88	108	107	103	89
Business Administration	52.02	185	163	162	192	160	177	180	213
Accounting	52.03	169	161	182	175	166	190	187	158
Financial Management	52.08	62	151	157	184	166	209	237	205
Mean Benchmark		189.2	190.2	190.4	188.1	208.0	206.2	200.9	183.3

TABLE B.10. UNDERGRADUATE STUDENT CREDIT HOURS PER FTE TENURED AND TENURE-TRACK FACULTY IN TWENTY-FOUR SELECTED DISCIPLINES: COMPREHENSIVE AND BACCALAUREATE INSTITUTIONS: FALL 1993, 1994, 1996, AND 1997.

DEPARTMENT/ PROGRAM		UG SCRH/ T-TT FTE Faculty COMP. Fall 1993	UG SCRH/ T-TT FTE Faculty COMP. Fall 1994	UG SCRH/ T-TT FTE Faculty COMP. Fall 1996	UG SCRH/ T-TT FTE Faculty COMP. Fall 1997	UG SCRH/ T-TT FTE Faculty BACC. Fall 1993	UG SCRH/ T-TT FTE Faculty BACC. Fall 1994	UG SCRH/ T-TT FTE Faculty BACC. Fall 1996	UG SCRH/ T-TT FTE Faculty BACC. Fall 1997
Communications	9.00	214	209	194	211	na	na	209	165
Computer and Information Sciences	11.00	211	181	180	209	na	162	213	228
Education	13.00	163	138	150	132	na	160	168	203
Engineering	14.00	153	122	159	132	na	na	na	na
Foreign Languages and Literature	16.00	209	198	194	181	na	138	152	160
English	23.00	228	215	215	217	na	191	187	191

	Code								
Biological Sciences	26.00	279	270	268	254	na	186	214	217
Mathematics	27.00	264	261	251	243	na	212	211	252
Philosophy	38.01	280	292	272	282	na	184	214	202
Chemistry	40.05	255	261	238	211	na	172	187	183
Geology	40.06	248	280	233	206	na	na	na	na
Physics	40.08	211	224	207	198	na	131	148	126
Psychology	42.00	305	288	283	254	na	218	229	272
Anthropology	45.02	298	320	338	289	na	196	na	na
Economics	45.06	255	252	263	292	na	184	209	190
Geography	45.07	353	347	299	312	na	na	na	na
History	45.08	306	295	282	258	na	219	215	185
Political Science	45.10	290	263	247	224	na	206	195	194
Sociology	45.11	326	327	308	297	na	227	253	242
Visual and Performing Arts	50.00	174	170	169	152	na	128	136	118
Nursing	51.16	131	127	115	112	na	na	na	na
Business Administration	52.02	225	218	228	212	na	190	146	178
Accounting	52.03	230	226	218	218	na	na	na	na
Financial Management	52.08	242	220	246	229	na	na	na	na
Mean Benchmark		243.8	237.7	231.5	221.9	na	194.0	193.3	194.5

TABLE B.11. TOTAL STUDENT CREDIT HOURS PER FTE TENURED AND TENURE-TRACK FACULTY IN TWENTY-FOUR SELECTED DISCIPLINES: RESEARCH AND DOCTORAL UNIVERSITIES: FALL 1993, 1994, 1996, AND 1997.

DEPARTMENT/ PROGRAM		Total SCRH/ T-TT FTE Faculty RESEARCH Fall 1993	Total SCRH/ T-TT FTE Faculty RESEARCH Fall 1994	Total SCRH/ T-TT FTE Faculty RESEARCH Fall 1996	Total SCRH/ T-TT FTE Faculty RESEARCH Fall 1997	Total SCRH/ T-TT FTE Faculty DOCTORAL Fall 1993	Total SCRH/ T-TT FTE Faculty DOCTORAL Fall 1994	Total SCRH/ T-TT FTE Faculty DOCTORAL Fall 1996	Total SCRH/ T-TT FTE Faculty DOCTORAL Fall 1997
Communications	9.00	188	210	222	227	214	200	211	225
Computer and Information Sciences	11.00	184	190	206	204	167	171	201	189
Education	13.00	160	155	156	151	171	173	168	157
Engineering	14.00	147	150	144	144	210	147	150	129
Foreign Languages and Literature	16.00	157	144	141	132	168	164	170	139
English	23.00	161	167	167	168	195	183	178	160

Biological Sciences	26.00	260	257	257	238	283	295	284	247
Mathematics	27.00	206	212	219	212	225	204	223	214
Philosophy	38.01	291	252	279	238	292	255	272	230
Chemistry	40.05	317	313	300	299	291	287	268	242
Geology	40.06	208	221	221	237	264	215	226	220
Physics	40.08	218	215	198	198	254	219	201	183
Psychology	42.00	295	287	281	283	286	271	236	222
Anthropology	45.02	245	281	269	246	278	277	247	242
Economics	45.06	236	252	278	268	278	244	246	232
Geography	45.07	325	297	300	271	339	322	301	304
History	45.08	294	270	256	258	316	289	267	242
Political Science	45.10	280	235	238	214	302	270	245	187
Sociology	45.11	313	288	282	298	352	331	301	255
Visual and Performing Arts	50.00	160	150	157	153	153	157	164	145
Nursing	51.16	132	146	110	123	131	137	155	124
Business Administration	52.02	237	212	235	265	229	226	218	249
Accounting	52.03	216	200	234	227	221	223	233	207
Financial Management	52.08	235	206	216	234	229	228	261	239
Mean Benchmark		227.7	221.3	223.6	220.3	243.7	228.7	226.1	207.6

TABLE B.12. TOTAL STUDENT CREDIT HOURS PER FTE TENURED AND TENURE-TRACK FACULTY: COMPREHENSIVE AND BACCALAUREATE INSTITUTIONS: FALL 1993, 1994, 1996, 1997.

DEPARTMENT/ PROGRAM		Total SCRH/ T-TT FTE Faculty COMP. Fall 1993	Total SCRH/ T-TT FTE Faculty COMP. Fall 1994	Total SCRH/ T-TT FTE Faculty COMP. Fall 1996	Total SCRH/ T-TT FTE Faculty COMP. Fall 1997	Total SCRH/ T-TT FTE Faculty BACC. Fall 1993	Total SCRH/ T-TT FTE Faculty BACC. Fall 1994	Total SCRH/ T-TT FTE Faculty BACC. Fall 1996	Total SCRH/ T-TT FTE Faculty BACC. Fall 1997
Communications	9.00	222	220	203	217	na	na	209	165
Computer and Information Sciences	11.00	227	200	196	227	na	162	213	228
Education	13.00	214	191	198	182	na	167	173	214
Engineering	14.00	167	149	177	141	na	na	na	na
Foreign Languages and Literature	16.00	211	202	195	182	na	138	158	160
English	23.00	236	220	222	223	na	191	200	192

Discipline	Code							
Biological Sciences	26.00	286	278	276	263	na	186	214	217
Mathematics	27.00	270	271	258	248	na	212	211	252
Philosophy	38.01	281	294	273	283	na	184	207	202
Chemistry	40.05	258	265	240	215	na	172	187	184
Geology	40.06	252	287	238	210	na	na	na	na
Physics	40.08	209	224	210	200	na	132	149	127
Psychology	42.00	323	306	299	271	na	218	229	278
Anthropology	45.02	301	325	342	297	na	196	na	na
Economics	45.06	262	262	276	304	na	184	211	192
Geography	45.07	360	354	304	322	na	na	na	na
History	45.08	313	302	284	263	na	219	216	187
Political Science	45.10	298	271	252	232	na	206	200	196
Sociology	45.11	332	329	310	300	na	227	254	243
Visual and Performing Arts	50.00	178	174	173	154	na	130	136	118
Nursing	51.16	143	141	136	121	na	na	na	na
Business Administration	52.02	250	248	251	235	na	197	189	178
Accounting	52.03	246	247	240	239	na	na	na	na
Financial Management	52.08	256	252	268	250	na	na	na	na
Mean Benchmark		254.0	250.5	242.5	232.5	na	195.1	197.4	196.1

TABLE B.13. UNDERGRADUATE ORGANIZED CLASS SECTIONS PER FTE TENURED AND TENURE-TRACK FACULTY IN TWENTY-FOUR SELECTED DISCIPLINES: RESEARCH AND DOCTORAL UNIVERSITIES: FALL 1993, 1994, 1996, AND 1997.

DEPARTMENT/ PROGRAM		UG Sections/ T-TT FTE Faculty RESEARCH Fall 1993	UG Sections/ T-TT FTE Faculty RESEARCH Fall 1994	UG Sections/ T-TT FTE Faculty RESEARCH Fall 1996	UG Sections/ T-TT FTE Faculty RESEARCH Fall 1997	UG Sections/ T-TT FTE Faculty DOCTORAL Fall 1993	UG Sections/ T-TT FTE Faculty DOCTORAL Fall 1994	UG Sections/ T-TT FTE Faculty DOCTORAL Fall 1996	UG Sections/ T-TT FTE Faculty DOCTORAL Fall 1997
Communications	9.00	2.1	2.0	1.8	1.8	2.6	2.4	2.2	2.1
Computer and Information Sciences	11.00	1.4	1.3	1.0	1.1	1.6	1.6	1.8	1.6
Education	13.00	1.4	1.1	0.9	0.9	1.4	1.5	1.5	1.2
Engineering	14.00	1.8	1.5	1.3	1.3	2.7	1.7	1.7	1.5
Foreign Languages and Literature	16.00	2.3	1.9	1.9	1.8	2.7	2.6	2.7	2.2
English	23.00	1.7	1.5	1.5	1.5	2.1	2.0	1.9	1.7

Discipline	Code								
Biological Sciences	26.00	1.4	1.1	1.1	1.1	2.0	2.0	1.9	1.6
Mathematics	27.00	1.6	1.4	1.4	1.3	2.1	1.8	1.9	1.8
Philosophy	38.01	2.2	2.0	1.9	1.8	2.2	2.3	2.5	2.4
Chemistry	40.05	1.7	1.0	1.0	1.1	2.1	1.7	1.5	1.3
Geology	40.06	1.8	1.4	1.4	1.5	2.6	2.0	1.9	1.6
Physics	40.08	1.6	1.3	1.2	1.1	2.3	1.6	1.5	1.5
Psychology	42.00	1.3	1.2	1.1	1.2	1.4	1.6	1.6	1.4
Anthropology	45.02	1.8	1.7	1.6	1.6	2.0	1.9	1.7	1.6
Economics	45.06	1.3	1.3	1.2	1.3	2.0	2.0	1.9	1.6
Geography	45.07	2.0	1.8	1.7	1.7	2.6	2.5	2.4	2.1
History	45.08	1.8	1.6	1.6	1.7	2.3	2.4	2.2	2.1
Political Science	45.10	1.7	1.5	1.5	1.4	2.1	2.4	2.2	1.8
Sociology	45.11	1.6	1.6	1.6	1.6	2.2	2.2	2.2	2.0
Visual and Performing Arts	50.00	2.7	1.9	1.8	1.9	3.0	2.9	2.7	2.2
Nursing	51.16	1.2	0.8	0.7	0.8	1.8	1.3	1.2	1.1
Business Administration	52.02	1.4	1.2	1.2	1.3	1.9	1.8	1.9	2.1
Accounting	52.03	1.6	1.5	1.5	1.4	2.0	2.1	2.2	1.7
Financial Management	52.08	1.3	1.2	1.2	1.3	1.8	2.3	2.8	1.9
Mean Benchmark		1.7	1.5	1.4	1.4	2.1	2.0	2.0	1.8

TABLE B.14. UNDERGRADUATE ORGANIZED CLASS SECTIONS PER FTE TENURED AND TENURE-TRACK FACULTY IN TWENTY-FOUR SELECTED DISCIPLINES: COMPREHENSIVE AND BACCALAUREATE INSTITUTIONS: FALL 1993, 1994, 1996, AND 1997.

DEPARTMENT/ PROGRAM		UG Sections/ T-TT FTE Faculty COMP. Fall 1993	UG Sections/ T-TT FTE Faculty COMP. Fall 1994	UG Sections/ T-TT FTE Faculty COMP. Fall 1996	UG Sections/ T-TT FTE Faculty COMP. Fall 1997	UG Sections/ T-TT FTE Faculty BACC. Fall 1993	UG Sections/ T-TT FTE Faculty BACC. Fall 1994	UG Sections/ T-TT FTE Faculty BACC. Fall 1996	UG Sections/ T-TT FTE Faculty BACC. Fall 1997
Communications	9.00	3.4	3.1	3.1	3.3	na	na	3.9	3.4
Computer and Information Sciences	11.00	3.2	2.8	2.7	3.2	na	3.0	3.3	3.7
Education	13.00	2.5	2.1	2.3	2.1	na	2.6	3.0	3.4
Engineering	14.00	3.3	2.0	2.3	2.2	na	na	na	na
Foreign Languages and Literature	16.00	3.5	3.6	3.5	3.6	na	3.0	3.3	3.3
English	23.00	3.1	3.1	3.1	3.2	na	2.7	3.0	3.2

	Code								
Biological Sciences	26.00	3.7	2.8	2.6	2.6	na	2.0	2.1	2.6
Mathematics	27.00	3.2	3.1	3.2	3.3	na	2.7	3.1	3.2
Philosophy	38.01	3.2	3.4	3.2	3.3	na	2.4	2.6	3.1
Chemistry	40.05	3.7	2.7	2.7	2.3	na	2.0	2.3	2.5
Geology	40.06	3.3	2.5	2.6	2.5	na	na	na	na
Physics	40.08	3.8	2.6	2.5	2.6	na	2.1	2.3	2.6
Psychology	42.00	2.9	2.7	2.9	2.8	na	2.7	2.7	2.8
Anthropology	45.02	3.2	3.1	3.4	3.3	na	2.6	na	na
Economics	45.06	2.8	3.2	3.0	3.2	na	2.8	2.8	3.3
Geography	45.07	3.4	3.3	3.6	3.2	na	na	na	na
History	45.08	3.2	3.2	3.2	3.2	na	2.7	3.0	3.2
Political Science	45.10	3.1	3.1	3.3	3.2	na	2.9	2.7	2.9
Sociology	45.11	3.2	3.1	3.2	3.3	na	3.0	3.1	3.2
Visual and Performing Arts	50.00	3.7	3.5	3.3	3.5	na	3.0	3.1	3.7
Nursing	51.16	2.2	1.5	1.2	1.6	na	na	na	na
Business Administration	52.02	2.7	2.6	2.6	2.5	na	3.4	3.2	4.1
Accounting	52.03	2.8	2.7	2.6	2.6	na	na	na	na
Financial Management	52.08	2.5	2.6	2.8	2.7	na	na	na	na
Mean Benchmark		3.2	2.9	2.9	2.9	na	2.9	2.9	3.2

TABLE B.15. TOTAL ORGANIZED CLASS SECTIONS PER FTE TENURED AND TENURE-TRACK FACULTY IN TWENTY-FOUR SELECTED DISCIPLINES: RESEARCH AND DOCTORAL UNIVERSITIES: FALL 1993, 1994, 1996, AND 1997.

DEPARTMENT/PROGRAM		Total Sections/ T-TT FTE Faculty RESEARCH Fall 1993	Total Sections/ T-TT FTE Faculty RESEARCH Fall 1994	Total Sections/ T-TT FTE Faculty RESEARCH Fall 1996	Total Sections/ T-TT FTE Faculty RESEARCH Fall 1997	Total Sections/ T-TT FTE Faculty DOCTORAL Fall 1993	Total Sections/ T-TT FTE Faculty DOCTORAL Fall 1994	Total Sections/ T-TT FTE Faculty DOCTORAL Fall 1996	Total Sections/ T-TT FTE Faculty DOCTORAL Fall 1997
Communications	9.00	2.4	2.4	2.3	2.4	3.0	2.8	2.7	2.7
Computer and Information Sciences	11.00	2.2	2.1	1.8	1.8	2.7	2.6	2.7	2.3
Education	13.00	2.7	2.4	2.2	2.3	3.1	2.9	2.9	2.9
Engineering	14.00	2.5	2.3	2.0	2.0	3.7	2.5	2.5	2.2
Foreign Languages and Literature	16.00	2.7	2.5	2.4	2.4	3.0	2.8	3.0	2.6
English	23.00	2.2	2.1	2.0	2.0	2.6	2.7	2.6	2.4

Biological Sciences	26.00	2.1	1.9	1.7	1.7	2.6	2.8	2.8	2.2
Mathematics	27.00	2.2	2.1	2.0	2.0	2.8	2.3	2.6	2.3
Philosophy	38.01	2.5	2.3	2.3	2.2	2.6	2.6	2.9	2.6
Chemistry	40.05	2.3	1.5	1.6	1.8	2.9	2.4	2.2	2.1
Geology	40.06	2.4	2.0	1.9	2.1	3.6	2.6	2.8	2.5
Physics	40.08	2.1	1.8	1.7	1.6	2.8	2.2	2.2	2.0
Psychology	42.00	2.0	2.0	1.8	1.9	2.4	2.6	2.6	2.1
Anthropology	45.02	2.2	2.2	2.1	2.2	2.7	2.8	2.5	2.3
Economics	45.06	2.1	2.1	1.8	1.9	2.6	2.5	2.4	2.3
Geography	45.07	2.6	2.3	2.2	2.2	3.1	3.0	2.8	2.7
History	45.08	2.4	2.1	2.1	2.2	2.9	3.1	2.7	2.7
Political Science	45.10	2.4	2.0	2.0	2.0	2.5	3.0	3.0	2.5
Sociology	45.11	2.2	2.1	2.0	2.2	2.5	2.6	2.7	2.5
Visual and Performing Arts	50.00	3.3	2.4	2.2	2.4	3.5	3.5	3.3	2.8
Nursing	51.16	2.1	1.5	1.6	1.6	2.3	2.0	2.2	1.7
Business Administration	52.02	2.2	2.0	2.0	2.2	2.5	2.6	2.5	2.5
Accounting	52.03	2.3	2.2	2.2	2.0	2.5	2.7	2.9	2.4
Financial Management	52.08	2.2	2.0	2.0	2.1	2.4	2.8	3.1	2.4
Mean									
Benchmark		2.3	2.1	2.0	2.1	2.8	2.7	2.7	2.4

TABLE B.16. TOTAL ORGANIZED CLASS SECTIONS PER FTE TENURED AND TENURE-TRACK FACULTY IN TWENTY-FOUR SELECTED DISCIPLINES: COMPREHENSIVE AND BACCALAUREATE INSTITUTIONS: FALL 1993, 1994, 1996, AND 1997.

DEPARTMENT/ PROGRAM		Total Sections/ T-TT FTE Faculty COMP. Fall 1993	Total Sections/ T-TT FTE Faculty COMP. Fall 1994	Total Sections/ T-TT FTE Faculty COMP. Fall 1996	Total Sections/ T-TT FTE Faculty COMP. Fall 1997	Total Sections/ T-TT FTE Faculty BACC. Fall 1993	Total Sections/ T-TT FTE Faculty BACC. Fall 1994	Total Sections/ T-TT FTE Faculty BACC. Fall 1996	Total Sections/ T-TT FTE Faculty BACC. Fall 1997
Communications	9.00	3.7	3.5	3.4	3.6	na	na	3.9	3.4
Computer and Information Sciences	11.00	3.4	3.2	3.1	3.5	na	3.0	3.3	3.7
Education	13.00	3.5	3.4	3.4	3.3	na	2.8	3.1	3.9
Engineering	14.00	3.6	2.9	2.8	2.7	na	na	na	na
Foreign Languages and Literature	16.00	3.5	3.6	3.5	3.7	na	3.0	3.4	3.3
English	23.00	3.4	3.4	3.3	3.4	na	2.8	3.1	3.2

Biological Sciences	26.00	4.1	3.1	2.8	2.9	na	2.0	2.1	2.6
Mathematics	27.00	3.4	3.3	3.3	3.4	na	2.7	3.1	3.2
Philosophy	38.01	3.2	3.5	3.3	3.3	na	2.4	2.7	3.1
Chemistry	40.05	3.8	2.9	2.9	2.6	na	2.0	2.3	2.6
Geology	40.06	3.4	2.7	2.6	2.7	na	na	na	na
Physics	40.08	3.8	2.7	2.6	2.7	na	2.2	2.4	2.6
Psychology	42.00	3.5	3.3	3.4	3.4	na	2.7	2.7	2.8
Anthropology	45.02	3.3	3.3	3.5	3.5	na	2.6	na	na
Economics	45.06	3.0	3.4	3.1	3.5	na	2.8	2.9	3.3
Geography	45.07	3.5	3.6	3.8	3.5	na	na	na	na
History	45.08	3.4	3.4	3.5	3.4	na	2.7	3.1	2.9
Political Science	45.10	3.3	3.3	3.3	3.4	na	2.9	3.0	2.9
Sociology	45.11	3.3	3.3	3.3	3.4	na	3.0	3.2	3.3
Visual and Performing Arts	50.00	4.0	3.7	3.5	3.6	na	3.0	3.0	3.7
Nursing	51.16	2.5	1.9	2.1	2.1	na	na	na	na
Business Administration	52.02	3.1	3.1	3.3	3.1	na	3.4	3.7	4.1
Accounting	52.03	3.2	3.1	3.0	3.0	na	na	na	na
Financial Management	52.08	2.8	3.1	3.4	3.1	na	na	na	na
Mean Benchmark		3.4	3.2	3.2	3.2	na	2.9	3.0	3.2

TABLE B.17. DIRECT INSTRUCTIONAL EXPENDITURES PER STUDENT CREDIT HOUR TAUGHT IN TWENTY-FOUR SELECTED DISCIPLINES: RESEARCH AND DOCTORAL UNIVERSITIES: FISCAL YEARS 1994, 1995, 1997, AND 1998.

DEPARTMENT/ PROGRAM	Direct Expense per SCRH Taught RESEARCH FY 1994	Direct Expense per SCRH Taught RESEARCH FY 1995	Direct Expense per SCRH Taught RESEARCH FY 1997	Direct Expense per SCRH Taught RESEARCH FY 1998	Direct Expense per SCRH Taught DOCTORAL FY 1994	Direct Expense per SCRH Taught DOCTORAL FY 1995	Direct Expense per SCRH Taught DOCTORAL FY 1997	Direct Expense per SCRH Taught DOCTORAL FY 1998
Communications	138	140	143	157	120	140	137	132
Computer and Information Sciences	179	178	173	170	150	153	143	141
Education	166	189	189	235	142	156	166	167
Engineering	317	317	333	395	263	306	304	332
Foreign Languages and Literature	107	137	154	165	117	128	130	124
English	108	108	110	122	96	105	107	111

Biological Sciences	160	192	213	261	129	153	148	167
Mathematics	110	127	126	144	92	112	118	113
Philosophy	105	109	117	123	100	114	117	136
Chemistry	153	162	186	205	137	172	185	197
Geology	177	173	194	208	153	207	155	159
Physics	206	230	229	249	144	176	176	178
Psychology	107	107	126	131	108	112	134	124
Anthropology	125	123	131	139	104	98	127	118
Economics	126	139	123	134	125	142	139	142
Geography	99	110	113	140	88	98	102	119
History	102	111	117	129	85	108	120	139
Political Science	105	126	138	160	98	120	142	172
Sociology	95	109	105	108	77	89	105	122
Visual and Performing Arts	193	180	186	205	167	179	183	193
Nursing	350	283	269	300	215	222	228	270
Business Administration	129	143	144	153	125	155	148	136
Accounting	138	152	139	155	133	157	167	161
Financial Management	158	175	169	174	131	149	163	174
Mean Benchmark	152	159	164	182	129	148	152	159

TABLE B.18. DIRECT INSTRUCTIONAL EXPENDITURES PER STUDENT CREDIT HOUR TAUGHT IN TWENTY-FOUR SELECTED DISCIPLINES: COMPREHENSIVE AND BACCALAUREATE INSTITUTIONS: FISCAL YEARS 1994, 1995, 1997, AND 1998.

DEPARTMENT/ PROGRAM	Direct Expense per SCRH Taught COMP. FY 1994	Direct Expense per SCRH Taught COMP. FY 1995	Direct Expense per SCRH Taught COMP. FY 1997	Direct Expense per SCRH Taught COMP. FY 1998	Direct Expense per SCRH Taught BACC. FY 1994	Direct Expense per SCRH Taught BACC. FY 1995	Direct Expense per SCRH Taught BACC. FY 1997	Direct Expense per SCRH Taught BACC. FY 1998
Communications	120	116	117	127	na	na	129	118
Computer and Information Sciences	131	138	127	119	na	279	210	203
Education	127	133	127	143	na	181	183	156
Engineering	234	254	236	282	na	na	na	na
Foreign Languages and Literature	126	117	115	141	na	199	150	186
English	99	97	95	100	na	142	119	135

Biological Sciences	120	114	110	121	na	175	196	151
Mathematics	101	94	95	105	na	154	128	97
Philosophy	100	91	91	95	na	181	173	146
Chemistry	143	134	131	157	na	214	213	189
Geology	127	112	137	137	na	na	na	na
Physics	160	160	158	160	na	246	261	235
Psychology	84	88	88	101	na	147	124	126
Anthropology	96	96	84	105	na	149	na	na
Economics	127	138	121	102	na	176	na	162
Geography	92	98	93	94	na	na	na	na
History	91	86	82	106	na	138	138	108
Political Science	107	110	111	121	na	134	143	160
Sociology	79	82	78	96	na	122	106	130
Visual and Performing Arts	154	171	164	175	na	254	215	207
Nursing	218	212	261	249	na	na	na	na
Business Administration	126	126	114	141	na	159	na	153
Accounting	141	140	140	151	na	na	na	na
Financial Management	135	155	135	157	na	na	na	na
Mean Benchmark	127	128	125	137	na	179	178	157

TABLE B.19. TOTAL DIRECT SEPARATELY BUDGETED EXPENDITURES FOR RESEARCH AND SERVICE IN TWENTY-FOUR SELECTED DISCIPLINES: RESEARCH AND DOCTORAL UNIVERSITIES: FISCAL YEARS 1994, 1995, 1997, AND 1998.

DEPARTMENT/ PROGRAM	Rscrh/ Service Expends/ T-TT FTE Faculty RESEARCH FY 1994	Rscrh/ Service Expends/ T-TT FTE Faculty RESEARCH FY 1995	Rscrh/ Service Expends/ T-TT FTE Faculty RESEARCH FY 1997	Rscrh/ Service Expends/ T-TT FTE Faculty RESEARCH FY 1998	Rscrh/ Service Expends/ T-TT FTE Faculty DOCTORAL FY 1994	Rscrh/ Service Expends/ T-TT FTE Faculty DOCTORAL FY 1995	Rscrh/ Service Expends/ T-TT FTE Faculty DOCTORAL FY 1997	Rscrh/ Service Expends/ T-TT FTE Faculty DOCTORAL FY 1998
Communications	5,610	1,600	7,252	2,984	1,165	3,620	2,636	553
Computer and Information Sciences	40,050	41,520	60,850	55,981	13,375	25,450	25,355	21,764
Education	37,015	17,030	25,610	30,699	15,835	21,745	31,350	13,336
Engineering	82,200	68,690	80,600	92,662	29,430	64,375	54,970	55,472
Foreign Languages and Literature	2,760	2,340	3,645	1,603	1,200	2,100	1,540	831
English	1,800	1,100	2,005	778	840	2,660	1,990	919

Biological Sciences	98,455	77,530	95,820	119,427	25,540	60,915	54,260	36,148
Mathematics	15,495	13,825	18,105	15,248	7,345	11,015	11,845	7,411
Philosophy	3,025	790	2,295	1,381	640	880	1,920	1,803
Chemistry	96,920	77,660	93,335	103,867	35,315	56,615	67,785	53,674
Geology	36,655	42,450	38,300	49,062	21,365	17,790	28,964	24,422
Physics	73,060	68,460	78,420	85,210	27,675	38,410	47,585	33,107
Psychology	33,950	25,830	31,835	35,781	7,625	9,995	12,080	19,202
Anthropology	11,750	12,315	17,630	12,491	9,480	11,150	12,455	15,959
Economics	10,855	3,620	8,700	7,274	1,235	2,645	2,855	3,094
Geography	24,755	19,400	40,880	38,242	3,620	9,295	10,360	12,043
History	4,240	1,720	2,200	1,624	1,425	3,600	3,590	2,309
Political Science	7,160	3,185	6,285	5,274	1,325	3,755	4,420	5,651
Sociology	20,405	12,340	11,670	15,621	4,760	6,250	9,560	6,374
Visual and Performing Arts	2,125	1,430	2,765	1,356	745	1,875	2,960	1,916
Nursing	17,770	9,760	25,925	28,587	3,115	8,315	11,780	11,251
Business Administration	11,805	2,450	4,340	4,606	1,805	4,925	4,210	4,640
Accounting	2,680	805	2,340	463	805	1,235	1,800	2,729
Financial Management	4,785	2,995	2,085	995	940	680	710	9,989
Mean Benchmark	26,889	21,202	27,621	29,634	9,025	15,387	16,958	14,358

TABLE B.20. TOTAL DIRECT SEPARATELY BUDGETED EXPENDITURES FOR RESEARCH AND SERVICE IN TWENTY-FOUR SELECTED DISCIPLINES: COMPREHENSIVE AND BACCALAUREATE INSTITUTIONS: FISCAL YEARS 1994, 1995, 1997, AND 1998.

DEPARTMENT/ PROGRAM	Rscrh/ Service Expends/ T-TT FTE Faculty COMP. FY 1994	Rscrh/ Service Expends/ T-TT FTE Faculty COMP. FY 1995	Rscrh/ Service Expends/ T-TT FTE Faculty COMP. FY 1997	Rscrh/ Service Expends/ T-TT FTE Faculty COMP. FY 1998	Rscrh/ Service Expends/ T-TT FTE Faculty BACC. FY 1994	Rscrh/ Service Expends/ T-TT FTE Faculty BACC. FY 1995	Rscrh/ Service Expends/ T-TT FTE Faculty BACC. FY 1997	Rscrh/ Service Expends/ T-TT FTE Faculty BACC. FY 1998
Communications	400	500	204	137	na	na	na	na
Computer and Information Sciences	475	3,725	5,130	423	na	0	0	na
Education	1,690	2,835	2,355	917	na	0	0	na
Engineering	2,855	17,150	24,120	4,269	na	na	na	na
Foreign Languages and Literature	120	236	82	20	na	30	0	na
English	135	450	330	167	na	5	25	na

Biological Sciences	3,170	7,355	7,300	4,328	na	2,270	390	na
Mathematics	1,020	1,030	1,795	769	na	1,855	180	na
Philosophy	25	125	50	46	na	0	0	na
Chemistry	3,315	5,755	5,240	3,287	na	3,930	11,705	na
Geology	2,615	4,810	4,960	1,572	na	na	na	na
Physics	3,530	8,310	8,835	3,154	na	4,375	2,880	na
Psychology	2,635	840	1,870	277	na	1,435	1,900	na
Anthropology	810	960	2,205	432	na	2,965	na	na
Economics	115	510	505	32	na	50	na	na
Geography	780	1,825	5,590	280	na	na	na	na
History	154	285	260	280	na	0	0	na
Political Science	535	1,145	915	142	na	290	65	na
Sociology	440	1,485	2,290	77	na	0	20	na
Visual and Performing Arts	190	210	280	168	na	85	5	na
Nursing	1,695	3,890	905	489	na	na	na	na
Business Administration	180	970	2,585	528	na	80	na	na
Accounting	40	165	60	290	na	na	na	na
Financial Management	85	470	110	0	na	na	na	na
Mean Benchmark	1,125	2,710	3,249	920	na	1,022	1,226	na

APPENDIX C

PARTICIPANTS IN THE DELAWARE STUDY

The following institutions have participated in the Delaware Study since its inception in 1992:

Appalachian State University (Boone, NC)

Arizona State University (Tempe, AZ)

Arizona State University-West (Phoenix, AZ)

Arkansas State University (Jonesboro, AR)

Auburn University-Main Campus (Auburn, AL)

Auburn University-Montgomery (Montgomery, AL)

Augusta College (Augusta, GA)

Averett College (Danville, VA)

Ball State University (Muncie, IN)

Baylor University (Waco, TX)

Black Hills State University (Spearfish, SD)

Bloomsburg University of Pennsylvania (Bloomsburg, PA)

Boston University (Boston, MA)

Bowling Green State University (Bowling Green, OH)

Bradley University (Peoria, IL)

Bridgewater State College (Bridgewater, MA)

Brigham Young University (Provo, UT)

Butler University (Indianapolis, IN)

California State University-Fresno

California State University-Long Beach

California State University-San Marcos

California State University-Stanislaus (Turlock, CA)

Carleton College (Northfield, MN)

Catholic University of America (Washington, DC)

Centenary College of Louisiana (Shreveport, LA)

Central Connecticut State University (New Britain, CT)

Charleston Southern University (Charleston, SC)

Christopher Newport University (Newport News, VA)

Clarion University (Clarion, PA)

Clarkson University (Potsdam, NY)

Clemson University (Clemson, SC)

Cleveland State University (Cleveland, OH)

Coastal Carolina University (Conway, SC)

College of Mount St. Joseph (Cincinnati, OH)

College of New Rochelle (New Rochelle, NY)

College of St. Elizabeth (Morristown, NJ)

College of the Holy Cross (Worcester, MA)

Creighton University (Omaha, NE)

Daemen College (Amherst, NY)

Dakota State University (Madison, SD)

Davidson College (Davidson, NC)

De Paul University (Chicago, IL)

De Pauw University (Green Castle, IN)

Delta State University (Cleveland, MS)

Drexel University (Philadelphia, PA)

Duquesne University (Pittsburgh, PA)

East Carolina University (Greenville, NC)

Eastern Michigan University (Ypsilanti, MI)

Eastern New Mexico University (Roswell, NM)

Eastern Washington University (Cheney, WA)

Elizabeth City State University (Elizabeth City, NC)

Fayetteville State University (Fayetteville, NC)

Florida Institute of Technology (Melbourne, FL)

Florida International University (Miami, FL)

Florida State University (Tallahassee, FL)

Furman University (Greenville, SC)

George Washington University (Washington, DC)

Georgetown University (Washington, DC)

Georgia Institute of Technology (Atlanta, GA)

Georgia Southern University (Statesboro, GA)

Georgia State University (Atlanta, GA)

Georgian Court College (Lakewood, NJ)

Grinnell College (Grinnell, IA)

Gwynedd-Mercy College (Gwynedd Valley, PA)

Hartwick College (Oneonta, NY)

Indiana State University (Terre Haute, IN)

Indiana University-Purdue University at Indianapolis

Indiana University (Bloomington, IN)

Iowa State University (Ames, IA)

Ithaca College (Ithaca, NY)

Jackson State University (Jackson, MS)

Jacksonville State University (Jacksonville, AL)

James Madison University (Harrisonburg, VA)

Kansas State University (Manhattan, KS)

Kennesaw State College (Kennesaw, GA)

Kent State University (Kent, OH)

La Salle University (Philadelphia, PA)

Lebanon Valley College (Annville, PA)

Longwood College (Farmville, VA)

Louisiana State University-Baton Rouge

Louisiana State University-Shreveport

Louisiana Tech University (Ruston, LA)

Loyola Marymount University (Los Angeles, CA)

Marist College (Poughkeepsie, NY)

Marshall University (Huntington, WV)

Marywood University (Scranton, PA)

McNeese State University (Lake Charles, LA)

Miami University (Oxford, OH)

Michigan State University (East Lansing, MI)

Michigan Technological University (Houghton, MI)

Mississippi State University (Mississippi State, MS)

Mississippi University for Women (Columbus, MS)

Mississippi Valley State University (Itta Bena, MS)

Montana State University-Bozeman (Bozeman, MT)

Moravian College (Bethlehem, PA)

Mount Saint Mary's (Emmitsburg, MD)

Muhlenberg College (Allentown, PA)

Nazareth College (Rochester, NY)

New York State College of Ceramics (Alfred, NY)

Niagara University (Niagra, NY)

Nicholls State University (Thibodaux, LA)

North Carolina A&T State University (Greensboro, NC)

North Carolina Central University (Durham, NC)

North Carolina State University (Raleigh, NC)

North Dakota State University (Fargo, ND)

Northeast Louisiana University (Monroe, LA)

Northeastern University (Boston, MA)

Northern Arizona University (Flagstaff, AZ)

Northern Illinois University (DeKalb, IL)

Northern Kentucky University (Highland Heights, KY)

Northern State University (Aberdeen, SD)

Northwestern State University of Louisiana (Natchitoches, LA)

Oakland University (Rochester, MI)

Oberlin College (Oberlin, OH)

Ohio State University (Columbus, OH)

Oklahoma State University (Stillwater, OK)

Old Dominion University (Norfolk, VA)

Oregon State University (Corvallis, OR)

Portland State University (Portland, OR)

Prairie View A&M University (Prairie View, TX)

Purdue University-Calumet (Calumet, IN)

Radford University (Radford, VA)

Rhode Island College (Providence, RI)

Rider University (Lawrenceville, NJ)

Rockhurst University (Kansas City, MO)

Rollins College (Winter Park, FL)

Rowan University (Glassboro, NJ)

Saint Edward's University (Austin, TX)

Saint Louis University (St. Louis, MO)

Saint Norbert College (DePere, WI)

Samford University (Birmingham, AL)

San Jose State University (San Jose, CA)

Siena College (Loudonville, NY)

Sonoma State University (Rohnert Park, CA)

South Dakota School of Mine and Technology (Rapid City, SD)

South Dakota State University (Brookings, SD)

Southeast Missouri State University (Cape Girardean, MO)

Southeastern Louisiana University (Hammond, LA)

Southern Illinois University-Carbondale (Carbondale, IL)

Southern Methodist University (Dallas, TX)

Southern University and A&M College (Baton Rouge, LA)

Southwest Missouri State University (Springfield, MO)

St. Bonaventure University (St. Bonaventure, NY)

St. Mary's University (San Antonio, TX)

State University of New York (SUNY)-Albany

SUNY-Binghamton

SUNY-Brockport

SUNY-Buffalo (College)

SUNY-Cortland

SUNY-Fredonia

SUNY-Geneseo

SUNY-Institute of Technology at Utica

SUNY-New Paltz

SUNY-Oneonta

SUNY-Oswego

SUNY-Plattsburgh

SUNY-Potsdam

SUNY-Purchase College

SUNY-Stony Brook

Sweet Briar College (Sweet Briar, VA)

Teachers College at Columbia University (New York, NY)

Temple University (Philadelphia, PA)

Tennessee State University (Nashville, TN)

Tennessee Technological University (Cookeville, TN)

Texas A&M University-Main Campus (College Station, TX)

Texas Tech University (Lubbock, TX)

Towson State University (Baltimore, MD)

Trinity College (Hartford, CT)

Troy State University (Troy, AL)

Tulane University (New Orleans, LA)

University of Alabama-Birmingham

University of Alabama-Huntsville

University of Alabama-Tuscaloosa

University of Alaska-Anchorage

University of Alaska-Fairbanks

University of Arizona (Tucson, AZ)

University of Arkansas-Little Rock

University of Arkansas-Fayetteville

University of California-Davis

University of Central Florida (Orlando, FL)

University of Charleston (Charleston, WV)

University of Colorado at Colorado Springs

University of Colorado at Denver

University of Dallas (Dallas, TX)

University of Dayton (Dayton, OH)

University of Delaware (Newark, DE)

University of Florida (Gainesville, FL)

University of Georgia (Athens, GA)

University of Hartford (West Hartford, CT)

University of Hawaii at Manoa (Honolulu, HI)

University of Houston-Clear Lake (Houston, TX)

University of Houston—Main Campus (Houston, TX)

University of Houston-Victoria (Victoria, TX)

University of Idaho (Moscow, ID)

University of Iowa (Iowa City, IA)

University of Kansas (Lawrence, KS)

University of Maine (Orono, ME)

University of Maine at Machias (Machias, ME)

University of Maryland-College Park

University of Massachusetts-Amherst

University of Miami (Coral Gables, FL)

University of Minnesota-Duluth

University of Mississippi (University, MS)

University of Missouri-Columbia

University of Missouri-Kansas City

University of Missouri-Rolla

University of Missouri-St. Louis

University of Montana (Missoula, MT)

University of Montevallo (Montevallo, AL)

University of Nebraska-Kearney

University of Nebraska-Lincoln

University of Nevada-Las Vegas

University of New Hampshire (Durham, NH)

University of New Haven (New Haven, CT)

University of North Carolina-Asheville

University of North Carolina-Charlotte

University of North Carolina-Chapel Hill

University of North Carolina-Greensboro

University of North Carolina-Pembroke

University of North Carolina-Wilmington

University of Northern Colorado (Greeley, CO)

University of Northern Iowa (Cedar Falls, IA)

University of Notre Dame (Notre Dame, IN)

University of Oklahoma (Norman, OK)

University of Oregon (Eugene, OR)

University of Pittsburgh (Pittsburgh, PA)

University of Pittsburgh-Bradford

University of Scranton (Scranton, PA)

University of South Alabama (Mobile, AL)

University of South Carolina-Columbia

University of South Dakota (Vermillion, SD)

University of South Florida (Tampa, FL)

University of Southern Mississippi (Hattiesburg, MS)

University of Southwestern Louisiana (Lafayette, LA)

University of Tennessee-Chattanooga

University of Tennessee-Knoxville

University of Texas-Austin

University of Texas-El Paso

University of Rio Grande-Ohio (Rio Grande, OH)

University of Utah (Salt Lake City, UT)

University of Vermont (Burlington, VT)

University of Virginia-Charlottesville

University of Washington (Seattle, WA)

University of West Alabama (Livingston, AL)

University of West Florida (Tampa, FL)

University of Wisconsin-Madison

University of Wisconsin-Whitewater

University of Wyoming (Laramie, WY)

Utah State University (Logan, UT)

Virginia Polytechnic Institute and State University (Blacksburg, VA)

Wake Forest University (Winston-Salem, NC)

Washington College (Chestertown, MD)

West Chester University (West Chester, PA)

West Georgia College (Carrollton, GA)

West Virginia University (Morgantown, WV)

Western Carolina University (Cullowhee, NC)

Western Kentucky University (Bowling Green, KY)

Western Michigan University (Kalamazoo, MI)

Western Washington University (Bellingham, WA)

Wichita State University (Wichita, KS)

William Paterson University (Wayne, NJ)

Xavier University of Louisiana (New Orleans, LA)

Youngstown State University (Youngstown, OH)

REFERENCES

America's Best Colleges, 1996. *U.S. News and World Report,* September 19, 1996, pp. 91–105.

Boyer, E. L. *Scholarship Reconsidered: Priorities of the Professoriate.* Princeton, N. J.: Carnegie Foundation for the Advancement of Teaching, 1990.

Boyer Commission on Educating Undergraduates in the Research University. *Reinventing Undergraduate Education.* State University of New York at Stony Brook, 1998.

Brinkman, P. T. "Higher Education Cost Functions." In S. A. Hoenack and E. L. Collins, eds., *The Economics of American Universities.* Albany, N.Y.: State University of New York Press, 1990.

Brinkman, P. T. "Factors That Influence Costs in Higher Education." *Containing Cost and Improving Productivity in Higher Education.* (C.S. Hollins, ed.) New Directions for Institutional Research, no. 75, San Francisco: Jossey-Bass, 1992.

Capaldi, E. D., and Lombardi, J. V. "The Bank." Unpublished paper. Gainesville, Fla.: University of Florida, March 2000.

A Decade of Performance. Gainesville, Fla.: University of Florida, Campaign for the University of Florida, 2000.

Goldberg, M. L., Maher, B. A., and Flattau, P. E. (eds.). *Research-Doctorate Programs in the United States: Continuity and Change.* Washington, D.C.: National Academy Press, 1995.

Hoenack, S. A. "An Economist's Perspective on Costs Within Higher Education Institutions." In S. A. Hoenack and E. L. Collins, eds., *The Economics of American Universities.* Albany, N.Y.: State University of New York Press, 1990.

Joint Commission on Accountability Reporting. *A Need Answered: An Executive Summary of Recommended Accountability Reporting Formats.* Washington, D.C.: American Association of State Colleges and Universities, 1996.

Joint Commission on Accountability Reporting. *JCAR Technical Conventions Manual.* Washington, D.C.: American Association of State Colleges and Universities, 1996.

Joint Commission on Accountability Reporting. *JCAR Faculty Assignment Reporting.* Washington, D.C.: American Association of State Colleges and Universities, 1997.

Middaugh, M. F. "Interinstitutional Comparison of Instructional Costs and Productivity, by Academic Discipline: A National Study." Paper delivered at the Annual Forum of the Association for Institutional Research, New Orleans, May 1994a.

Middaugh, M. F. "Interinstitutional Comparison of Instructional Costs and Productivity, by Academic Discipline: A National Study." Paper delivered at the Annual Meeting of the Society for College and University Planning, San Francisco, July 1994b.

Middaugh, M. F. "Closing in on Faculty Productivity Measures." *Planning for Higher Education,* 1995, 24(2), 1–12.

Middaugh, M. F. "How Much Do Faculty Really Teach?" *Planning for Higher Education,* 1998, 24(2), 1–11.

Middaugh, M. F., and Hollowell, D. E. *Examining Academic and Administrative Productivity Measures.* New Directions for Institutional Research: Containing Costs and Improving Productivity in Higher Education, no. 75. San Francisco: Jossey-Bass, 1992.

Middle State Association of Colleges and Schools, Commission on Higher Education. *Characteristics of Excellence in Higher Education: Standards for Accreditation.* Philadelphia, Penn.: Middle States Association of Colleges and Schools, 1994, p. 17.

National Center for Education Statistics. *Instructional Faculty and Staff in Higher Education Institutions: Fall 1987 and Fall 1992.* Washington, D.C.: U.S. Department of Education, Office of Educational Research and Improvement, 1997.

National Commission on the Cost of Higher Education. *Straight Talk About College Costs and Prices.* Phoenix, Ariz.: The Oryx Press, 1998.

National Science Board, Science and Engineering Indicators, 1998. Arlington, Va.: National Science Foundation, 1998. (http://www.nsf.com)

Research Associates of Washington. *Higher Education Revenues and Expenditures.* Washington, D.C. Research Associates of Washington, 1991.

Rosovsky, H. "From the Belly of the Whale." *Pew Policy Perspectives,* Sept. 1992, 4(3), pp A1–A8; B1–B4.

Sapp, M., and Tamares, L. "A Monthly Checkup: Key Success Indices Track Health of University of Miami." *NACUBO Business Officer,* March 1992, 25(9), 24–31.

Sax, L. J., Astin, A. W., Arredondo, M., and Korn, W. S. *The American College Teacher: National Norms for the 1995–96 HERI Faculty Survey.* Los Angeles: Higher Education Research Institute, University of California at Los Angeles, 1996.

South Carolina Commission on Higher Education. *Performance Funding: A Report of the Commission on Higher Education to the General Assembly.* Columbia, S.C., 1997.

Zemsky, R., and Massy, W. "Cost Containment: Committing to a New Economic Reality." *Change,* 22(6), 16–22, 1990.

SUPPLEMENTARY READINGS

Anderson, R. E., and Meyerson, J. W. (eds.). *Productivity and Higher Education: Improving the Effectiveness of Faculty, Facilities, and Financial Resources*. Princeton, N.J.: Peterson's Guides, 1992.

Caplow, T., and McGee, R. J. *The Academic Marketplace*. New York: Basic Books, 1998.

Creswell, J. W. *Faculty Research Performance: Lessons from the Sciences and the Social Sciences*. ASHE-ERIC Higher Education Report No. 4. Washington, D.C.: Association for the Study of Higher Education, 1985.

Creswell, J. W. (ed.). *Measuring Faculty Research Performance*. New Directions for Institutional Research, no. 50. San Francisco: Jossey-Bass, 1986.

Cuthbert, R. (ed.). *Working in Higher Education*. Buckingham, England: The Society for Research into Higher Education & Open University Press, 1996.

Davis, J. S. *College Affordability: A Closer Look at the Crisis*. Washington, D.C.: Sallie Mae Education Institute, 1997.

Graham, H. D., and Diamond N. *The Rise of American Research Universities: Elites and Challengers in the Postwar Era*. Baltimore: The Johns Hopkins University Press, 1997.

Groccia, J. E., and Miller, J. E. (eds.). *Enhancing Productivity: Administrative, Instructional, and Technological Strategies*. New Directions for Higher Education, no. 103. San Francisco: Jossey-Bass, 1998.

Hoenack, S. A., and E. L. Collins (eds.). *The Economics of American Universities: Management, Operations, and Fiscal Environment*. Albany, N.Y.: State University of New York Press, 1990.

Huber, R. M. *How Professors Play the Cat Guarding the Cream: Why We're Paying More and Getting Less in Higher Education*. Fairfax, Va.: George Mason University Press, 1992.

Jones, L. W., and Nowotny, F. A. (eds.). *An Agenda for the New Decade*. New Directions for Higher Education, no. 70. San Francisco: Jossey-Bass, 1990.

Keller, G. *Academic Strategy: The Management Revolution in American Higher Education.* Baltimore: The Johns Hopkins University Press, 1983.

Lynton, E. A., and Elman, S. E. *New Priorities for the University: Meeting Society's Needs for Applied Knowledge and Competent Individuals.* San Francisco: Jossey-Bass, 1987.

Pazandak, C. H. (ed.). *Improving Undergraduate Education in Large Universities.* New Directions for Higher Education, no. 66. San Francisco: Jossey-Bass, 1989.

Sallie Mae Education Institute. *College Affordability: Parents' Views on the Value of a College Education and How They Pay for It.* Washington, D.C., 1997

Taylor, B. E., and Massy, W. F. *Strategic Indicators for Higher Education: Vital Benchmarks and Information to Help You Evaluate and Improve Your Institution's Performance.* Princeton, N.J.: Peterson Guides, 1996.

Wergin, J. F. (ed.). *Analyzing Faculty Workload.* New Directions for Institutional Research, no. 83. San Francisco: Jossey-Bass, 1994.

INDEX